Resurgent Africa

Resurgent Africa

Structural Transformation in Sustainable Development

Banji Oyelaran-Oyeyinka

ANTHEM PRESS

Anthem Press
An imprint of Wimbledon Publishing Company
www.anthempress.com

This edition first published in UK and USA 2021
by ANTHEM PRESS
75–76 Blackfriars Road, London SE1 8HA, UK
or PO Box 9779, London SW19 7ZG, UK
and
244 Madison Ave #116, New York, NY 10016, USA

First published in the UK and USA by Anthem Press in 2020

Copyright © Banji Oyelaran-Oyeyinka 2021

The author asserts the moral right to be identified as the author of this work.

All rights reserved. Without limiting the rights under copyright reserved above, no part of this publication may be reproduced, stored or introduced into a retrieval system, or transmitted, in any form or by any means (electronic, mechanical, photocopying, recording or otherwise), without the prior written permission of both the copyright owner and the above publisher of this book.

British Library Cataloguing-in-Publication Data
A catalogue record for this book is available from the British Library.

Library of Congress Control Number: 2020936155

ISBN-13: 978-1-83998-175-3 (Pbk)
ISBN-10: 1-83998-175-X (Pbk)

This title is also available as an e-book.

CONTENTS

List of Illustrations — vii
Foreword — ix
Preface — xiii
Abbreviations — xvii

   Introduction — 1

1. Understanding the Pathways of Africa's Economies — 11
   1.1 Introduction — 11
   1.2 Oil- and Mineral-Dependent Economies — 13
   1.3 Agriculture- and Resource-Dependent Economies — 18
   1.4 State of Economic Diversification in Selected African States — 21
   1.5 Summing Up — 25

2. Growth Pathway: Skipping the Industrial Phase in Africa — 27
   2.1 Introduction — 27
   2.2 Structural Transformation — 29
   2.3 Putting the Service Cart before the Industrial Horse — 30
   2.4 Industrialization Policies in Africa's Pathways — 35
   2.5 Putting Numbers to the Narrative — 40
   2.6 Neither Agriculture nor Manufacturing — 46
   2.7 Summing Up — 49

3. Losing the Urban Advantage — 51
   3.1 Introduction — 51
   3.2 Urban Opportunities and Challenges — 55
   3.3 Seizing the Urban Advantage in Africa — 58
   3.4 Putting Numbers to the Narrative — 60
   3.5 Summing Up — 68

4. Pathways to Productivity Growth in Africa — 71
   4.1 Introduction — 71
   4.2 Putting Numbers to the Narrative — 77
   4.3 Summing Up — 82

5.	Pathway to Employment Creation	89
	5.1 Introduction	89
	5.2 Unemployment and Underemployment in Africa	91
	5.3 Putting Numbers to the Narrative	96
	5.4 Summing Up	103
6.	Pathways of Urban Living Standards	105
	6.1 Introduction	105
	6.2 Putting Numbers to the Narrative	109
	6.3 Statistical and Econometric Analysis	111
	6.4 The Differential Impacts of Growth on the African Urban Consumer	122
	6.5 Summing Up	127
7.	Conclusions and Recommendations: Mapping Africa's Growth Pathways	129
	7.1 Introduction	129
	7.2 The Structural Transformation Pathways	131
	7.3 Can a Services-Led Growth Pathway Prosper Africa?	137
	7.4 Making a Case for Industrial Manufacturing in Africa	140
References		147
Index		157

ILLUSTRATIONS

Figures

1.1	Structure of sample economies in 2017	21
2.1	Comparative analysis of structural change in African countries	30
2.2	Value-added share in Botswana	31
2.3	Value-added share in Nigeria	32
2.4	Value-added share in South Africa	32
2.5	Value-added share in Tunisia	33
3.1	Economic growth and urbanization in sub-Saharan Africa	61
3.2	Human Development Index and degree of urbanization in African countries	64
3.3	Labor productivity and degree of urbanization in African countries	65
5.1	Wealth growth in sample countries (set 1)	97
5.2	Wealth growth in sample countries (set 2)	97
5.3	Shifts of shares for main economic sectors	98
5.4	Shifts in agriculture, manufacturing and services employment	100
6.1	Labor productivity and urbanization	116
6.2	Urbanization and living standards	120

Tables

3.1	Degree of Urbanization and Living Standards	63
4.1	Average Decomposition of Labor Productivity Growth from 1991 to 2013	79
5.1	Shift of Value-Added Share in Mining, Utilities and Construction	100
5.2	Change in Employment Share: Mining, Utilities and Construction	102
6.1	Urbanization and Structural Transformation in Ethiopia	112
6.2	Urbanization and Structural Transformation in Ghana	112

6.3 Urbanization and Structural Transformation in Morocco   113
6.4 Urbanization and Structural Transformation in Senegal   113
6.5 Urbanization and Structural Transformation in Zambia   114
6.6 Comparative Statistics   126

FOREWORD

This book makes very important contributions to the discourse of an important theoretical concept: the notion of structural transformation. It uses a rich data set and sound theoretical framing to explain the variety of ways in which structural transformation relates to employment, industrialization, productivity growth, urbanization and poverty reduction. It enriches the debate on how societies are transformed from agrarian economic structures to modern industrial structures, and more significantly the attainment of sustainable social and economic development.

Another important set of analytical findings coming out of this book is the establishment of an explicit relationship between the manufacturing capacities of nations and the eventual transition to high-value services. While the emergent Fourth Industrial Revolution seems to be blurring the boundaries of the three key sectors, namely, agriculture, industry and services, the author demonstrates the inevitable acquisition of manufacturing capacity as a necessary condition for sustainable structural transformation. Clearly, the rate of growth of manufacturing and value added does not just undergird economic growth; it is a strong prerequisite for mastering industrial agriculture and services sectors.

The book shows that while both agriculture and manufacturing value added (MVA) and exports are important drivers of real economic growth, Africa's participation in the global market of manufactures is negligible when compared to other developing countries. Its contribution to continental gross domestic product (GDP), which stands at 11 percent, represents lower ratios than those of other developing regions such as East Asia and Pacific (23 percent of GDP) or South Asia (16 percent of GDP) (African Economic Outlook, 2017).

Not surprisingly, the impact of MVA on real economic growth has been weaker than that of services in Africa. In other words, not only has industrialization not taken a firm root in the region, but sub-Saharan Africa has also been skipping the manufacturing phase of development. The central message of this book is that Africa is unlikely to witness shared and inclusive economic growth and development without industrialization.

Fortunately, over the last decade, industrialization has been back on Africa's economic policy agenda. The leadership of the region understands the imperative of industrialization, with at least half of African countries having put industrialization policies in place. What these countries seem to understand is that for as long as they lack industrial capabilities, there will be no breaking away from the dependency on commodities.

The broad regional agenda to achieving Africa's development goals include the African Union's (AU's) Vision 2063 Goal of "A Prosperous Africa Based on Inclusive Growth and Sustainable Development," which recognizes industrialization at the driving force, and NEPAD's "*Industrialization*, Science, Technology and Innovation" as one of its four main work streams. Notably, industrialization features prominently in the African Union Commission's (AUC's) First 10-Year Implementation Plan (2014–23).

In other words, despite the difficulties encountered in promoting industrialization, these renewed articulation of industrial policies indicate that confidence in the manufacturing sector as an engine of growth remains, and we must therefore continue to support African countries to implement industrial policies.

For example, the African Development Bank (AfDB) Group's *Industrialize Africa* High Five (H5) strategy sets out a clear and robust path to promote diversification and industrial development of African economies through investment in transformative flagship programs, supportive policy, institutions, infrastructure, access to markets and capital, competitive talents, capabilities and entrepreneurship.

Under the *Industrialize Africa* High 5 priority, the AfDB is working with our development partners to support industrial enterprises of all sizes to promote productivity along international value chains. The Bank has invested in high-value industrial projects that promote manufacturing; for example, between 2016 and 2018 the total average approvals for *Industrialize Africa* were valued at US$2.34 billion. In 2018, 1.2 million people benefited from investee projects (of which half were women). Additionally, we catalyzed funding into private sector industrial projects valued at US$357 million in Nigeria, Guinea and Mauritania, among others.

The Bank also supported private equity funds in manufacturing to invest and build capacity of African small- and medium-sized enterprises (SMEs): It channeled long-term innovative finance and technical assistance to African banks in order to boost lending to transformative sectors, particularly SMEs. This includes US$450 million to trade financing, directly linked to industrialization, and enabled 154,000 owner-operators and micro, small and medium enterprises (MSMEs) to benefit from access to financial services (81 percent of beneficiaries were in low-income countries) through various programs.

Institutional funding of approximately EUR 474 million was provided to public sector lending for institutional and budget support linked to industrialization and manufacturing. This includes EUR 180 million budget support to Morocco's industrialization strategy in 2017 and EUR 268 million for the second phase of Morocco's industrialization strategy in 2019.

We are aware that the growth of modern African agriculture and its role as a driver of economic growth rates, alongside improved levels of social development, will be sustained only if productivity changes are based on widespread economic diversification. The Bank is therefore investing heavily in transformational agro-industrial processing, which is coded in the notion of *Special Agro-Industrial Processing Zones* (SAPZs). The agro-industrial sector is a subset of the manufacturing sector that processes raw materials and intermediate products derived from agriculture, fisheries, livestock and forestry. The SAPZs are designed to concentrate agro-processing activities within areas of high agricultural potential. They are to cluster and enable *agricultural producers, processors*, aggregators and distributors to operate *in the same vicinity* to reduce transaction costs and share business development services for increased productivity and competitiveness. The components include (i) infrastructure (energy, water, roads, and information and communications technology (ICT)), (ii) value chain support to commodities with high agricultural potential and (iii) promotion of investment from private agro-industrialists/entrepreneurs.

Clearly, the achievement of development goals including specifically the attainment of higher living standards will therefore depend on how well the agro-processing sector performs. Remarkably, out of the 28 African countries growing above 4 percent GDP per capita in the period 2000–16, close to 70 percent, about 19 of them, recorded agricultural GDP growth of more than 3 percent per year in the same period. Notably, Ethiopia, Nigeria and Rwanda made significant progress in this respect.

Again, the Bank is investing explicitly in the sector because the region has been lagging in export performance and losing international markets. Africa has traditionally performed well in the export of raw agricultural materials, but it has lost much of this space at the same time as it has also been overtaken in the export of semi-processed and agro-processed goods. Asian countries that spectacularly experienced the Green Revolution have been able to sustain a rapid transition out of poverty due to increase in productivity in their agricultural sector. This process points to successful structural transformation, where agriculture through higher productivity provides food, labor and even savings to the process of urbanization and industrialization. Clearly, a vibrant agriculture raises labor productivity in the rural economy, pulls up wages and gradually eliminates the worst dimensions of absolute poverty. In the course of time, there will be a gradual decline in the relative importance of traditional agriculture to the overall economy, as the industrial and service sectors grow even more rapidly, partly through stimulus from a modernizing agriculture and migration of rural workers to urban jobs.

I believe Africa will benefit from structural change as other regions have if it pays close attention to modernizing the agricultural sector and turn agriculture into big business. This is because while African countries have comparative assets in raw agricultural production, they have lost and continue to lose comparative advantage in agro-products due to their relatively lower capabilities in industrial manufacturing. In the context in which global trade has shifted from bulk agricultural raw material to the production and trade in high-value products and foods, the future belongs to countries that process and add value. African countries will therefore need to invest massively in innovative agricultural practices and technologies that foster high productivity, and in processing techniques that are knowledge-based.

While congratulating the author on a well-researched book, I recommend it to scholars, policy makers and students of development alike.

Dr. Akinwumi Ayodeji Adesina
President, African Development Bank
Abidjan
September 2019

PREFACE

I have always been intrigued by the underlying reasons behind the stark differences between the rich and poor countries as well as that between rich and poor households, communities, towns and cities. I have been curious to understand why developed nations got wealthy and why poor nations lagged. As a young graduate I was very much involved with my country's industrialization efforts, especially the development of Nigeria's iron and steel and other industrial plants. The failure of these initiatives further heightened my curiosity and eventually led me to seek answers when I went off to pursue my doctorate degree at the Science and Technology Policy Studies Unit (SPRU), University of Sussex, in the United Kingdom. I wrote my thesis applying development economics framework on "Technological Capability Acquisition: The Steel Industry in Nigeria." While my focus in the early days was on the technological dimension of industrial capability acquisition, I was always fascinated by the writings of Simon Kuznets and Arthur Lewis on structural change.

Several years later, working as a consultant for the United Nations Economic Commission for Africa (UNECA), I expressed my thoughts in a report as follows: "The industrial development process in the Twentieth Century is one in which backward countries and regions have employed extant technologies to overcome the wide gaps between them and the industrial forerunners. The key to the successful industrialization of countries that are now referred to 'late-comers' had been not only been willingness to imitate but also more importantly the will to learn" (UNECA 1997). In other words, technology transfer demands explicit investment on the part of the learner in order to acquire both formal and tacit knowledge. While the former is fairly easily acquired in the short term, the latter is the product of long-term learning-by-doing, expensive process of heuristics and the establishment of institutions of some sort that is a repository of institutional memory.

For the most part, African countries have neither redeemed their developmental promise nor fulfilled the great potential that natural resources and large deposit of minerals, petroleum and agricultural resources conferred. A number of African countries are endowed with a large population, a potential supply of skilled manpower and ready domestic market. Yet, despite the excitement over their economic potential at independence, most remain stuck in the low-income category.

The difference in the level of development between countries lies in the extent of diversification of their production structures, which result from a shift of labor from low-productivity agricultural activities to more productive industrial sectors. Development, in this sense, means the creation of backward and forward sectoral linkages, based on cumulative processes and incentives generated by recurrent imbalances between sectors (Hirschman, 1958); in short, development means structural change.

The Arthur Lewis thesis that formalized the structural transformation theory in his book *Theory of Economic Growth* (1955) follows from Simon Kuznets's (1965)[1] tradition, who did not actually formalize his thesis. The central concern of Lewis's book is to "provide an appropriate framework for studying economic development" (p. 5); it zeroes in on the notion of growth in per capita output. This is the idea of both individual and broader national productivity, which I have taken up in this book. Another concern in *Theory of Economic Growth* is the issue of contemporary challenge in Africa, the idea of growth with little development (improvement in the quality of life and unemployment). The book puts it in uncertain terms: "It is possible that output may be growing, and yet the mass of the people may be becoming poorer" (p. 5).

In this book I make the case for the industrial manufacturing pathway that makes possible large gains in economies of scale that is often not realized in subsistence agriculture or low-level services (Cornwall, 1977). As a large part of the literature points out, technological change and innovation are largely concentrated in the manufacturing sector and diffusing from there to other economic sectors such as the service sector (Rosenberg, 1982; Winter and Nelson, 1982).

Manufacturing generates linkage and spillover effects that are far more prominent and widespread in diverse industrial manufacturing compared with agriculture or mining. The notion of inter-linkage and their effects was made popular by Hirschman (1958), who analyzed the direct backward and forward linkages in production; this has come to include other interactive relations between different sectors and subsectors.

The African approach to income generation and export earning has locked its industrial trajectory into a pathway whereby countries have become mere feeders of raw material into the economies of advanced countries as it was

---

[1] Economists such as Chennery and Syrquin, Johnston, Mellor and Timmer have advanced on Kuznets's thesis.

in the colonial times. The colonial structures, institutions and infrastructure left behind decades after countries gained independence were adverse and still remain unsupportive of manufacturing-driven industrialization. Most of these countries continue to rely on extractive industries that formed the basis of colonial economies by which they mostly export primary goods with little value addition. If Africa is to meet the sustainable development goals of eradicating poverty by 2030, the structures of the economies have to undergo faster structural shifts.

My profound thanks to my wife and children for always supporting my scholastic efforts. My gratitude goes to my academic collaborators, particularly Kaushalesh Lal, Sampa Paul and Adedoyin Liwaji. My deep appreciation to Anthem Press for the many conversations that made this book a better one.

"Cover design by Selom Dossou".

I thank Victor Oladokun and Abike Sawyerr for editorial assistance. My deep gratitude to my wife and children for always providing a supportive environment in the pursuit of my academic interests.

ABBREVIATIONS

ADB	Asian Development Bank
AEO	African Economic Outlook
AfDB	African Development Bank
AIDA	Accelerated Industrial Development of Africa
AUC	African Union Commission
CAGR	compound annual growth rate
CSIS	Center for Strategic and International Studies
DFID	Department for International Development
DRC	Democratic Republic of the Congo
DU	degree of urbanization
EAC	East Africa Community
ERP	Economic Recovery Program
EU	European Union
FDI	foreign direct investment
GDP	gross domestic product
GGDC	Groningen Growth and Development Centre
GNP	gross national product
GSGDA	Ghana Shared Growth and Development Agenda
GVA	gross value added
HDI	Human Development Index
ICT	information and communication technology
IFAD-IFPRI	International Fund for Agricultural Development and the International Food Policy Research Institute
ILO	International Labour Organization
IMF	International Monetary Fund
IPAP II	The Industrial Policy Action Plan II
ISI	import substitution industrialization
KES	Kenyan Shilling
LDCs	least developed countries
LR	likelihood ratio
LS	living standards

MFP	multifactor productivity
MSMEs	micro, small and medium enterprises
MVA	manufacturing value added
NBS	Nigeria Bureau of Statistics
NEPAD	The New Partnership for Africa's Development
NIE	newly industrializing economies
OEC	The Observatory of Economic Complexity
OECD	Organisation for Economic Co-operation and Development
OLS	ordinary least squares
PPP	purchasing power parity
PVH	Phillips Van Heusen
RRD	rural development model
SADC	Southern Africa Development Community
SAP	Structural Adjustment Programme
SAPZs	Special Agro-Industrial Processing Zones
SC	structural change
SDG	Sustainable Development Goal
SIDA	The Swedish International Development Cooperation Agency
SMEs	small- and medium-sized enterprises
SPRU	Science and Technology Policy Studies Unit
SSA	sub-Saharan Africa
ST	structural transformation
TFP	total factor productivity
UNCTAD	The United Nations Conference on Trade and Development
UNDESA	The United Nations Department of Economic and Social Affairs
UNDP	United Nations Development Programme
UNECA	United Nations Economic Commission for Africa
UNHABITAT	UN-Habitat: United Nations Human Settlements Programme
UNIDO	The United Nations Industrial Development Organization
UNU-WIDER	The United Nations University World Institute for Development Economics Research
USDA	The United States Department of Agriculture
VA_AGR	value-added share by agriculture
VA_IND	value-added share by industry
VA_MAN	value-added share by manufacturing
VA_SER	value-added share by services
WDI	World Development Indicators
WTO	World Trade Organization

INTRODUCTION

African economies have recorded significant growth in output; however, growth has not been enough to lift its teeming population out of poverty, stem growing unemployment and bridge the significant income divide within cities and between rural and urban areas. Jobless growth has resulted in poor standard of living even in the face of relatively impressive GDP growth. To understand the dynamics of recent development in Africa, this book draws on Arthur Lewis's (1954) "dual" thesis as well as recent scholarship on structural change (SC) (McMillan and Rodrik , 2011), which posits that where modern and traditional sectors coexist as in the case of African countries, there is the potential for capital and labor to move from low-productivity to high-productivity sectors through the process of SC that fuels economic growth and raises productivity. The rise in productivity and growth through these movements results in resource allocation efficiency gains, even when within-sector productivity is not changing significantly.

Central to discussions on the nature of structural transformation (ST) of economies is the rapid rate of urbanization fueled by a combination of natural birth within cities and migration of rural dwellers to urban centers. Conventional wisdom suggests that industrialization and urbanization proceed in tandem; however, when this takes place in the absence of industrialization and manufacturing production, large swathes of cities are turned into slums while informal economies with little prospects for productivity growth proliferate. Additionally, African economies have been characterized by jobless growth. Urbanization has produced a mixture of wealth conjoining with a conundrum of sprawls, slums and sickness. Africa's current population stands at close to 1.2 billion, and will reach about 1.689 billion (16 percent of world total) by 2030 if we assume a growth rate ranging between 2.0 percent and 2.5 percent. The driver of the rapid changes is high fertility in countries, such as Nigeria, the United Republic of Tanzania, Democratic Republic of the Congo (DRC), Ethiopia and Uganda, whose contribution to total growth is quite significant. In addition is the rapid decline in urban mortality rates and increased life expectancy that complement equally rural–urban migration, thereby fueling urban growth.

The motivation for this book, therefore, is to better understand how ST connects with human well-being measured by income, employment and equity. In the *conventional* ST model, two dynamic processes are observed, namely, "the rise of new industries (i.e. economic diversification) and the movement of resources from traditional industries to these newer ones. When the first component is absent, sustainable industrialization is likely absent and economic development is weak. Without the second, productivity gains do not diffuse in the rest of the economy."[1] Our objective in this book is therefore concerned with understanding SC dynamics and how it affects job creation, living standards and the efficiency of productive cities through manufacturing productivity growth that benefits majority of citizens. We therefore conceptualize sustainable ST in Africa as one in which economic growth is inclusive, driven by sustainable urbanization, undergirded by industrial manufacturing. This process generates widespread employment, resulting in rising living standards, and bridges the widening divide in society.

What the historical evolution of ST in Africa tells us is that growth will not translate automatically into human development, which begs the question: Are there pathways for SC that better address the aspirations of today's low-income countries and are differently formulated to ensure equity, mass employment and poverty? This book will likely not answer all these questions, but it will take account of and analyze issues of social outcomes resulting from ST. As Islam and Iversen (2018) observed, under the 2030 Agenda, explicit policy instruments may be necessary to address the poverty and hunger challenges of our time. Spontaneous SC may not fully address social objectives, but much research will be required to understand the underlying dynamics of the relationship of ST and social outcomes.

There are three unique contributions of this book. First, our analysis deepens the understanding of what we term *unconventional* pathways of ST: manifested in patterns of jobless growth, which suggests economic growth that does not necessarily lead to employment; the dominance of services at the expense of the manufacturing industry explaining the regress in Africa's industrial sector; and occurrence of structural shift without improvement in labor productivity.

Second, the book articulates the close connection of economic ST and human well-being codified among others in the process of urbanization, which describes the movement of people between the urban and rural areas and the implication for manufacturing. The analysis that seeks to determine possible associations between urbanization and GDP per capita, on the one hand, and between urbanization and labor productivity, on the other, is novel.

---

[1] Margaret McMillan and Dani Rodrik (2011), paper prepared for a joint International Labour Organization-World Trade Organization (ILO-WTO) volume.

It is an attempt to fill a gap in empirical studies because little effort has been made to determine the relationship between urbanization and ST.

To be sure, scholars such as Chenery et al. (1986), in their formulation of development, did point out the importance of several characteristic features of the development process, including physical/human capital, patterns and changes in consumer demands, rising urbanization and demographic transition.[2] However, recent discourse hardly ties these together conceptually as socioeconomic concerns are not seen as an integral part of ST analysis. According to Islam and Iversen (2018: 21), "The implicit assumption has been that once per capita income rises (as a result of GDP growth, attained through structural change), the social goals will also be achieved." As this book demonstrates, explicit policy design is required to deal with issues of jobless growth and widening inequality as "increases in aggregate or per capita income do not always ensure achieving the social development goals."[3] We therefore proceed in this book to analyze in detail the social dimensions of, and connection to, ST. These are important concerns for Africa's long-term development because sustainable urbanization and industrialization are not just closely connected but are key drivers of economic change. The book provides initial analyses on the relationships between ST and social development as well as preliminary recommendations for policymakers on the need to adopt a new approach to Africa's sustainable development.

Third is the use of relatively advanced statistical techniques to quantify SC. In the estimation of composite score of SC, the following sectors were included: agriculture, mining, manufacturing, utilities, construction, "trade, restaurants and hotels services," "transport, storage and communication services," and "finance, insurance, real estate and business services."

We collected relevant data for selected African countries including Nigeria, Ghana, South Africa, Kenya, Rwanda, Ethiopia, Botswana, Uganda and Tunisia; geographic location and stage of development are the determinants for the selection of these countries. The data for the study are drawn from various sources such as Groningen Growth and Development Centre (GGDC), World Development Indicators (WDI), United Nation Development Programme (UNDP), and country-specific sources. Value-added and employment data

---

[2] H. B. Chenery (1979), *Structural Change and Development Policy*, London: Oxford University Press; H. B. Chenery, Sherman Robinson, Moshe Syrquin (1986), *Industrialization and Growth: A Comparative Study*, Washington, DC: World Bank.

[3] There is also the broader critique by Amartya Sen leveled against per capita GDP as an indicator of well-being. Sen defines development as "freedom" and recommends to focus on the "functionings" that an individual wants to perform and his or her "capability" to actually do so, as the main indicator and goal of development. See Sen (1985 and 1989). We are not getting into those deeper issues here.

come from GGDC, while GDP per capita and degree of urbanization (DU) were taken from WDI. Human Development Index (HDI) is the proxy measure of economic development and the data for the same come from UNDP. The other data related to poverty draw on country-specific sources

The estimation of SC was carried out in three stages. In the first stage, composite score of the share of all sectors was generated. This was done using factor analysis technique, an advanced statistical tool used for variable reduction situations. The criterion used for extraction of factors is the number of factors rather than eigenvalues. Only a single factor was opted in the factor analysis. After obtaining the composite score, the next step was to measure the variability of the score over the sample period. Standard deviation was used to estimate variability. In the third stage, these deviations were standardized on a 100-point scale. The SCs recorded by the sample economies on a 100-point scale are used in the book.

In sum, this book attempts to connect key drivers of economic development with outcomes of economic growth. It provides an in-depth analysis and knowledge on Africa's diversified economies by establishing relationships between industrialization trends, rates of urbanization, urban living standards, income growth and employment in Africa.

The organization of the book is as follows:

Chapter 1

It provides insight into the pathways of Africa's diversified economies by articulating the ways by which drivers of growth, namely, industrialization, urbanization and ST, influence Africa's economic growth. It discusses how mineral and oil dependence on the one hand and economic diversification on the other tend to create different economic growth scenarios over time, and the ways these regimes differentially impact on employment and living standards. The evidence established how poor diversification in factor-endowed economies, especially oil and mineral exporters, has strongly determined growth pathways in sub-Saharan Africa (SSA). The outcomes include underinvestment in human capital, high-income inequalities, vulnerability to external price shock and diminished employment opportunities for skilled workers, overconsumption and other externalities.

The analyses confirm that mineral dependency creates enclave economies in contrast to manufacturing-based economies. The latter foster continuous learning and in building technological capabilities while promoting investment in and production of goods and services. The former create limited employment opportunities as excessive capital and labor resources are directed toward primary production in the exhaustible mineral sector. Analyses of Africa's transition economies identified expanding intra-African trade as key to future growth through improved infrastructure and regulatory systems. In all, there is need for the continent to leverage on its strength by including its teeming youthful population, agricultural resources, as the region has 60 percent of the world's uncultivated arable land, and higher rate of return on foreign investment, among others, for its economic growth.

Chapter 2

Throughout history, almost all countries and regions have followed a conventional path of growth and development. Countries start with agriculture and move surplus labor into industry, which has higher productivity and subsequently transit into services. The book provides detailed evidence of what McMillan and Rodrik (2011) rightly describe as "premature deindustrialization." The chapter provides insight into Africa's growth pathway, which shows that countries are skipping the industrial phase. The literature is replete with accounts of the struggles by African countries to industrialize and stay in the path of industrial development. In large part their performance has been disappointing. Conventional economic transformation associated with the migration of labor out of the rural agricultural sector into the urban industrial sector has been rare. Empirical analysis shows Africa to have the highest average GDP share for services among developing regions, meaning that economic growth is being steered essentially by service-led ST, while industrial manufacturing is skipped.

We show that Africa's urbanization has proceeded without ST because Africa has not experienced its own "Green Revolution"; the region experiences continued low yield on food crops and grains, while little industrial food processing takes place. Equally, Africa's dominant services' growth is found to be largely growth-reducing because labor is shifting into low-productivity and informal-service subsectors. The estimation of SC in relation to living standard reveals how rapid growth of African economies has been accompanied by rising poverty, widening inequality, low employment rates and growing rates of unemployment, establishing that employment creation and structural economic transformation are among the two major challenges at the forefront of current African growth and development strategies.

Chapter 3

Cities are the loci of production and innovation; they are where citizens leverage the urban advantage. The urban advantage refers to the abundance of goods and services, amenities and varieties of opportunities, including social and business networks largely absent in rural areas (UN-Habitat, 2010). The deviation from the conventional pattern of growth implies loss of significant parts of the urban advantage. Consistent with recent evidence (Jedwab et al., 2013), we show that urbanization could occur without change in labor productivity, especially in the case of African economies, specifically natural resource exporters. Natural resource exporting countries tend to urbanize without significantly increasing their GDP share of manufacturing output. It is worth noting that the most urbanized countries in our sample export natural resources: oil (Angola, Gabon and Nigeria), diamonds and/or gold (Botswana, Liberia and South Africa). In these countries, the urbanization process occurs without significant change in the economic structure.

According to conventional wisdom, economies are expected to modernize as the agricultural sector becomes productive and countries urbanize, but this differs from the African urban reality. The decline in productivity in industry and manufacturing has been the major reasons for the unsustainable urbanization process and stagnant economic development. Although the DU varies in countries, the linkages between urbanization and economic development suggest that the association is positive in all countries.

The chapter points to the imperative of seizing the urban advantage and to redress the situation whereby cities have transformed into *consumption cities*; that is, cities with a large share of workers in less-productive sectors rather than *productive cities* where industries and manufacturing play a larger role in the local economy. In sum, the chapter establishes that urbanization in Africa is not associated with industrialization and has not led to ST as envisioned. This finding calls for well-designed urban policies to attenuate the inefficiencies associated with consumption cities.

Chapter 4

The lack of economic progress has in part been a result of Africa's lack of endogenous industrial capabilities to produce and compete with emergent economies. Africa's consumers tend to have abandoned their "used-to-be-thriving" industrial activities in exchange for low-cost Asian imports. The rise of Asian giants, and most poignantly China with large-scale production capacity, has combined with other internal factors to deindustrialization in the African continent. These internal factors include lack of basic infrastructure, unfavorable geography, long-neglected energy and transport infrastructure and relatively poor industrial skills. On the bright side, strong growth in the African region, rising wages in China and improvements in the policy and institutional context provide a unique opportunity that African countries should utilize to attract investment in value-added manufacturing.

This chapter discusses to some depth the pathways to productivity growth in Africa through dynamic industrial policy and renewed state investments in infrastructure, human capital and sustainable energy. Although the economic progress of several African countries can be attributed to the rise of the services sector as they "jumped" the manufacturing phase, we argue that a continual shift toward labor- and skill-intensive industrial activities is the most effective way to engage excess labor and enhance worker productivity.

Labor productivity is generally low in Africa compared to other developing regions and it is partly attributed to poor educational quality and shortage of skilled manpower. Empirical evidence confirms that productivity increase could be attributed to ST and varying factors at individual, enterprise and national levels. However, analyses of African economies over two decades show that labor has been relocated from one low-productivity activity (agricultural sector) to another (low-level services), which is evidenced by a negative labor productivity growth. This suggests that development policies adopted by African states appear to have fostered an undesirable SC, which led to movement of labor in the wrong direction.

We suggest improvement of productivity in Africa's manufacturing sector as a way to achieve dynamic and sustainable industrialization through innovation and technological advancement, foreign direct investment (FDI), investment in human capital, investment in physical capital and infrastructure and establishment of relevant institutional framework.

Chapter 5

The chapter examines ST and the nature and shifts of employment. The emergence of modern sectors is expected to result in movement of labor from the traditional sector of agriculture to industry. In conventional ST models, it is expected that surplus labor from low-value-added sectors will be fully absorbed in new sectors, resulting in employment creation. The chapter describes the relationships between structural economic transformation and employment by demonstrating how this relationship impacts development and growth for African economies. Employment results in economic development, as it allocates the workforce into sectors with the highest growth potential and productivity, creates an environment for social welfare to flourish and enables a rise in living standards and minimum-wage employment, among others. Employment dynamics in relation to youth and gender and the skill root of employment and development is discussed.

The analysis reveals that SC contributes significantly to wealth creation, and the relationship between the two is linearly positive. The association of employment and SC is however not straightforward because while SC contributes to wealth creation, it does not necessarily guarantee employment creation. Although the lack of skill-based opportunities in the manufacturing sector often results in unemployment and underemployment in urban areas, structural unemployment is more a result of lack of demand, requiring a combination of demand and supply-side policy responses, among others.

Chapter 6

This chapter analyzes industrial pathways and how they determine urban living standards in relation to poverty and inequality. It discusses industrial origins of rising living standards and mechanisms for getting Africa out of poverty. The link between manufacturing, sustainable urbanization and living standards and their relationship to poverty in Africa is also examined. Skills of workforce, poverty and productivity growth as drivers of employment in the process of ST are analyzed.

As countries industrialize, and workers are pulled out of low-productivity sectors, there is a rise in economy-wide productivity and an increase in the total proportion of workers with higher skills and competences migrating to higher-income wages in manufacturing. Rise in employment and skill-based wages reduce poverty indirectly through positive employment effect on economic growth. The corresponding rise in income as a result of increased levels of employment stimulates spending, thereby creating further demand and investments. Clearly, structural shift from agriculture to industry is a pathway out of poverty because it creates diverse avenues for wage employment.

The prerequisite is that countries need to put in place appropriate human development policies to build industrial skills workforce operating in high-value-added activities. A resurgent African economy will thrive on strengthening the skill base of cities, ensuring sustainable urbanization and continuing investment in science and technology education.

Chapter 7

This concluding chapter summarizes the findings of the various chapters. The key finding is that when countries engage with policies that deepen ST in ways that foster economic and industrial diversification, the broad outcome is quantitative improvements in total factor productivity, which in turn lead to socioeconomic development and rise in living standards. In this book we analyze the relationships between SC, industrialization, urbanization and the resulting socioeconomic outcomes in African countries.

The central theme of the book is ST, while the analytical subthemes that make up the book are key variables of productivity growth, industrialization, urbanization, poverty and employment. When capital and labor move from low-productivity to high-productivity sectors, SC fuels economic growth and raises productivity. African countries with "dual" economies, modern and traditional sectors, have the potential to significantly increase their productivity and growth through these movements, resulting in resource allocation efficiency gains, even when within-sector productivity is not changing much. The book uses labor productivity as another measure of productivity, that is, total-factor productivity cannot be used due to lack of data.

The main sources for productivity growth are the adoption of advanced technologies or upgradation of skill of the workforce. Both these inputs are expected to result in higher productivity. Therefore, productivity growth could be treated as an outcome of technology transfer or development of endogenous skills through training and learning.

The chapter concludes by making a case for manufacturing in Africa as the surest pathway to development.

Chapter 1

UNDERSTANDING THE PATHWAYS OF AFRICA'S ECONOMIES

1.1 Introduction

Africa's economic growth pathways are being shaped by three powerful drivers that are linked together in very complex ways, namely, industrialization, urbanization and ST. However, Africa's industrial evolution, as well as urbanization dynamics, tends to not follow conventional wisdom. While some countries are clearly skipping the industrial phase, with their economic growth being led by the services sector, others have deindustrialized over time. These three drivers in turn significantly influence and shape the speed and quantum of three highly desired outcomes, namely, economic growth, employment and living standards.

According to the African Development Bank (AfDB, 2019), economic growth in SSA was estimated at 2.3 percent for 2018. This was down from 2.5 percent in 2017, keeping economic growth below population growth for the fourth consecutive year. Although it was expected that regional growth would rebound to 2.8 percent in 2019, it remained below 3 percent since 2015 (World Bank, 2019). In 2016, when the continent's economic growth was projected to fall to 1.6 percent, non-oil producers recorded relatively strong GDP growth. The best-performing countries include Ethiopia, Rwanda, Côte d'Ivoire, Senegal and Tanzania. These countries escaped the volatility associated with the commodity crash and continued to grow at annual average growth rates of over 6 percent (World Bank, 2016).

The slowdown in aggregate economic performance has been a result of the weak performance of the region's largest economies, namely, Nigeria and South Africa, as their combined output is half that of the continent's. This resulted from fall in oil prices from over $100 to less than $50 per barrel since mid-2014, which affected Nigeria's GDP output combined with poor manufacturing output, due in large part to power outages, and in South Africa, the initial drop (which rebounded later) in mining and manufacturing output.

Clearly, poor diversification, especially in oil and mineral exporters in SSA, was a strong factor determining the evolutionary pathways of their growth. These countries have evolved as enclave economies in which factor endowments pattern the evolution of core institutions leading, for instance, to high-income inequalities, the rise of what one may describe as "consumption cities" where average income lags far behind cost of living. Enclave economies are created by a combination of local political interest and foreign investment in oil and mineral resources with a strong export orientation. The sectors of oil, gas and mineral, in particular, are characterized by "extensive scale economies" requiring exacting technological capabilities in investment and production.[1]

Enclave-driven institutional structures are found in mineral-producing countries of Africa such as Zambia, Nigeria, South Africa, Ghana and Angola. The resource profile of enclave economies exhibits broadly similar characteristics, consisting of plentiful land to support plantations (tea, coffee, banana and sugar) or minerals (copper, gold, diamond, iron ore and bauxite). Capital and technology intensiveness are normally higher than average in setting up mineral processing complexes and, therefore, are skill requirements. While specialization grows, the imperative for manufacturing through alternative industrial organizations such as SMEs is reduced. Institutions supporting the enclave production system often get locked in, with a strong exclusionary effect. Alternative modes of industrial organization are foreclosed, and the dominant institution exhibits persistence and self-reinforcing attributes.

However, African countries present a highly diverse landscape of economic growth scenarios ranging from the relatively highly industrialized to largely agriculture-led countries.

In effect, African countries are following different economic pathways based on their resource endowments, policies and geographical and historical realities. As our analyses show in the different chapters that follow, most countries seem to have followed an involuntary service sector development route as a driver for growth; a more than cursory look reveals that this was not a predetermined choice. Policy statements and plans in different countries recognized industrial manufacturing and the need to diversify the economy as their preferred pathway. African countries, for the most part, looked to Asian economies that have undergone huge economic transformations, that is, fast economic growth and major employment shifts from agriculture to

---

[1] This necessary conjunction of domestic and international partnerships is referred to as "disproportionate political influence" and "extensive-scale economies" by S. L. Engerman and K. L. Sokoloff (1997). In *How Latin America Fell Behind*, ed, S. H. Haber, Stanford, CA: Stanford University Press, pp. 260–304.

the manufacturing sector, for inspiration. The central assumption had been that manufacturing, followed at a future date by the services sector in that sequence, has been the direction for dynamic growth for much of Asia over the past two decades. This rapid industrialization, supported by high savings and investment rates and export-oriented policies, was expected to manifest in the African experiences. However, the nature of sector evolution, the sequence and, in some cases, the pace of growth within the continent had been different. The performance of different sectors of the two regions have been different, and one will assume the differences in the technological, policy and institutional structures governing various sectors of the economies as the explanatory variables of the differential performances across countries.

The preference for manufacturing is its superior productivity growth whereby a typical worker in manufacturing produces four times more output than the average farm worker in agriculture. In the same manner, the average worker in services such as construction or wholesale and retail trade tend to produce far higher outputs several folds than the worker in manufacturing. However, this must be understood within the capability and educational context: a computer software or electronic engineer is not to be compared with a farmer with no education; the skill set required in the typical services sector is qualitatively higher than that of the farmer. A rice farmer and a bank accountant are essentially different factors of production, as one cannot be transformed into another without substantial investment of time and resources. But a farmer can transform more easily into a production worker in a garment factory, thereby multiplying her/his wages.

Consequently, in SSA, SC has not always followed the conventional pathway underpinned by industrialization, but the service-led path has not compensated for the "jumping of industry" in terms of superior wealth generation. For the most part, African countries have fallen far behind and tend to be several times poorer compared with their Asian counterparts. Broadly, Africa's employment shares in industry and services were 8 percent and 28 percent, while GDP shares were 29 percent and 54 percent, respectively. Productivity was 9 times higher in non-agriculture than in agriculture, but then overall labor productivity was 2.5 times lower than that in Asia, the productivity gap being lower in agriculture (1.4 times) and industry (1.1 times) than that in services (2.5 times).

1.2 Oil- and Mineral-Dependent Economies

As observed above, a sizeable number of SSA countries exhibit high mineral dependence. In 2014, diamonds accounted for 86 percent of Botswana's export revenues (UNCTAD, 2017). In Ghana, exports are dominated by gold, which accounts for 45 percent of exported goods, and cocoa beans, which account for 25.6 percent of total exports. Growth was recorded in Ghana's GDP from 4.4 percent in 2009 to 7.7 percent in 2010 and 13.6 percent in 2011 due to high prices of gold and cocoa with a sound macroeconomic management (The United States Department of Agriculture (USDA), 2012). Thus, Ghana exhibits a high dependence on mineral resource and a medium level of agricultural dependence. Agricultural products account for Kenya's principal exports. Tea contributed to 45 percent of all domestic exports, followed by horticulture's 29.8 percent contribution in 2017. Other export products include coffee and fish, signifying a highly agricultural-dependent economy (Muraguri et al., 2018). Nigeria exhibits the highest level of oil dependence in our sample, with crude oil accounting for an 81.1 percent share of the country's total exports in the third quarter of 2018 (Nigeria Bureau of Statistics (NBS), 2018). Although South Africa is also a mineral-dependent economy, it does export a broader array of minerals including platinum, coal, ferroalloys, iron ores and concentrates, diamonds, petroleum oils and manganese ores.

In contrast, Asian economies are heavily manufacture-focused. Broadcasting equipment, computers, office machine parts, integrated circuits and telephones accounted for 25.4 percent of Chinese exports in 2018; the exports of China have increased during the past five years at an annual rate of 2.5 percent (OEC, 2018). Hong Kong's exports in 2009 were similarly dominated by various manufactured goods including machinery and transport equipment (55.9 percent) and miscellaneous manufactured articles (23.7 percent). Indeed, machinery and transport equipment also accounted for the largest shares of exports in the Republic of Korea in 2009 at 56.8 percent, in Singapore in 2009 at 51.9 percent and in Thailand in 2010 with 42.2 percent of total exported goods.

According to the African Economic Outlook (AEO) (OECD, 2013: 14), "Taking together agricultural commodities, timber, metals and minerals, and hydrocarbons, natural resources have accounted for roughly 35 percent of Africa's growth since 2000. Resource-based raw and semi-processed goods accounted for about 80 percent of African export products in 2011, compared with 60 percent in Brazil, 40 percent in India and 14 percent in China.

Similarly, most greenfield foreign direct investment (FDI) in Africa went to resource-related activities. The balance of the growth was contributed by SCs, as will be shown in Section 1.2.1. The lack of sector diversification is due in part to poor linkages because the oil sector is generally dominated by large-scale operations and transnational corporations that do not have substantial connections with other economic sectors. Oil production is an "enclave sector" that therefore produces very few spillover benefits to other sectors in the economy, or even within the sector itself.

Another important consequence of the enclave economy is the limited employment opportunities as excessive capital and labor resources are directed toward primary production in the exhaustible mineral sector. The oil industry especially employs a highly specialized group of professionals and is highly capital- and technology-intensive, but precluding widespread employment. Oil dependence combined with the inability of the country to add value to these resources by refining its own crude oil or producing other petroleum-based products has further diminished employment opportunities for its teeming graduates. Thus, the inability to capitalize on mineral products beyond extraction often leads to missed opportunities for skilled workers such as engineers, scientists, researchers, environmentalists, accountants and lawyers, among others.

Again, large investments in the oil and mineral sector by transnational corporations have in fact competed for the use of other natural resources, such as land and water, a factor that further reduced agricultural development opportunities. It indirectly impacts employment in rural areas, particularly if they affect small-scale agriculture that otherwise would provide employment for a significant share of the labor force. For instance, in Nigeria's Niger Delta region, due to oil spillage and pollution, fishing activities have been reduced, effectively foreclosing access to gainful employment for some, destroying prospects of long-term local economic development.

Additionally, oil- and mineral-dependent economies are externally dependent on, and thus vulnerable to, external price shocks, which originate from global commodities markets. Oil dependence tends to encourage overconsumption during peak return periods that is unsustainable across time with high price volatility. In Nigeria, the 1970s was a period whereby revenue from oil exports was greater than the country's imports. The government at this time had accrued huge short-, medium- and long-term loans, with which it funded unproductive projects and a part was misused through corruption. When the oil crisis ensued, and the oil market was depressed, earnings from oil began to decline. Coupled with high debt levels, by 1985, over 33 percent of export earnings were meant for debt service.

External relationships of mineral-dependent economies are very different from the pattern seen with manufactured exporters. Much of upstream activities in the petroleum value chain, for example, oil refineries or petrochemicals processing, tends to be carried out in developed countries. This production linkage limits the value that developing countries can capture from their mineral resources and reinforces the lack of sector diversification by focusing economic activity entirely on extraction with little investment in manufacturing. An additional trend in oil-dependent countries is underinvestment in human capital (specifically education), which is a result of the lack of demand in the mineral sector for broader sets of educated, skilled labor.

As noted by the United Nations Research Institute for Social Development, conclusions drawn from comparing education investment in countries with varying degrees of resource wealth (based on the assumption that those without mineral wealth would have a greater demand for labor productivity and thereby human capital in non-mineral sectors) have however been contested on measurement grounds, as well as the use of indicator variables. Nonetheless, only very few countries, such as Botswana, were found to have used mineral rents to increase investments in education.[2]

Though there is a great deal of variety among oil-dependent economies, and similarly within agriculture- and manufacture-dependent economies, there are important trends within each typology that are worth further attention, particularly as they pertain to economic development and social welfare consequences.

However, while Africa has benefited immensely from price rise in oil and high demand in commodity over the past decade—for instance, oil price rose from less than $20 a barrel in 1999 to more than $145 in 2008, natural resources brought in just about 30 percent of Africa's GDP growth from 2000 through 2008—close to 70 percent was derived from other sectors, including wholesale and retail, transportation, telecommunications and manufacturing (McKinsey Global Institute, 2010).

1.2.1 Can Natural Resources Be a Pathway for Sustainable Growth?

Some analysts have suggested that natural resources could be a basis for structural transformation, but there are serious questions around this assumption. As we have observed earlier, enclave economies provide limited platform for mass employment and are as well subject to volatilities in the commodity markets. The natural resource sector could be a pathway to driving structural transformation through four channels: (i) as linkage and diversification into adjacent activities; (ii) as a source of employment for large numbers of low-skilled workers and consequently also the source of demand for potential new products from new activities, (iii) as a source of government revenue, mainly from extractive industries, but industrial agriculture can be important too, which can then be invested in creating the right conditions and pushing structural transformation and (iv) by attracting foreign investment that brings capital and know-how (AfDB, OECD, UNDP and UNECA, 2013: 22). Foreign investment is a pointer to sectors with the most potential. However,

---

[2] https://reliefweb.int/report/world/africas-mineral-economies-breaking-their-dependence-mining.

the primary sector needs the right environment of institutional and policy contexts to succeed, often like conditions that apply to manufacturing.

There a lengthy work of literature that argues that countries and regions possessed of abundant natural resources, and more particularly nonrenewable resources, minerals and fuels, will experience less growth in other sectors and consequently less development (McMillan and Rodrik, 2011: 3).

The enclave character of natural resource products and the resulting absence of linkages ensure that any rise in the share of natural resources exports will further constrain development elsewhere, particularly in modern manufacturing.

Africa's oil and gas exporters have accumulated the greatest amount of wealth and have the region's highest GDP per capita; on the negative side, they tend to experience lock-in into single commodities production and export and are therefore vulnerable to the lack of diversification of their economies. This group—Algeria, Angola, Chad, Congo, Equatorial Guinea, Gabon, Libya and Nigeria—comprises the core mineral and oil producers, and export of petroleum has been their mainstay over decades. Oil price surge has raised export revenues significantly and the three largest producers (Algeria, Angola and Nigeria) earned $1 trillion from petroleum exports from 2000 through 2008, compared with just $300 billion in the 1990s (McKinsey Global Institute, 2010). In the main, these economies have not deepened industrial sectors and in part this makes the case that mineral-dependent countries tend to have difficulties using resource revenues to build dynamic industrial sectors. While extra revenue helps to prevent balance of payment deficits, reduce budget deficits and build foreign-exchange reserves, it tends to give false comfort of assured prosperity, until another cycle of commodity crash.

All sectors of the economy in these countries remain closely tied to minerals, or petroleum export prices. Manufacturing and services account for just one-third of GDP—less than half their share in the diversified economies. The experience of emerging-market oil exporters outside Africa illustrates the potential for greater diversification. In Indonesia, manufacturing and services account for 70 percent of GDP, compared with less than 45 percent in Algeria and Nigeria—even though all three countries have produced similar quantities of oil since 1970.

Nigeria serves as an example of an African oil exporter that has begun the transition to a more diversified economy. Natural resources have accounted for just 35 percent of Nigeria's growth since 2000, and manufacturing and services are growing rapidly. Banking and telecoms, in particular, are expanding, thanks to a series of economic reforms. Since 2000, the number of telecom subscribers in Nigeria has increased from almost zero to 63 million, while banking assets have grown fivefold.

Equally, the economic evolution of Ghana is symptomatic of a country that is largely dependent on natural resource exports such as cocoa, mining (mostly gold) and timber. Its manufacturing and service sectors, on the other hand, have remained small and/or unproductive. Economic growth in the immediate postindependence period was driven by import substitution industrialization and an increasing role of government in the economy. As with most commodity-dependent countries, the GDP and employment shares of industry have remained stagnant over the past five decades, and, worse still, in the late 1970s and early 1980s the sector witnessed a contraction. In 2010, it accounted for 13.5 percent of GDP and around 10.8 percent of employment.[3]

From independence, the government in Ghana identified industrialization as the sole source for development. Different governments invested massively based on this assumption all through the 1960s and 1970s, but there was only the slightest rise in the GDP and employment shares of manufacturing (Jedwab and Osei, 2012). Productivity increased, but this rise was not sustainable as it did not represent a SC of the economy but reflected biased public policies. When per capita income declined after 1976, the entire manufacturing sector contracted, and productivity dropped. It was only following the structural adjustment program (SAP) in 1983 that manufacturing production was successfully resumed. Yet, the fact that manufacturing productivity in 2010 was about the same as in 1970 confirms the lack of ST in this subsector. Manufacturing exports have also remained very low due to high wages relative to productivity (Teal, 1999).

1.3 Agriculture- and Resource-Dependent Economies

Africa's transition economies—Cameroon, Ghana, Kenya, Mozambique, Senegal, Tanzania, Uganda and Zambia—have lower GDP per capita than the countries in the first two groups but have begun the process of diversifying their sources of growth. These countries are diverse: some depend heavily on one commodity, for example, copper in Zambia or aluminum in Mozambique. Others, like Kenya and Uganda, are already more diversified.

In these economies, the agriculture and resource sectors together account for as much as 35 percent of GDP and for two-thirds of their exports. However, they increasingly export manufactured goods, particularly to other African countries. Successful products include processed fuels, processed food, chemicals, apparel and cosmetics. As these countries diversified, their annual

---

[3] Industry in Ghana consists of four sectors: manufacturing, public utilities (water, gas and electricity), mining and quarrying (gold, bauxite, manganese and diamonds) and construction.

real GDP growth accelerated from 3.6 percent a year in the 1990s to 5.5 percent after 2000.

Expanding intra-African trade will be one key to the future growth of the transition economies, because they are small individually, but their prospects improve as regional integration creates larger markets. If these countries improve their infrastructure and regulatory systems, they could also compete globally with other low-cost emerging economies. One study found that factories in the transition countries are as productive as those in China and India, but that the Africans' overall costs are higher due to poor infrastructure and regulation—problems that the right policy reforms could fix. The local service sectors (such as telecommunications, banking and retailing) in the transition economies also have potential. While they are expanding rapidly, their penetration rates remain far lower than those in the diversified countries, creating an opportunity for businesses to satisfy the unmet demand.

1.3.1 Least Developed and Rural Economies

The economies in this category—the Democratic Republic of the Congo, Ethiopia, Mali and Sierra Leone—are still relatively poor, with GDP per capita of just $353—one-tenth that of the diversified countries. Some, such as Ethiopia and Mali, have meager commodity endowments and large rural populations. Others, devastated by wars in the 1990s, started growing again after the conflicts ended. But many economies, such as that of Ethiopia, are now growing very fast. The three largest (the Democratic Republic of the Congo, Ethiopia and Mali) grew, on average, by 7 percent a year since 2000, after not expanding at all in the 1990s. Even so, their growth was erratic at times and could falter again.

The economies of most of the least developed countries (LDCs) are dominated by low-productivity agriculture and petty service activities. Both industrial activities and services are becoming slowly more important for the LDC group. However, the types of industrial activities that are expanding are mining, the exploitation of crude oil and, in some cases, the generation of hydropower; types of services that are expanding are petty trading and basic commercial services.

The share of manufacturing value added in total GDP was only 11 percent in 2000–3, and almost 40 percent of the total manufacturing value added of the LDCs as a group was in one country, Bangladesh. Over the ten-year period between 1990–93 and 2000–3, the share of manufacturing in total value added declined in 19 out of 36 LDCs, and it stagnated in another two. During the 1990s, the share of medium- and high-technology manufactures in total manufacturing value added also declined for half of the LDCs, for which data are available. In a few LDCs there has been an increase in the relative share of manufactures in total value added. This has generally been associated with the expansion of garment exports based on special preferences associated with the now-expired Agreement on Textiles and Clothing.

Primary commodity exports accounted for approximately 70 percent of LDC merchandise exports during 2000–3. During that period, processed minerals and metals constituted a lower share of total mineral and metal exports than 20 years earlier (down from 35 percent to 28 percent), and processed agricultural goods also constituted a lower share of total agricultural goods exports (down from 23 percent to 18 percent). On the positive side, the share of dynamic agricultural products (those with an income elasticity of demand greater than one) has risen between 1980–83 and 2000–3 from 19 percent to 39 percent.

Low-technology, medium-technology and high-technology manufacture exports from the LDCs are expanding much more slowly than such exports from other developing countries. The share of such exports in total merchandise exports was only 4 percent during 2000–3, the same share as 20 years earlier. The export structure of the LDCs as a group is nevertheless diversifying away from primary commodities through the expansion of labor- and resource-intensive exports, and services exports, notably tourism. Such diversification is, however, not occurring in all countries and 31 remain primary-commodity dependent.

Although the individual circumstances of these economies differ greatly, their common problem is a lack of the basics, such as strong, stable governments and other public institutions, good macroeconomic conditions and sustainable agricultural development. The key challenges for this group will include maintaining the peace, upholding the rule of law, getting the economic fundamentals right and creating a more predictable business environment. These countries can also hasten their progress with support from international agencies and new private philanthropic organizations that are developing novel ways to tackle poverty and other social issues.

In a more stable political and economic environment, some of these countries could tap their natural resources to finance economic growth. The Democratic Republic of the Congo, for example, controls half of the world's cobalt reserves and a quarter of the world's diamond reserves. Sierra Leone has about 5 percent of the world's diamond reserves. Ethiopia and Mali have 22 million and 19 million hectares of arable land, respectively. If these countries could attract businesses to help develop their resources, they could push their economies upward on the path of steadier growth.

If recent trends continue, Africa will play an increasingly important role in the global economy. By 2040, the continent will be home to one in five of the

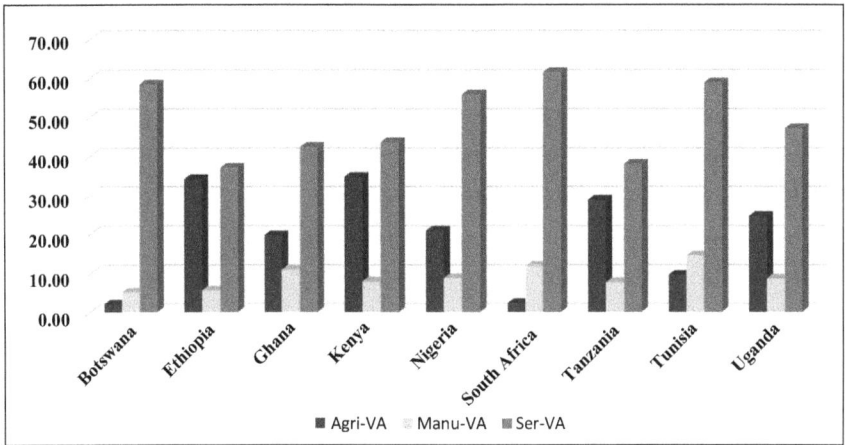

Figure 1.1 Structure of sample economies in 2017
Source: World Development Indicators

planet's young people, and the size of its labor force will top China's. Africa has almost 60 percent of the world's uncultivated arable land and a large share of the natural resources. Its consumer-facing sectors are growing two to three times faster than those in the OECD7 countries. The rate of return on foreign investment is higher in Africa than in any other developing region. Global executives and investors cannot afford to ignore this. A strategy for Africa must be part of their long-term planning.

1.4 State of Economic Diversification in Selected African States

This book focuses on SC and socioeconomic development in Africa. A sample of nine countries representing the continent has been included in the study to demonstrate the association between SC and socioeconomic development. The geographical location and stage of development are the driving forces behind the selection of these countries. The structural composition, that is, share of value added to GDP by various sectors of the sample countries in 2017, is presented in Figure 1.1.

The contribution of the services sector is highest in South Africa, as seen from the figure. Hence the detailed analysis of South Africa is presented in the following subsection. Of the remaining eight countries, Botswana and Tunisia follow the same pattern in terms of structure of the economies while the remaining countries, that is, Ethiopia, Ghana, Kenya, Nigeria,

Tanzania and Uganda, follow a different pattern. In the first set of countries, the contribution of agriculture is lowest, followed by the manufacturing sector. In the second group of countries the reverse is the case as contribution of the manufacturing sector is lowest followed by agriculture. The following subsections present in-depth analyses of the different countries.

1.4.1 South Africa

South Africa enjoys a very different status in terms of economic development in the continent. The sectoral contributions to GDP in 2017 were 2.29, 11.86 and 61.49 percent for agriculture, manufacturing and services, respectively. The South African economy is the second-largest, and one of the most diversified economies, in Africa. The economy's GDP grew at an average of 2.3 percent after negative GDP growth in 2009 due to the global financial crisis. Its economic success is based in part on its extraordinary mineral wealth. With a well-established manufacturing base, which was developed in the early twentieth century and strongly linked to traditional sectors, such as agriculture and mining, South Africa's manufacturing base is a key driver of economic growth and diversification. This is illustrated by the presence of industries, such as agro-processing, metals and leather, as well as construction and engineering specifically geared for mining, geological projects and financial services, that also often specialize in local sectors.

New sectors such as the automobile industry and call centers have opened in recent years with strong government support. Tourism is also seen as an important component of the country's economic development, as a result of its spillover effects in developing infrastructure (roads and airports especially), construction of hotels and other facilities, job creation and image-building for the country.

Ranked at 67th position out of 140 countries in 2018, and attaining the second spot in Africa after Mauritius, the South African economy is deemed as the second-most competitive economy in Africa. According to the same index, it tops the list in financial market and business sophistication, technological readiness and market size and performs very well in innovation. These are some of the factors responsible for South Africa's well-diversified economy. Its financial sector, for example, ensures relatively easy access to credit and this in turn fuels the growth of business and enterprise, key engines of economic growth and innovation.

South Africa's economy is, however, facing problems of high unemployment rates attributed in part to the decline in the tradable sectors, especially manufacturing, which employs low-skilled labor intensively (OECD, 2015).

1.4.2 Kenya

Kenya represents the set of countries where the contribution of agriculture is more than manufacturing. The sectoral contribution to the GDP of Kenya by agriculture, manufacturing and services in 2017 was 34.64, 7.90 and 43.62 percent, respectively. The Kenyan economy is based on traditional sectors such as agriculture and tourism. Due to lack of economic diversification, the political turbulence in 2008 badly affected Kenya's tourism, at a time when agricultural growth was slowing down. The economy has since experienced an average growth of 5.6 percent. Drought, climate change and worries about food security are ongoing challenges facing the Kenyan economy. However, its strong private sector has played a major role laying a foundation for stronger growth in services, which have been largely driven by traditional sectors and its geostrategic location in East Africa.

Kenya's economy is dominated by services and agriculture. Agriculture directly generates 31 percent of national GDP, 61 percent of total employment and 28 percent of total export earnings. Major agricultural exports include tea, coffee and horticulture. The main processed agricultural exports include fruits/vegetables, fats/oils and tobacco. As of 2017, the sector was valued at KES 2.3 trillion, and contributed about 33 percent to 36 percent of GDP. Overall, the agriculture sector has grown at an average of 4.8 percent between 2012 and 2016, slightly below growth across the Kenyan economy. This growth rate is on par with or ahead of countries in the region that had a similar mix of agriculture, manufacturing and services for the period 2012–16, including Rwanda (5 percent) and Uganda (2 percent) (IFAD-IFPRI, Kenya Value Chain Validation report, 2018).

The services sector has been quite strong. Kenya's strategic location between the Indian Ocean and the regional hinterland accords it many opportunities for trade and investment, although this location's usefulness depends also on a good transportation network. The country is, however, still faced with problems related to infrastructure, particularly in respect to the crucially important transportation and energy sectors. The private sector, traditional sector, newly discovered resources (oil in Turkana and gas off the coast) and geostrategic location have been identified as the country's drivers for diversifying the economy.

1.4.3 Tunisia

Tunisia represents the set of countries where the contribution of agriculture is less than manufacturing. The contribution of value added to GDP by agriculture, manufacturing and services sectors in 2017 was 9.54, 14.49 and

58.82 percent, respectively. A long-established, growing and well-educated middle class is a key backbone of the Tunisian economy. Since the late 1980s, Tunisia has undertaken macroeconomic policies and structural reforms designed to transform the country into a market-driven economy with a liberalized trade regime. Average GDP between 1999 and 2009 was 5 percent. However, since 2009 the country has experienced a GDP growth of 2 percent. Key drivers for Tunisia's diversification are geographic location allowing for easy access to the European, Middle Eastern and African markets and enabling its companies to link into the European Union (EU) supply chains, good business climate, infrastructure and highly skilled human resources to drive economic diversification. Its thriving sectors include tourism, services, manufacturing, tourism, ICT and business process outsourcing services.

Tunisia has taken advantage of its proximity to Europe to create an economic program that is geared toward integration with the EU economy. For example, 72 percent of Tunisia's exports and 69 percent of its imports are with the EU (OECD and UN, 2011). According to the OECD and UN (2011), Tunisia identified four industrial sectors as priorities and each is already exporting more than EUR 1 billion worth of products: aeronautical and automotive components; ICT/offshoring; textile, leather and shoes; and food processing. These newly developing sectors are rapidly evolving toward becoming platforms for further diversified growth.

The government also established capacity-building programs across all sectors and tourism, which is well suited to Tunisia's circumstances. Tunisia ranked 35th in the world in terms of competitiveness, according to the 2011 World Competitiveness Report, but dropped to 87th out of 140 in 2018. This was due to decreasing employability in relation to higher level of education for women and youth, resulting in growing outward migration of youth from these regions, thereby posing a growing threat to Tunisia's long-term economic competitiveness. Inflation also saw acceleration from 4.2 percent in December 2016 to 7.8 percent in June 2018, coupled with currency depreciation, administered energy price increases, wage inflation and credit growth (World Bank, 2018). Prior to the decline, Tunisia's trade policies helped it to become more competitive in international markets. It signed an association agreement with the EU in 1995, which sought to remove trade barriers for industrial goods, with ongoing negotiations for the service and agriculture sectors. In addition, Tunisia became the first country in the Mediterranean area to enter into a free-trade area with the EU. It is also undertaking an Upgrading Program that aims to make Tunisian private-sector enterprises globally competitive and includes training and infrastructure upgrading among other things.

1.5 Summing Up

This chapter sets the stage for the other five chapters. It shows that Africa's economic growth pathways are being shaped by three powerful drivers, all interlinked in very complex ways, namely, industrialization, urbanization and structural transformation. In this book we will show that Africa's industrial evolution, as well as urbanization dynamics, tends to not follow conventional wisdom. This nonconventional path results in many countries skipping the industrial phase rather than moving seamlessly from agriculture to industry, their economic growth being led by the services sector while others have deindustrialized over time. These three drivers in turn influence and shape the speed and quantum of three highly desired outcomes, namely, economic growth, employment and living standards. However, African countries present a highly diverse landscape of economic growth scenarios ranging from the relatively highly industrialized to largely agriculture-led countries.

The book argues for the centrality of industrial capability building, given the lengthy literature that argues that countries and regions possessing abundant natural resources, and more particularly nonrenewable resources, minerals and fuels, will experience less growth in other sectors and consequently less development.

Chapter 2

GROWTH PATHWAY: SKIPPING THE INDUSTRIAL PHASE IN AFRICA

2.1 Introduction

Attempts at industrialization by all regions of the world hacks back to the success first of Great Britain, followed by Western Europe and thereafter North America during the nineteenth and early twentieth centuries. The academic literature seems to agree that although the early industrializing countries started out at different stages of growth, they followed more or less a similar format of change that led to their transformation. Marked by the shift from a subsistence/agrarian economy toward more industrialized/mechanized modes of production, the hallmarks of industrialization include technological advancement, widespread investments into industrial infrastructure and a dynamic movement of labor from agriculture into the manufacturing sector (Lewis, 1978; Romer, 1986; Todaro, 1989).

Broad consensus exists that a dynamic process of industrialization is fundamental to the overall economic development of countries, because it promotes growth-enhancing structural change, which is the gradual movement of labor and other resources from agriculture to manufacturing, as accompanied by increases in productivity. Manufacturing is central to ST because the degree of industrialization is related to the per capita income of countries. Given that productivity is higher in manufacturing than in agriculture, the transfer of resources into manufacturing should normally provide a basis for higher rates of productivity-induced growth structures. The nexus of industrial growth and urbanization is therefore vital to our understanding of economic growth and living standards in modern cities.

Typically, rural economies make far less demand on infrastructure, but in contradistinction to the agriculture-dominated rural societies, urban industrial settings demand more but yields higher development dividends because manufacturing pathway is a faster road to capital accumulation. This is particularly so in spatially concentrated manufacturing (cluster agglomeration) compared with spatially dispersed agricultural activities. Capital intensity is equally high for sectors linked closely to urban manufacturing such as mining, utilities, construction and transport and much lower in agriculture and services. Capital accumulation is one of the aggregate sources of growth; therefore, as the share of manufacturing rises, aggregate growth contribution increases.

Urbanization in developing countries typically is a mixture of wealth conjoining with a conundrum of sprawls, slums and sickness. Africa's current population stands at close to 1.2 billion, and will reach about 1.689 billion (16 percent of world total) by 2030 if we assume a growth rate of between 2.0 percent and 2.5 percent. The driver of the rapid changes is high fertility in countries, such as Nigeria, the United Republic of Tanzania, DRC, Ethiopia and Uganda, whose contribution to total growth are quite significant. In addition is the rapid decline in urban mortality rates and increased life expectancy that complement rapid rural–urban migration, thereby fueling urban growth.

Africa was 40 percent urban in 2010 and is expected to reach 60 percent by 2050, with the urban dwellers increasing from 400 million to about 1.26 billion (The United Nations Department of Economic and Social Affairs (UNDESA), 2015a), while its cities contribute between 50 percent and 70 percent to the continent's GDP (UN-Habitat, 2015: 8). This contribution, however, says nothing about the absolute level of its wealth and the shape and structure of its economies. Urban Africa is made up of *consumption cities*; its skills and knowledge are largely wasted. Africa's consumer spending largely by its urban households amounted to US$860 billion in 2008, which was more than that in India or Russia and was projected to grow to US$1.4 trillion by 2020. The continent's largest consumer markets, each exceeding US$25 billion, are Cairo, Alexandria, Cape Town, Johannesburg and Lagos. Durban, Khartoum, Luanda and Pretoria are among the markets in the US$15–US$25 billion range; while a range of rising urban markets of around US$10 billion per year include Dakar, Ibadan, Kano, Rabat, Nairobi and Addis Ababa. ST aligned to these urban markets will be spurred by emerging "home-grown" companies able to compete locally and in global markets.

A consumption city ships its employment potential to other producing countries, while due to lack of wealth creation its spatial structures are dominated by informal economic transactions, urban sprawl, rising inequality and unmitigated formation of slums. Because of lack of planning and poor manufacturing production capacities, African cities have evolved into import-dependent enclaves with its elites affecting to a consumerist and unsustainable lifestyles that feed on natural resources dependency.

Alternatively, a paradigmatic change in the consumption–production nexus attended by sustainable urbanization as a driver of Africa's transformation will lead to more sustainable future pathways for the region. As we express it in a different paper, this requires a transition of rural–urban landscapes that structure both rural and urban economy, ecology and society in ways that reward the present generation with higher quality of life but without endangering and diminishing the living standards of future generations. It was emphasized that "this structural shift is underpinned by proper planning, supported by enforceable laws that bring about rapid economic progress and the equitable development of citizens. When rural-urban shift is properly managed alongside industrialization and planned urban space, it tends to lead to higher productivity and, eventually, rising living standards and better quality of life" (Oyeyinka and Lal, 2015).

2.2 Structural Transformation

ST is characterized by the transition of an economy from low-productivity and labor-intensive economic activities to higher-productivity and skill-intensive activities. The driving force behind ST is the change of productivity in modern sector, which is dominated by manufacturing and services. Structural change is equally attended by the movement of the workforce from labor-intensive activities to skill-intensive urban-based ones. The key constraint to the movement of labor from rural to urban space is the lack of opportunities in skill-intensive sectors such as manufacturing. When labor migrates to cities with little or no opportunities, available labor is underemployed or employed inefficiently.

Asia is an example of the standard story of urbanization with ST. Successful Asian economies typically went through both a green revolution and an industrial revolution, with urbanization following along as their economic activity shifted away from agricultural activities. In contrast, Africa offers a perfect example of urbanization without ST. This is because there has been little evidence of a Green Revolution in Africa. Its food yields have remained low. There has also been no industrial revolution in Africa. Manufacturing and services were 10 percent and 26 percent, respectively, for Africa, but 24 percent and 35 percent for Asia, and African labor productivity was 1.7 times and 3.5 times lower in industry and services, respectively (Oyeyinka and Lal, 2017).

The data used in the computation of structural change are from 1991 to 2017, subject to the availability of full series. Figure 2.1 depicts ST in African countries..

In Uganda, the share of agriculture was seen to decline from 52.82 percent in 1991 to 25.26 percent in 2013 (compound annual growth rate (CAGR): −4.03 percent). During the same period, share of the services sector changed from 34.82 percent to 53.98 percent (CAGR: 2.32 percent). Such a drastic change in structure is captured by showing the highest structural change. On the other hand, the share of agriculture in Tanzania witnessed

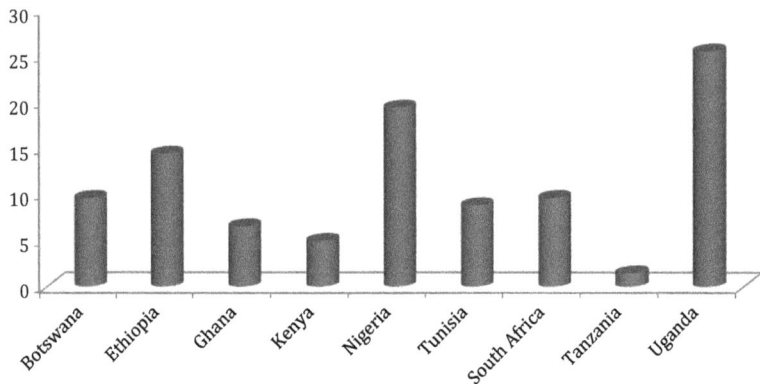

Figure 2.1 Comparative analysis of structural change in African countries
Source: Scores computed from World Development Indicators online database

declining trend from 36.07 percent to 29.15 percent during 1991–2011 (CAGR: −1.36 percent), and other sectors with reasonable percentage of share did not experience much change, which is shown as lowest structural change.

Nigeria experienced second-highest structural change due to the decline in the share of the mining sector and saw a decrease from 52.61 percent in 1991 to 28.17 percent in 2011 (CAGR: −3.14 percent), and the share of agriculture increased from 24.88 percent to 37.69 percent (CAGR: 2.66 percent) during the same period. The share of trade in the services sector also grew at the rate of 2.54 percent and attained the value of 21.25 percent in 2011. Such a major change in shares of mining, agriculture, and trade services resulted in second-highest change in the structure of the Nigerian economy.

2.3 Putting the Service Cart before the Industrial Horse

Almost all countries and regions have followed fairly similar path of growth and development. Countries start with agriculture and move surplus labor into industry, which has higher productivity and subsequently transit into services. China in the past six decades has followed such a trajectory as with the earlier Asian high performers, notably Japan, South Korea and Taiwan. For the most part, there has been a lack of data on Africa's growth trajectory and, for the more industrial countries, partly a lack of interest in understanding models on services-led growth. Knowledge on the sustainability of a services-led growth is important if we are to chart the strategic directions for African economies that are prematurely deindustrializing and being principally transformed into services economies.

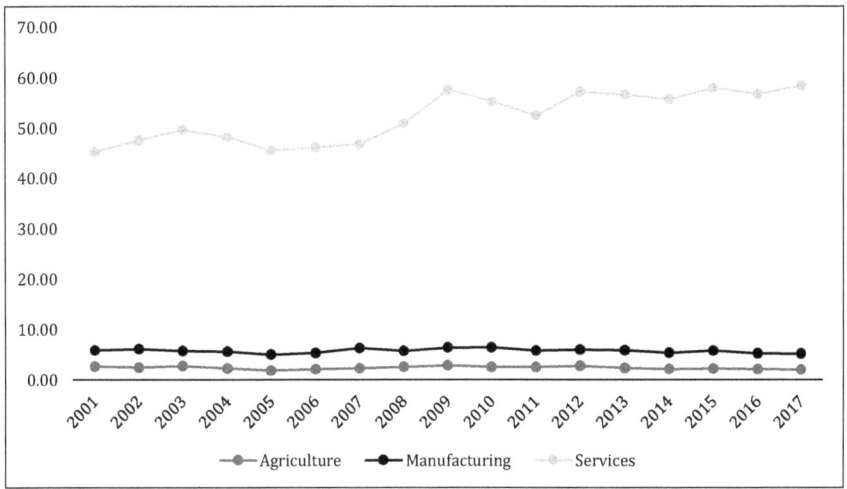

Figure 2.2 Value-added share in Botswana
Source: WDI online

Conventional growth paths have countries first developing from agrarian societies into manufacturing as the logical sequence of ST. This is the result of a long-held belief that manufacturing contribution to growth is derived largely from the fact that it is a higher-productivity activity compared to both agriculture and services. However, there are contrary realities in the African growth narrative whereby development is being driven by an ever-expanding services sector over the past decade.

Evidence across most countries in Africa indicates that economic growth is being steered essentially by growth in the services sector, indicating the possibility of a services-led ST, in addition to income surges resulting from increase in commodity trade across borders (Oyeyinka and Lal, 2017). Other than services contribution, local policy reforms, global commodity boom and emerging Asia's insatiable demand for primary products to which Africa is home, have stimulated domestic growth in output and employment. In any case, Africa's current realities bring to light the need to prioritize service sector development as a driver for growth in other tradable sectors of developing economies.

The service-led economic development is demonstrated by Botswana, Nigeria, South Africa and Tunisia, among the sample countries. The value-added share of each sector in these countries is presented in Figures 2.2 to 2.5.

According to a 2015 Report on the development potentials of tertiary activities on the continent, the services sector in Africa accounts for about

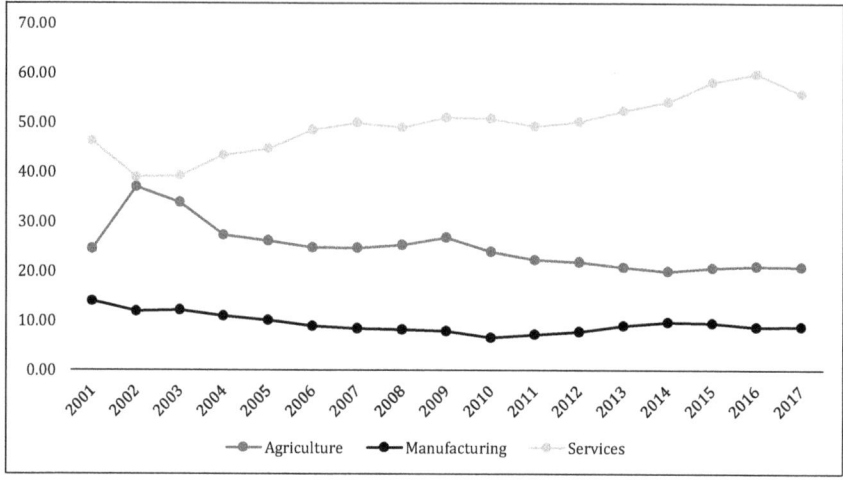

Figure 2.3 Value-added share in Nigeria

Source: WDI online

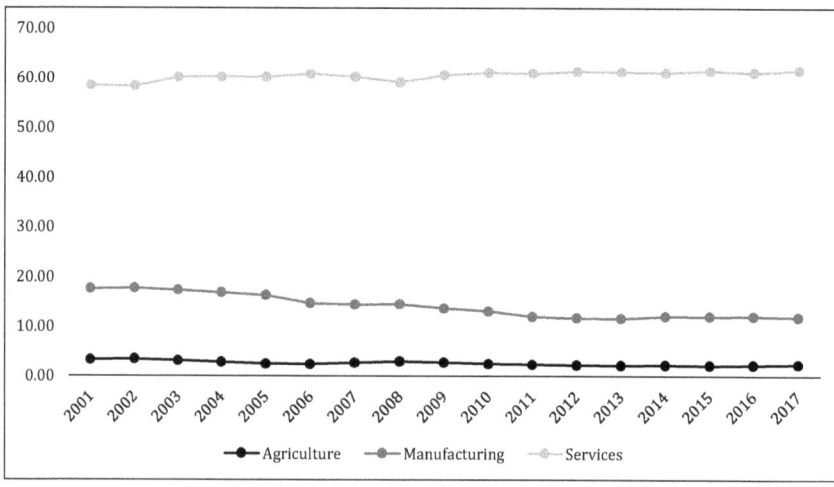

Figure 2.4 Value-added share in South Africa

Source: WDI online

50 percent of total output on the average (UNCTAD, 2015a). In some countries, the contribution of the services sector to total output goes over 70 percent. Transport, storage and communications subsectors have been growing most rapidly among other sectors and they undergird economic development

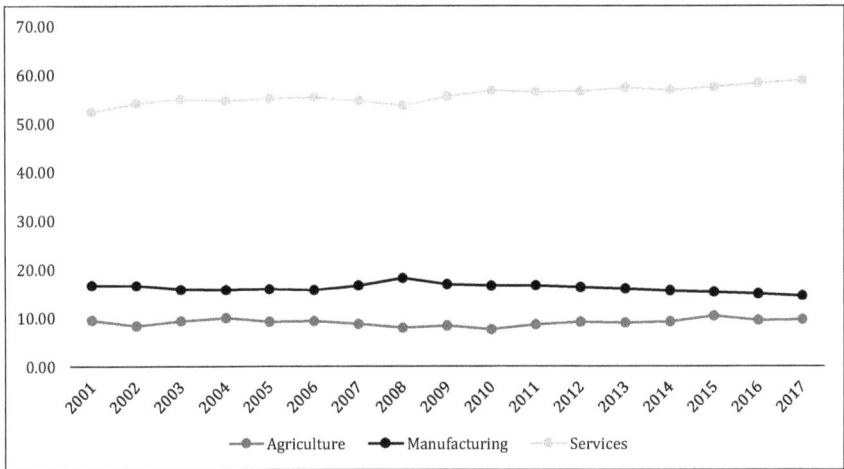

Figure 2.5 Value-added share in Tunisia
Source: WDI online

in Africa. Growth of services averaged over 5 percent during the decade 2002–12. While the average share of services in Africa's real output increased from 45 percent in 2004 to 49 percent in 2012, the share of manufacturing in total output decreased in most African countries over the same period (with 30 countries experiencing declining manufacturing contribution to real output). This incidence indicates that the growth in services is neither characterized by sufficient backward and forward linkages with manufacturing activities, nor is there evidence of complementarities between service sectors and manufacturing sectors.

Much of the arguments for a services-led growth rely on findings from more advanced economies that argue for the services sector as growth enhancing. In the African experience, what we are witnessing is a dominant services growth that is more growth-reducing because labor is shifting into low-productivity subsectors—largely low-level ICTs, wholesale and trade, incipient tourism and financial and banking services.

Another set of studies show inter-sectoral linkages based on input–output to justify the sustainability of services-led growth in countries such as India with stronger linkages between industry and services than between agriculture and services (Hansda, 2005). This of course is not surprising given the relatively stronger industrial base of India compared with African countries with very shallow manufacturing bases.

Compared with global growth in services, Africa's growth in services more than doubled the global average during 2009–12. However, Africa's growth in services was lower at 4.6 percent than the developing countries' average at 5.4 percent. In effect, Eastern and Western African subregions experienced stronger growth in services than other subregions. The transport, storage and communications subsector grew at a rate of 5.8 percent; wholesale trade, retail trade, restaurants and hotels subsector grew at a rate of 5.0 percent; and other activities grew at a rate of 4.0 percent during the period. In Burundi, Chad, the Congo, Côte d'Ivoire, Equatorial Guinea, Ethiopia, Ghana, Nigeria, Rwanda and Togo, services sector grew fastest at a rate of over 8 percent, driven largely by domestic demand. Only two countries, Ethiopia and Rwanda, were services exports-dependent during the period (UNCTAD, 2015a).

However, with respect to employment contribution, agriculture remains the largest employer of labor on the African continent, even though the services sector currently accounts for 32.4 percent of total employment on the average. While the share of services employment varies from country to country, it is pertinent to note that services sector accounts for as much as two-thirds employment in some African countries. Over the next 15 years to the decade of the 2030, the spiraling rate of urbanization in Africa, coupled with its population structure, and rising incomes are factors expected to trigger further expansion of the services sector.

In spite of the impressive growth of Africa's service sector over the past decade, a greater concern is that most of the thriving subsectors are nontradable services. This further limits Africa's contribution to global trade in services, a meager 2.2 percent contribution. Challenges confronting the development of Africa's services sector include high energy and transportation costs, regulatory and policy bottlenecks, and primary-sector dependence, which limits investment toward developing the services sector potentials. There is also a growing need to make service infrastructure in Africa accessible, qualitative, affordable and competitive (UNCTAD, 2015).

The transition from a low-income economy to a middle-income economy very often takes place when a traditional agricultural economy enters the early stages of industrialization. Although this transition brings about significant changes to the form and contents of production, its nature as a labor-based activity remains largely unchanged. In the same way that traditional agriculture is characterized by repetitive labor, the early stages of industrial production mainly involve introducing and copying the creations and inventions of others, with little self-innovation taking place in the labor process.

The transition from a middle-income economy to a high-income economy, on the other hand, takes place when an economy progresses from the early stages of industrialization to the advanced stages of industrialization. As a leap from repetitive labor to creative labor, this transition must be founded on the widespread occurrence of independent innovation. Different levels of repetitive labor and creative labor and the occurrence of qualitative change are distinct to certain stages of economic development. These are the factors that determine the transition to a different stage of economic and social development. Grasping this essential relationship gives us the fundamental means to interpret many of the problems that occur in the middle-income stage.

In industrial growth, learning-by-doing labor is manifested as extended reproduction. Following advancements in science and technology after the Second World War, developed countries began to restructure their industries at an accelerated rate and export capital and technology abroad. Through an integration of capital, technology, labor and the market, less developed economies were able to utilize their lower labor costs to emulate productive modes that had already been established in developed countries. Due to the absence of complex and creative activities in their production, these economies were able to achieve rapid development and give rise to seemingly miraculous economic growth.

However, after entering the middle-income stage of development, some countries failed to realize the nature of their current stage of development. They believed that the transition from the middle-income stage to the high-income stage was a straightforward process of quantitative industrial development, and they neglected the qualitative differences that define different stages. Unaware of the deeper issues that lay behind their "miracles," blind optimism convinced them that the transition to a high-income economy could be achieved in the same way that production could be copied. On this basis, they set out to emulate high-income countries politically, economically and socially without discretion. However, the result was far from what they expected.

2.4 Industrialization Policies in Africa's Pathways

Industrial policy is any government measure, or set of measures, to promote or prevent structural change (Curzon, 1981). Industrialization policies are instruments initiated by government to encourage the growth of manufacturing sector and other sector of the economy with a view to promote productivity-based growth. Industrialization policies are selective interventions aimed to adjust the structure of production toward more sectors that are expected to offer a better prospect for economic growth (Pack and Saggi, 2006). Industrialization policies always come in the form of vision document to enhance efficiency and to promote productivity growth in manufacturing sector (Chang, 2011). It is a government-sponsored economic program bringing private and public sectors together for technological advancement and industrialization (Reich, 1991) and providing rules and procedures that govern the growth and pattern of industrial activity. Some of the major objectives of industrialization policy in any country are (i) to promote rapid industrial development, (ii) to enhance balanced industrial structure, (iii) to prevent concentration of economic power and (iv) to enhance balanced regional growth.

Over time, studies on economic growth have evidently revealed that before industrialization policies could achieve their full course in any country or region, ST must come to play (Nixson, 1990). Development economists also established that ST plays an important role and constitutes one of the main components in the process of economic development. In the economic system, ST reallocates resources from low-productivity activities to high-productivity activities to generate an increase in productivity growth and increase manufacturing contribution to GDP (Atiyas, 2015). It also changes the sectoral composition of output and employment contributing with a view to boost economic growth and increased utilization of underutilized resources, especially labor (The United Nations Industrial Development Organization (UNIDO), 2015).

Countries with economic powers have driven their economies over time with ST featuring shifts from primary production, such as mining and agriculture, to manufacturing; and in manufacturing from natural-resource-based to more sophisticated, skill- and technology-intensive activities (UNIDO, 2009). This is evident in advanced industrial nations that have over time consolidated structural change with industrialization policies leading to changes in their industrial structure. They move their economies from low-productivity sectors to more sophisticated production sectors and at the same time establish their first mover status. Since 1945, developing economies have been struggling with the process of industrialization (Szirmai, 2009), while most African countries remain on the margins of global industrial players. Despite the fact that a lot of policies have been initiated in the recent past, also at a point supplemented with structural change, all these efforts have not driven industrialization in Africa. The rest of this section will examine industrialization policies in African states and how these policies have been driven by ST to have better understanding of potential pathways to progress.

The significance of industrialization in economic growth and development cannot be overemphasized. Industrialization generates higher skill levels of employment opportunities, facilitates deeper links across agricultural and service sectors, between rural and urban economies and between consumer, intermediate and capital goods industries (Marti and Ssenkubuge, 2009). Considering the dynamic role of manufacturing in economic development, virtually all advanced countries of today support, protect and develop their industries through specific policies and institutions (Chang, 2005).

In Africa, despite decades of development assistance, preferential trade arrangements and experiments with diverse trade and industrial policies, the developmental contribution of the industrial sector is still very low to its potential (Lall and Wangwe, 1998). At present, Africa is the least industrialized region of the world as its share in global MVA has declined in most sectors over time. While advanced regions of the world have increased their share of non-oil exports over the past two decades, almost two-thirds of Africa's merchandise exports are still accounted for by agricultural, fuel and mining products (Marti and Ssenkubuge, 2009).

In the early years of independence, most African states favored a state-led development strategy with industrialization a focal point of their development plan. This was expected to facilitate the transformation of economic structure to modern industrial economies and transform their economies from poor primary-commodity-based ones into upper middle-income-based ones. As at that period, import substitution policy was the prevailing industrialization strategy in most developing countries. In the early 1960s, Zambia, Tanzania and Nigeria implemented the import substitution policy on a large scale, followed by Ghana and Madagascar, among other countries (Mendes et al., 2014). Up until the 1980s, import substitution was the only industrialization strategy in most African states, particularly in the other sub-Saharan countries. During that era, significant growth was recorded in the manufacturing sector. In DR Congo, the average annual growth rate of the industry between 1948 and 1959 was 11 percent; in Zimbabwe, the average annual growth rate was 8.7 percent, between 1948 and 1963; in Nigeria, 6 percent between 1950 and 1957; and in Kenya, 5 percent between 1956 and 1963. With regard to Zimbabwe, between 1945 and 1965, the share of manufacturing in GDP rose from almost 3 percent to 20 percent, while that of the mining sector fell from approximately 13 percent to 7 percent, and agriculture, from 20 percent to 12 percent (Stoneman, 1982).

In the 1980s, 25 years after focusing on industrialization strategy through import substitution, the share of African manufacturing sector was small in the regional economy accounting for only 7.5 percent of GDP in 1983. In several countries, the share of manufacturing in GDP, compared to that in the 1960s, even decreased, indicating the process declined over time (Iheduru, 1999). Although there were variations across countries, the annual growth rate of MVA fell to 2 percent in most sub-Saharan countries in the first half of the 1970s and was negative in the second half (UNIDO, 1983). In this same period, African governments' external borrowing from various bilateral and multilateral donors was heavy, especially the Breton Woods Institutions, the World Bank and the IMF, in order to finance wealth creation and to jump-start the industrialization process. This situation led to the accumulation of large amounts of debt. As a result, African countries suffered huge balance of payment deficits since most of its GDP/gross national product (GNP) proceeds go to servicing foreign debt.

In the late 1970s, it became apparent that industrialization was not feasible in Africa with the Import Substitution Industrialization (ISI) model, which was attributed to the low level of physical and human capital accumulation, prevalence of unskilled labor, slow pace of industrialization and increased dependence on developed countries for manufactured goods. This was also coupled with associated economic difficulties, high rates of inflation, unmanageable balance of payments and fiscal deficits and associated oil shocks, World Bank and IMF alongside other bilateral and multilateral donors introduced SAP through policy conditions to reorientate and strategize development and industrialization in African countries (Mumo, 2010).

In early 1980s, most African countries adopted another industrialization policy called "Structural Adjustment Program," which places emphasis on trade liberalization, deregulation and privatization, aimed at integrating into global markets and attracting private investment to replace state interventions/public ownership and also to support infant industries (Mumo, 2010). During this period, most African countries experienced a bad economic situation, due to reduction in tariffs and quotas, reformation and devaluation of exchange rates, reduction in state ownership, dissolution of marketing boards, lack of access to foreign finance, resuscitation of agricultural sector, fiscal and financial reform through contractive macroeconomic policies such as budget cuts and increase in interest rates (Tregenna, 2009).

Also during this period, research shows that SAPs, which were supposed to stimulate the growth of industrial sector through attraction of foreign capital, failed in their course except in resource-extractive sectors (Elhiraika, 2008). Though the earlier industrialization policy (ISI) had poor performance in growth and innovation, SAP has a negative effect on the process of technological accumulation (Chang, 2009). Lall (1995) also opined that SAP failed totally in technological advancement, manufacturing performance, skills improvement, higher productivity, and increased value added in the agro-industry in African states. On the policy front, the failure of Africa's industrialization can also be attributed to the inability of African policy initiatives to find the right balance between the state and the market (Rodrik, 2015).

After a long period of economic stagnation during 1975–95, African states, SSA in particular, experienced economic growth. Since the turn of the millennium, African economies have averaged GDP growth rates of 5.6 percent per annum (AfDB, 2012). Countries such as Angola and Equatorial Guinea, which are both oil-rich, have the current leading economies, while resource-scarce regions, such as East Africa, have also grown at unprecedented rates, making Africa's growth a continent-wide phenomenon. Since the 1990s, most African states have been managing monetary, fiscal and trade policies more successfully to avoid the macroeconomic instabilities experienced in the past (Fosu, 2013).

Africa's economic boom could in part be attributed to the increasing international demand for resources, which led to a sustained upward trend of prices. In 2002, mineral prices surged, and in 2006 prices for agricultural commodities also rose sharply (Morris et al. 2012). This benefited SSA, which is particularly well-endowed with oil and mineral resources and has the world's largest reserves of underexploited agricultural land. Export revenues rose from US$100 billion in 2000 to $420 billion in 2011 (World Bank, 2013), while FDI tripled from $15 billion in 2002 to $46 billion in 2012. Most of the FDI was targeted to extractive industries.

ST also increases investments in construction industry, transportation sector, electricity, real estate, telecommunication and water infrastructure. Furthermore, export revenues and capital inflows spurred income growth and domestic consumption. Increase in consumer spending also attracted investment in the retail sector, especially in countries with growing urban middle classes, such as Nigeria, Kenya and Ghana. Africa's economic expansion is thus largely built on extractive industries and increased public and private expenditure, and it is also associated with revenues from extractive industries, real estate, construction and consumer goods.

Despite the different policies, very little structural change was witnessed in Africa. Agriculture sectors' share in GDP is still higher than that in any other region, although the services sector currently contributes the higher share to GDP, and both sectors are characterized as low-productivity sectors. Thus, the main structural change of the past decades has been a shift of labor force from low-productivity agriculture to low-productivity non-tradable services. Mining and oil and gas industries are highly productive, accounting for 75.9 percent of regional exports (World Bank, 2013), but they employ less than 1 percent of the region's workforce (McKinsey Global Institute, 2012).

MVA as a percentage of GDP declined from 15 percent in 1990 to 10 percent in 2008 (UNIDO and UNCTAD, 2011). SSA's shares of global manufacturing output and exports are dismally low and have stagnated over the period 1990–2005 (UNIDO, 2009). While other regions' manufacturing sector have benefited immensely from globalization, African states have experienced negative, or even a declining-productivity, structural change for the past two decades in the sense that productive sectors shrank as a share of GDP, and drift of labor from higher to lower productivity sectors and to informality (McMillan and Rodrik, 2011). The region's lack of manufacturing industry is not just a reflection of low per capita GDP.

Historically, for several reasons, growth has been associated with structural change in the direction of manufacturing. Manufacturing tends to be more productive than other sectors. In Africa, labor productivity in manufacturing is on average more than twice that in agriculture (McMillan and Rodrik, 2011). At the same time, manufacturing tends to be labor intensive, particularly at early stages of industrial development, and can, therefore, absorb part of the surplus of workers who flock to the cities in search of work. Some estimates show that close to 80 percent of the sub-Saharan African workforce is employed in low-productivity, low-income jobs, either in small-scale agriculture or the informal economy. Thus, there is a great need for productive urban employment. Manufacturing is also associated with greater product sophistication, which led to higher per capita GDP growth (Hausmann et al. 2007; UNIDO, 2009).

Lastly, manufacturing is associated with diversification, which cushions price volatility. Sub-Saharan African exports tend to be highly concentrated in a narrow range of products and are thus particularly vulnerable to external shocks. Altogether, SSA's growth process is socially exclusive. The main driver of growth in some countries—the oil and mining industry—employ very few people and have hardly any productive forward and backward linkages. Moreover, incomes earned from extractive industries are typically regressive. Manufacturing and modern services, which could potentially integrate a larger part of the workforce in productive jobs, have not yet benefited from increased consumption. The largest part of the workforce is still stuck in smallholder agriculture and petty trading, where productivity is very low. All this suggests that sub-Saharan African countries need to push for ST. The region faces the challenge of kick-starting productivity-driven and labor-absorbing economic development.

2.5 Putting Numbers to the Narrative

To better understand the extent to which industrialization policies have driven ST in African states, the chapter examines the experiences at country levels. The African countries examined are Uganda, Botswana, Ghana, Kenya, Nigeria, South Africa and Tanzania.

2.5.1 South Africa

Up until 2007, much of the industrialization policies in South Africa were centered around privatization and trade liberalization, which failed to deliver long-term investment, growth and employment. In 2007, two key industrialization strategies, New Growth Path and the Industrial Policy Action

Plan II (IPAP II), were initiated to change the course of industrialization in South Africa. The new growth path policy was initiated to address the issues surrounding unemployment, inequality and poverty, through strategy implementation and creation of five million jobs by 2020, restructuring the South African economy to improve performance in relation to labor-intensive and an improved growth rate. Five key job drivers were identified to create jobs: public investment in infrastructure, targeting of labor-absorbing activities (agriculture, mining, manufacturing, services), taking advantage of new opportunities in emerging economies, nurturing rural development and regional integration. However, priorities were given in creating employment in agriculture, mining, Green economy, manufacturing, tourism and services.

Also IPAP II was launched with a view to address South Africa's unsustainable growth path and to ensure stronger cohesion exists between macro- and microeconomic policies that relate to exchange and interest rates, inflation and trade balance requirements, alignment of skills, and technology and innovation policies to sector priorities. This industrial action plan emerged with a framework and objectives to facilitate diversification beyond traditional commodities and non-tradable services, long-term intensification of South Africa's industrialization process and movement toward a knowledge economy; to promote more labor-absorbing industrialization path with emphasis on tradable labor-absorbing goods and services and economic linkages that catalyses employment creation; to promote a broader-based industrialization path characterized by the increased participation of historically disadvantaged people and marginalized regions in the mainstream of the industrial economy; and to contribute to industrial development on the African continent, with a strong emphasis on building its productive capacity. Conversely, during the consensus of these policies, South Africa's level of industrialization improved.

The advent of this policy saw sectoral contribution to GDP in agriculture declined from 3.89 percent in 1991 to 2.55 percent in 2013, and the share of the manufacturing sector trailed similar drift of agriculture as it declined from 21.43 percent in 1991 to 18.00 percent in 2013. At the same time, the services sector, which had a share of 36.23 percent in 1991, grew at the rate of 1.95 percent annually, resulting in its increased share of 52.63 percent as at 2013. In terms of employment, the industrialization policy results in a decline of employment share in the agricultural sector, which stood at 20.85 percent in 1991 and fell to 16.08 percent in 2013 in the manufacturing sector; there was a negative growth rate of employment share of −0.43 percent, while employment share of the services sector grew from 38.87 percent in 1991 to 47.80 percent in 2013 with annual growth rate of 1.05 percent. High growth rate of 5.22 percent was recorded in finance, insurance, real estate and business services followed by trade, restaurants and hotel services with growth rate of 2.19 percent.

2.5.2 Kenya

The onset of industrialization in Kenya can be traced to the 1960s and 1970s when ISI strategies were initiated, which led to export-led industrialization. In this regime, government provided an enabling platform through provision of incentives for increase in exportation and establishment of export promotion council and export procession zones authority in 1992 and 1996, respectively. In order to foster an increase in efficiency, privatization and liberal economic reform were launched through SAP in the 1990s, which afterward had little contribution to the performance of the country. As a result, economic recovery strategy was instituted during 2003–2007 with a view to improve competitiveness in the manufacturing sector and transform the country from a low-income to industrialized middle-income country.

Through medium-term plan Vision 2030, manufacturing was to increase its contribution to GDP by 10 percent annum, while the contribution of manufacturing to GDP declined from 11.2 percent in 2004 to 10.4 percent in 2012; the industrial sector experienced similar drift as its contribution to GDP declined from 18.2 percent in 2004 to 10.4 percent in 2012. There was an increase in the share of contribution to GDP in the agricultural sector from 28 percent to 29.3 percent during 2004–2012, while the service sector maintains an average of 53 percent contribution to GDP during the period. Vis-à-vis employment, the agricultural sector in Kenya remained the largest employer (45.68 percent) in 2013, though employment declined at the rate of −1.92 percent annually. At the same time, share of employment in manufacturing grew at the rate of 4.26 percent and became triple in 2013 (13.83 percent) to what it was in 1991 (5.62 percent). Similarly, employment share of the services sector grew at the rate of 2.78 percent, and remained the second largest employer in 2013 (31.58 percent).

2.5.3 Nigeria

In Nigeria, industrial development initiatives come in three phases from postindependence to date. The first stage (1960–85) featured ISI strategy with a view to foster technological advancement, reduce imports and to increase foreign exchange. During this period, the Indigenization Decree (1972) was enacted targeted at promoting indigenous participating in productive sectors of the economy. Conversely, this policy did not succeed in import displacement and shift control of sectors to Nigerians. The second phase (1986–99) witnessed the launch of export-led industrialization and SAP in order to improve value added in the primary sector by ensuring that commodities were processed before exportation. Trade policies were also instituted to promote exportation of locally manufactured goods. Also this era experienced privatization and liberalization, which in due course encouraged dumping thereby affecting production capacity of the domestic industries to manufacture. Evidently, the adoption of SAP results to deindustrialization and widespread unemployment in Nigeria also decline in contribution to GDP from 9.9 percent in 1983 to 4 percent by 1993. The third phase of industrial development in Nigeria featured foreign private-sector-led initiatives to improve the economic landscape and increase contribution of the manufacturing sector to GDP.

However, several policies were put in place to accomplish this, some of which include outright bans on importation of goods with adequate local substitutes, formulation of legal framework for local content in the industrial sector and creation of sustainable programs for small and medium enterprises. Even with all these policies, the share of agriculture to GDP still experienced an increasing trend. The share of agriculture, which stood at 24.88 percent in 1991, increased to 39.72 percent in 2013 at an annual growth rate of 2.66 percent. The share of the services sector also increased significantly at a similar rate (2.59 percent) to that of agriculture, resulting in 28.38 percent in 2013. Up till now, the share of the manufacturing sector is relatively low. It declined during 1991–2013 from 4.26 percent to 3.56 percent.

Also in the share of value added and employment, Nigeria is the only sample economy where the share of value added and employment in agriculture increased during 1991–2013; with value-added growth of 2.66 percent, the share of employment grew at the rate of 0.72 percent, resulting in its of 62.67 percent share in 2013. Share of employment in service and manufacturing sectors declined during the period though the value-added share of the services sector recorded a positive growth rate.

2.5.4 Ghana

Since 1957 when Ghana gained independence, several policies and programs have been initiated to stimulate industrial development, to promote large-scale capital-intensive manufacturing enterprises in the country and to raise living standards of the citizenry. Against the background, the state launched the ISI policy in order to solve the problems of inadequate domestic market, private capital formation and to regularize international trading systems. In 1983, the Economic Recovery Program (ERP) was launched following a decade of unprecedented economic decline caused by external shocks, adverse macroeconomic policies and natural disasters. This policy was to reverse the declining trend of the economy and to put it back on the path of growth through monetary and fiscal reform to reduce the level of inflation; rationalization of exchange rate to stimulate exports, and to redirect resources toward the more productive sectors of the economy with a focus on the promotion of economic efficiency and resource allocation; and expansion of the productive capacity of the economy (Ewusi, 1987).

During this period, radical import liberalization was implemented, and subsequently local industries encountered severe resource and management constraint. The share of manufacturing in GDP and the share of its contribution to employment drastically declined, and this eventually led to widespread poverty in the country. In order to restructure the economy and promote small-scale industries in the country, the government came up with different economic growth initiatives. The Poverty Reduction Strategy was launched in 2003–2005, followed by Growth and Poverty Reduction Strategy during 2006–2009 and then the Ghana Shared Growth and Development Agenda (GSGDA) 2010–13. With all these policies, agriculture contributes almost one-third to GDP during 1991–2012 with a decreasing rate of −1.07 percent annually, resulting in 25.68 percent share in 2013. Share of the services sector to GDP also increased during the period with annual growth rate of 0.73 percent. Consequently, its share increased from 33.10 percent in 1991 to 37.38 percent in 2013. At the same time, the share of the manufacturing sector declined from 11.86 percent to 8.51 percent during this sample period. Correspondingly, in the employment share, there was a decline of employment in agriculture (−1.64 percent), which resulted in a loss of its position as the largest employer (55.43 percent in 1991) of the services sector in 2013. The services sector employment grew at the rate of 2.45 percent and became the largest (39.22 percent) in 2013. Among services subsector, employment in "finance, insurance, real estate and business services" recorded the highest growth (8.48 percent), followed by "trade, restaurants and hotels services" (5.10 percent).

2.5.5 Botswana

Before the advent of globalization, the main industrialization policy in operation for Botswana was the import substitution model launched in 1984, which eventually led to export-oriented industrialization in 1998 due to increasing intensity of international competition and globalization and the great urge for economic diversification from minerals to the industrial sector, among other sectors. This policy is still in operation up till now. Nevertheless, the performance of the industrial sector, particularly the manufacturing sector, is not very satisfactory. The manufacturing sectoral contribution to GDP has declined drastically; the share of agriculture, which stood at 3.89 percent in 1991, declined to 2.59 percent in 2013. On the other hand, the services sector performed extremely well by increasing its share from 23.88 percent in 1991 to 50.17 percent in 2013. Regarding ST in employment, the agricultural sector had the largest share of total employment with 37.78 percent in 2013. Also, the services sector made tremendous success in employment growth at the rate of 1.83 percent and remained the second-highest employer (35.20 percent) in 2013, while in the manufacturing sector, although value-added share grew at the rate of 0.27 percent annually, employment grew at the rate of 1.19 percent.

2.5.6 Tanzania

After independence in 1967, Tanzania embarked on industrialization centered on import-substitution strategy with a view to achieve the primary aim aligned with other countries. With the advent of intensive international trade and globalization export-oriented strategy was later adopted. In 2003, Tanzania came up with a National Trade Policy for competitive and export-led growth. However, the country faces stiff competition within the two communities—East Africa Community (EAC) and Southern Africa Development Community (SADC)—and outside the communities. With the introduction of the policy, the share in Tanzanian manufacturing increased from 8.38 percent in 1991 to 10.58 percent in 2013 with an annual growth rate of 1.11 percent. Although the share of agriculture in Tanzania declined during the period, the rate of decline is not very high (−1.36 percent annually). Its share changed from 36.07 percent to 28.36 percent. Similarly, the services sector experienced a moderate growth rate of 0.18 percent, resulting in its shift of share from 30.02 percent to 31.43 percent.

In terms of employment, the agriculture sector is still the largest employer. Its share of employment changed from 85.77 percent in 1991 to 69.21 percent in 2013. The rate of decline in employment share in the sector was −1.06 percent. Whereas, the employment share of the other two sectors recorded positive growth, that is, manufacturing 4.97 percent and services 3.28 percent. Like other African economies, the employment in "finance, insurance, real estate and business services," "transport, storage and communication" and "trade, restaurants and hotels" grew at the rates of 10.56 percent, 8.98 percent and 6.27 percent, respectively. Although the services sector in Tanzania recorded a positive growth rate, its share in employment remained very low (15.70 percent) in 2013.

2.6 Neither Agriculture nor Manufacturing

Industrialization is recognized as a stimulant of economic development as it accounts in large part for the considerable divide between the rich and the poor countries, as well for the significant differentials in wealth within countries. The level of industrialization is commonly measured by manufacturing employment or output share to GDP even as it is crucial to trade and investment across countries of the world. Industrialization simply reflects the structural shift or resource reallocation from low productive sector (agriculture) to high productive sector (manufacturing), and it is believed to be pivotal in economic transformation and the transition from stagnation to growth.

Economic structural change can be described as quantifiable structural shift (GDP or employment share of economic sectors explained by the level of development). This phenomenon involves observable economic transformation coupled with notable changes to the relative contribution of different sectors, in terms of production and factor use. The landmark point of an economy is when the share of employment in agriculture declines at a faster rate than the share of agriculture in GDP; when this occurs, labor productivity between the agricultural and nonagricultural sectors ceases to exist in the final stages of the transformation process. A substantial and prominent gap, which appears between labor productivities in the agricultural and nonagricultural sectors, precedes the convergence of labor productivities among sectors leading to inter-sectoral income inequalities and concentration of poverty in the agricultural sector (Lele, 2014).

The growth of sectors is highly influenced by governance roles that include the provision of high-quality infrastructure, establishment of regulatory frameworks and industrial policies, subsidies and taxation. Development plans were formulated by several African countries after independence, which imitated current-day discussion of industrial policy.[1] Enabling policies that result in the process of capital accumulation, structural change and technological progress brings economic transformation, thus requiring the strengthening of government capabilities (Ohno and Ohno, 2012; UNCTAD, 2006). East Asian countries that are successful today also faced the weak policy capability currently being experienced by African countries but overcame through dynamic capability development;[2] thus giving credence to the important role of governance and institutions. African economies have much to learn from successful cases that enhanced capital formation and the promotion of technological capability accumulation.

---

[1] E.g., Nigeria formulated successive five-year development plans since 1962, which was interrupted by the country's Civil War (1969–72).
[2] Focused hands-on endeavors to achieve concrete objective.

Economic backwardness of the latecomer[3] economies is implied in a variety of ways: the absence of strong and competent state institutions, weak entrepreneurial business firms, the somewhat low level of skill of engineers and technical personnel and nonexistence of well-educated and abundant low-cost managers (Amsden, 1989; Amsden and Chu, 2003). These reasons indicate that the weaker an economy is, the greater the coordination role of public agencies required, and the more backward a country is, the harsher the justice meted out by market forces. State action is not easy to define but it is necessary and required to build the capacity of African states to deal with the multifaceted requirements of ST.

Since the 1960s, African countries have been struggling on industrial path of development, and over the past three decades, these countries have experienced a disappointing performance in economic growth due to radical changes in development policies (Sundaram et al., 2011). In the early stage of postindependence period, most African countries started promoting industrialization with emphasis on autonomy and self-dependency with a view that industrialization would quicken the transformation of African countries from agrarian to modern economies, create employment opportunities, raise incomes and standards of living and reduce vulnerability to trade shocks resulting from dependence on primary commodity exports.

African countries also adopted several models of industrialization some of which included import substitution model (ISI); rural development model (RRD) from 1970s to 1980s; the SAP, which was in early 1980s; and the adoption of the Accelerated Industrial Development of Africa (AIDA) policy. Since 1970, there has been no significant change in the MVA of African states. MVA of GDP in Africa was 12.3 percent during 1970–74, 8.5 percent during 1975–79, 9.9 percent during 1980–84, which increased to 13.1 percent during 1985–89, declined to 12.7 percent during 1990–94, increased again to 13.3 percent during 1995–99, declined to 12.2 percent during 2000–2004, declined further to 10 percent during 2005–2009 and eventually to 9.6 percent during 2010–13 (UNIDO, 2016).

Examples of countries that witnessed decline in the share of MVA in total GDP during 1990–94 and 2000–2004 were South Africa, Mauritius, Cameroon, Zambia, Zimbabwe, Cote d'Ivoire and Kenya. South Africa recorded 24 percent MVA in 1990 and 19 percent in 2004, while Zambia reported 36 percent MVA in 1990, which declined to 11 percent in 2004; Kenya reported 12 percent in 1990, which declined to 11 percent in 2004. A stagnant share of 6 percent, 10 percent, 12 percent, 7 percent, 19 percent

---

[3] We define "latecomer" as a country that is late to meeting up certain key capabilities compared with both the forerunners at the global frontier as well as competitors.

and 9 percent MVA in total GDP between 2000 and 2004 was experienced in Botswana, Ghana, Burundi, Rwanda, South Africa and Tanzania, respectively (World Bank, 2015). Countries like Ethiopia, Kenya, South Africa, Swaziland, Madagascar, Lesotho and Mauritius had an increase in the relative share of manufacturing in total value added. This has generally been associated with the expansion of garment exports based on special preferences associated with the now-expired Agreement on Textiles and Clothing (Chemengich, 2010; Páez et al., 2010).

Industrialization can be measured by total share of employment in manufacturing sector. Over the years, African states have experienced continuing decline in the share of employment in manufacturing sector. During 1970–74, the share of employment in manufacturing sector, which was 20.3 percent, dropped to 17.9 percent during 1975–79, 16.1 percent during 1980–84, 15.4 percent during 1985–89, 14.5 percent during 1990–94, 13.7 during 1995–99, 12.5 percent during 2000–2004, 11.4 percent during 2005–2009 and 10.7 percent during 2010–13 (UNIDO, 2016).

Another dimension of the industrialization process in Africa is its sectoral share in GDP (i.e., manufacturing, mining and construction). The share of manufacturing in Africa's GDP rose from 9.88 percent during 1970–79 to 10.55 percent during 1980–89. Between 1990 and 1999, it fluctuated before experiencing an increase in subsequent years. It declined to 9.09 percent during 1995–99 from 9.29 percent during 1990–94; subsequently, it increased from 9.83 percent in 2000–2005 to 10.58 percent in 2006, 10.59 percent in 2007, 13.6 percent in 2008 and 12.9 percent in 2009 (UNECA, 2011).

Another parameter for measuring manufacturing performance is the value of commodity export (i.e., manufactured goods in global industrial exports). This indicator reveals that the share of manufactures exports of SSA declined from 1.12 percent during 1970–71 to 0.60 percent during the 1975–76 period (Fransman, 1982). Also, primary commodity exports accounted for approximately 14 percent of Africa's merchandise exports during 2002–12. During this period, the region's total merchandise exports (in value terms) grew at an average annual rate of 14 percent, rising from $100 billion to $400 billion. Much of this impressive performance was driven by the region's natural resources, underpinned by the commodity price boom of 2003–2008. Oil, metal and other mineral exports increased from $56 billion in 2002 to $288 billion in 2012, and oil exports alone accounted for over half of the goods exported in 2012 (World Bank, 2013).

Despite the promotion of industrialization policies by African states and the African Union Commission (AUC), industrialization has not taken a smooth course in most African countries. Though the role of ST in industrialization and economic development has been established, industrialization has not taken its place to enable ST in most African countries. Structural change requires the building up of new capabilities through learning, which is fostered and implemented through government policies and actions.

Although government intervention is sometimes subject to corruption, abuse and inefficiency, government failure to intervene may be as detrimental to development as market failure (Amsden, 2007: 94). The necessity is therefore about how the state should play a role, and the requirements for such roles to be effectively played. The more industrialized countries of East Asia and Latin America have addressed market imperfections, using extensive diverse but context-based industrial policies to support the development process through ST (Oyeyinka, 2012: 242). However, the latecomer faces evident the reality that "backwardness has been relatively greater" that demands from it, it requires more intensive effort by the state and actions that translate to policy competence.

2.7 Summing Up

African economies are characterized by dominance of low-productivity agriculture and petty service activities, the rise of a group of consumer-based industrial activities and services at the expense of manufacturing, an average low share of MVA in total GDP, heavy reliance on resource-based exports, which makes the region highly vulnerable to shocks in commodity prices, among others. These commodities are nonrenewable and are being depleted at a very rapid rate, thereby posing a threat to future growth and sustainability. With the current rate of 40 percent of urban dwellers in Africa, which is projected to rise to 60 percent by 2050, urbanization in African cities has been driven by natural resources exports rather than by industrial or agricultural revolution. This neither provides widespread employment nor inclusive wealth creation.

ST will only happen in Africa when there is an attendant investment in skill development, particularly in areas that have kept the continent behind other developing regions. In this regard, Africa needs to harness its natural resources to build skills for its youthful population in order to achieve its development objectives and secure a place in the global value chain. An enlightened population is important to Africa's global engagement in trade and commerce. ST also presupposes a transformed relationship between state and citizens; therefore, the fight against corruption and nepotism, human rights violations and poor stewardship of the economy, among others, needs to be won.

African countries have been growing at a relatively fast rate since the beginning of the new millennium, which in turn has led to improvements in several areas such as trade, mobilization of government revenue, infrastructure development, and the provision of social services. Historically, much of sub-Saharan countries adopted a package of policies aimed at either stimulation of economic growth or stabilization and adjustment in return for multilateral and bilateral loans. During the two decades of SAPs in Africa, several questions related to the appropriateness and efficacy of such measures was raised. Economic growth driven by various industrial development strategies has been considerable in several developing countries over the past decades. The Asian Tigers and the Newly Industrializing Economies (NIEs) have set such considerable standards of dynamic growth, showing that catching up with the traditionally viewed industrial leaders is possible.

Overall, economic transformation, which is often known to be associated with the migration of labor out of rural agricultural sector into the urban industrial sector, has not been strongly experienced in the African context during most of the first five decades of their independence. Driven by urbanization and decades of neglect of agriculture, most countries in the region have seen rapid labor migration out of a stagnating agriculture sector into an informal services sector—with even lower productivity levels. The contribution to overall economic productivity has therefore been negative.

Zero to negative growth in the industrial sector has led to the absorption of the growing labor force by the informal services sector, which has been expanding at a rapid pace; the agriculture sector, on the other hand, has shrunk faster than is normal under successful transformation. Africa also has the highest average GDP share for services among developing regions. The GDP share of the service sector in Africa is only slightly lower than the average share of Latin American countries, which have an average per capita income that is nearly eight times higher than the African average. This imbalance in sectoral growth has delayed ST and slowed productivity and income growth across Africa.

Job-rich growth and structural change are fundamental to addressing inequality in the long term as leaving large swathes of society in the mire of unemployment is costly to economies and societies. Unemployment lowers growth and productivity and throws the economy into an inefficiency cycle. Due to the strong association between lower levels of inequality in developing countries and sustained periods of economic growth, long-run sustainability is required to sustain equality. Other factors such as the role of the state in long-run growth, governance, state capacity and skills are required. But low inequality is a necessary condition.

Chapter 3

LOSING THE URBAN ADVANTAGE

3.1 Introduction

Urbanization is closely linked with the process of ST and industrialization. ST refers to the reallocation of economic activities across the three broad sectors (agriculture, manufacturing and services) that are associated with productivity increase and economic growth. As countries urbanize, their economies modernize toward highly productive sectors such as industries and manufacturing. The analysis of ST and productivity changes are key to understanding the mechanisms behind urbanization. Reversely, analyzing urbanization is essential to understand the causes of SC.

In traditional growth patterns, ST and urbanization are deeply interrelated. Both phenomena are characterized by the same movement of labor from the rural and agricultural sectors to the manufacturing and urban sectors. This process normally translates into higher productivity levels and overall economic growth. However, the observed lessons from developed countries does not seem to apply to all developing countries, where urbanization is often not accompanied by industrialization. The example of African countries is particularly striking. Africa's transformation trajectory is very dissimilar to the conventional pattern of growth whereby sustainable urbanization proceeds with transformation from agriculture to productive manufacturing. Contrarily, African cities are crowded with migrants from rural areas with little skill sets and mostly engaged in low-value services rather than high-value manufacturing.

Recent empirical evidence indicates that ST could occur without change in labor productivity, especially in the case of African economies. Most importantly, this situation is common in natural resource exporters (Jedwab et al., 2013). Many African countries tend to specialize in the export of natural resource, which constrain conventional transitions experienced in industrialized settings. Natural resource–exporting countries tend to urbanize without significantly increasing their GDP share of manufacturing output. It is worth noting that the most urbanized countries export natural resources: oil (Angola, Gabon and Nigeria), diamonds and/or gold (Botswana, Liberia and

South Africa). In these countries, urbanization takes place without significant change in the economic structure. A recent analysis looked at ST and productivity growth in eleven sub-Saharan countries during the past 50 years (McMillan et al., 2014). It suggests that the early postindependence period had brought an augmentation of manufacturing activities due to the reallocation of resources, resulting in economic growth. However, in the following period from the mid-1970s to the 1980s, the process of SC attenuated. While growth rebounded in the 1990s, workers relocated to the services industries rather than the manufacturing and industrial sectors.

A recent empirical study by Jedwab et al. (2013) found that countries for which exports of natural resources account for more than 10 percent of GDP constitute the great majority of the countries that urbanized without ST. For the same urbanization rate, cities in natural resource exporting countries have a lesser share of manufacturing and tradable services. In 2015, around 48 percent of the Nigerian population lived in cities, and manufacturing accounted for 9.5 percent of GDP in the African country. For the same urbanization level, manufacturing accounted for 32 percent in 2009 in China. The GDP per capita associated to the same urbanization level was US$4,100 in China compared to US$2,550 in Nigeria (World Bank, 2011). This shows that urbanization has not enhanced manufacturing and wealth in Nigeria—an oil exporter country—in the same way as it did in China that has known a great economic success over the past decade. This is explained by the fact that large export surplus obtained in these countries are used to import food and manufactured goods. Therefore, the composition of urban employment varies considerably between resource-exporters and non-exporters (Jedwab et al., 2013).

African countries, and particularly resource-exporter countries, tend to experience the emergence of "consumption cities" in which a large share of workers is employed in non-tradable services, including commerce, transportation or personal and government services. These types of cities are different from "production cities" that have more workers in more productive sectors such as manufacturing and high-value services, according to traditional patterns. For example, it is estimated that Angola's urbanization rate was 15 percent before the discovery of oil in the 1960s compared to 60 percent in 2010. Although oil accounts for over half of GDP, the sector only employs around 10,000 workers (Gollin et al., 2016). "Consumption cities" tend to have higher poverty rates and higher shares of population living in slums. On the contrary, "production cities" have a larger share of workers in industrial sectors like manufacturing or in tradable services like finance. For example, in cities of resource-exporter countries such as Luanda, Lagos and Libreville, the portion of workers in manufacturing is lower compared to that of Johannesburg, Seoul or Kuala Lumpur, although these cities have similar levels of urbanization.

While Africa has urbanized to the same level as Asia over the past decades, Asian labor productivity was 1.9 times and 2.3 times higher in industry and services, respectively (Gollin et al., 2016). This is because African cities lack opportunities in skill-intensive and productive activities such as manufacturing that constraint labor movement from rural to urban areas. Consequently, new migrants constitute labor that is unemployed or underemployed. This absence of industrialization translates into the phenomenon of urbanization without growth. While cities are the driving force for economic development in conventional model of growth, urbanization seems to occur in the absence of economic growth in most sub-Saharan African countries (Oyeyinka and Lal, 2016).

Additionally, the phenomenon of *ghost towns* and *ghost cities* is also on the rise in Africa and coincides with the existence of consumption cities. The term "ghost towns" refers to towns that were once prosperous but damaged and abandoned as a result of wars, conflicts, famine or forced migration. Residents of these towns evacuated to supposedly safer cities but are relocated to slums in which living conditions are decidedly appalling, while other parts of the ghost cities are empty because they are unaffordable. Ghost cities refer to cities where no person or few people live due to high cost of housing and services in a predominantly poor country. This is the case of Kilamba, 30 km from the capital, Luanda in Angola, where the real estate market is dysfunctional and where many buildings are empty due to the prohibitive costs of houses. In this consumption city, part of the housing stock is regarded as an investment rather than a shelter.

The rich could afford to buy apartments in the new estates but do not care about leaving them empty because the tax system does not give any incentive not to do so. This is true in the case of Kilamba City, as it is in Abuja and Lagos in Nigeria, although the latter are not representative of the ghost city that Kilamba is. Another example is Nairobi, which also has an expensive housing market while one-fourth of the population lives in slums. New real estate development projects are increasing in the city, leaving the poorest behind. Although this phenomenon is not widespread in the entire region, it is likely to characterize other African cities if the same urbanization pattern continues.

Unarguably, urbanization is one of the most significant global trends of the twenty-first century. In 2008, for the first time in history, the global urban population outnumbered the rural population. As at 2018, 55 percent of the world's population were living in urban areas. This figure was less than 20 percent only one century ago. Urban population is expected to further increase at an unprecedented rate, with 68 percent of the world population projected to be living in urban areas by 2050 (UNDESA, 2018). Most of this growth is expected to occur in developing nations, which will contribute to 90 percent of the world urban population growth. African cities have grown rapidly in the recent past. At the end of the twentieth century, Africa's urban population was 35 percent and today it stands at 41 percent. As at 2018, urban areas contained 472 million people, and this is expected to double over the next 25 years. The global share of African urban residents is projected to grow from 11.3 percent in 2010 to 20.2 percent by 2050 (Center for Strategic and International Studies (CSIS), 2018). Although Africa is currently the least urbanized continent, with only 41 percent of urban population, it is the fastest urbanizing. The growth from the past decade is expected to continue at an even increasing rate. African urbanization is entering a critical phase where many cities will be doubling in size and playing a significant role in the national economy. For instance, Africa is currently home to three of the world's megacities, defined as cities hosting more than 10 million inhabitants, including Cairo, Lagos and Kinshasa. By 2030, three more are expected to emerge. These are Dar es Salaam, Johannesburg and Luanda, which are each projected to surpass the 10 million mark (United Nations Department of Economic and Social Affairs (UNDESA), 2014).

Although urbanization brings about many challenges, it offers great potential for growth and development both at the local and national level. Past experiences have shown that economic growth and rising living standards have gone hand in hand with urbanization. Currently, cities are said to account for about 70 percent of global GDP (World Bank, 2009). In most countries, the contribution of their cities to their national GDP far exceeds their contribution to the total country's population. Economic activities in urban areas account for as much as 55 percent of the GDP in low-income countries, 73 percent in middle-income countries and 85 percent in high-income economies (UN-Habitat and Department for International Development (DFID), 2002). This indicates that urban workers are more productive than their rural counterparts. According to projections, the productivity level of urban workers is going to increase further, with 80 percent of future global economic growth attributed to cities alone (Swedish International Development Cooperation Agency (SIDA), 2006).

Despite the disproportionate economic contribution of urban areas and their high level of productivity, urbanization is often ignored in development policy or not duly integrated in development strategies and plans. This neglect is especially prevalent in Africa where urbanization has been associated with growing urban poverty and unemployment. This has led numerous policy makers in Africa to formulate policies to halt rapid urbanization. However, studies have shown that the level of urbanization and GDP per capita is positive (Fay and Opal, 2000). Countries with higher GDP growth experienced faster urbanization, and rapid urbanization came hand in hand with higher growth in industries and services. This is primarily because urbanization and ST are two processes that go hand in hand and mutually reinforce one another. Urbanization is a powerful force for transformation as it enables agglomeration that facilitates industrial productions and economies of scale.

This chapter analyzes urban dynamics and potential. It highlights the flip side of rapid urbanization and how national economies might miss out on the gains from the urban advantage. It also examines the phenomenon of "consumption cities" and absence of industrialization in urban centers. Finally, the chapter provides recommendations on seizing the urban advantage in Africa to achieve SC and economic growth.

3.2 Urban Opportunities and Challenges

Throughout history, in rich as well as poor countries, urbanization has been closely associated with economic development. No nation has grown to middle income without urbanizing, or to high income without vibrant cities (Harvey, 2009). This is because economic and social development is intimately related to urban areas, which have been indispensable to achieve productivity gains. As a result, the increase of urban population has not only generated the resources for infrastructure and services that are shared within cities but has also significantly increased labor productivity. Therefore, continued urbanization represents a virtuous circle that enhances productivity increase and, in turn, higher national income.

A century of experience indicates that as developing countries move up the income ladder, labor increasingly moves from the agricultural to the industrial and services sectors. Workers leave their villages and their agrarian occupations to move into larger and denser settlements in which productivity is higher and where concentration and agglomeration matter. Unlike the rural sector, proximity plays an important role within urban spaces to access not only markets for goods and services, but also ideas and knowledge (Harvey, 2009). Due to scale economies, workers in cities are more productive compared to the same unit of labor in the rural sector, and they earn a higher income level. Consequently, urbanization theorists see cities as a space that represents an opportunity to earn higher income for excess labor from rural areas (Lewis, 1954). Due to higher levels of productivity, cities experience higher economic outcomes and employment opportunities, which translate into greater prosperity at both the local and national levels.

Agglomeration economies and external economies of scale are the main principles that explain why people in larger cities are more productive than those located in small towns or rural areas. It is fundamental to understand how agglomeration economics explains the higher productivity level of larger cities. According to the New Economic Geography, firms particularly benefit from agglomeration economies as it enables them to be close to other firms. This in turn reduces their transaction costs and allows them to gain from network effects, such as shared information (Ellisson et al., 2010; Turok and McGranahan, 2013). Being located in close proximity promotes positive externalities among economic agents, such as the reduction of business costs, as well as improved interaction and knowledge spillovers (Turok, 2004). Urban areas also provide giant market places, which facilitate trade and commerce, making the production of many goods and services more efficient (UN-Habitat, 2012). In addition to this, the benefits of agglomeration economies include proximity to a large labor pool, suppliers, customers and competitors within the same industry, and firms in other industries (Turok and McGranahan, 2013).

Due to the advantages of agglomeration economy, economic growth and rising living standards ordinarily proceed in tandem with urbanization. Therefore, there has been a puzzle regarding Africa's rapid urbanization and why it has not been accompanied by greater economic dynamism. Some scholars regard Africa as a major exception to the urbanization-development nexus. Past studies found no relationship between urbanization and development in Africa. However, recent studies reveal that countries with higher GDP growth experienced faster urbanization and that rapid urbanization go hand-in hand with higher growth in services. A counterfactual of an Africa without urbanization is one with even slower economic growth, greater GDP per capita losses, and increases in poverty (Harvey, 2009).

In Africa, the rising number of urban dwellers creates large centers for consumption and represents considerable market opportunities favoring businesses. This enhances job creation and increases productivity due to the concentration of commercial and industrial activities, boosting growth and development. There is also proof that African cities improve human development and enhances living standards as they improved access to infrastructure. Education levels, health conditions and sanitation of urban dwellers are also better than their rural counterparts. Figures show that the higher the urban population share, the higher the life expectancy at birth and the higher school enrollments (Arouri et al., 2014).

3.2.1 The Flip Side of Rapid Urbanization

Over the past two decades, Africa has been experiencing the fastest urbanization rate compared to other regions of the world. In 2015, the annual urban population growth rate was 4.1 percent in SSA as opposed to 2.3 percent in

East Asia and 1.4 percent in Latin America (World Bank, 2011). This fast-paced growth of African cities is not limited to the number of people but also extends to the size of cities. Many challenges arise from the rapidity of this process in African countries, which counteracts the benefits gained from urbanization.

In theory, urbanization is caused by pull factors such as better access to jobs, basic services and social safety nets. However, African cities tend to be the results of push factors from rural conflicts and rural degradation (UN-Habitat, 2012). While cities have the potential to spur growth and development, inadequate infrastructure and poor planning or management has posed enormous challenges to urban dwellers in Africa. For instance, it is estimated that Africa's enormous infrastructure deficit requires US$178 billion a year to service adequate growth and service delivery (Vollgraaff and Thukwana, 2018). Most of this infrastructure investment is needed in cities despite municipal government's limited financial capacity. Much of all cities are under-resourced to fulfill their potential as drivers of national economic development, while the key drivers of productivity found in urban areas have been neglected by African governments (Gollin et al., 2016).

The rapid urbanization of Africa mostly arises from the influx of migrants from rural areas. The extensive rural–urban migration for people seeking economic opportunities in cities put significant strains on resources and infrastructure of African cities. However, the inflow of migrants has outpaced the creation of jobs in the formal economy, and the informal economy has been the major source of employment for these newcomers. Urbanization in Africa is therefore associated with a significant increase of the informal sector. Over the past decades, informal work has accounted for 66 percent of urban employment in SSA (ILO, 2015a). This has considerable repercussions as the informal sector is both less productive and tends to reduce economic growth in developing countries. Furthermore, in terms of living standards, workers employed in the informal sectors are more likely to be worse off in terms of salary and working conditions than those working in the formal economy.

In addition to rapid rural to urban migration, cities in Africa are poorly regulated and planned, which further encourages informality and illegality. The rapid proliferation of slums is the most visible sign of the challenges caused by urbanization and is explained by the cities' lack of resources to meet basic needs such as housing. While slums are not specific to Africa, the continent has the highest share of urban slum dwellers. In 2014, more than a half of urban dwellers in SSA lived in slums, as opposed to one-fourth in East Asia and close to one-third in South Asia (World Bank, 2011). In certain African cities, slum inhabitants make up a large proportion of the urban residents. For example, in Nairobi, around a quarter of the population live in sprawling slums (UN-Habitat, 2012). This poses multiple threats to the health and safety of the new migrants and those already residing in slums as the living and safety conditions tend to be worse in urban slums than in rural areas. This type of informal settlements is associated with the lack of water and sanitation and insecurity of tenure that especially affects the most vulnerable. In 2015, 60 percent of the urban population in SSA did not have access to improved sanitation facilities (World Bank, 2011).

This is accentuated by urban primacy that characterized the urbanization process of Africa. In 2015, 28.4 percent of the urban population were living in each country's largest city, as opposed to 22.8 percent in Latin America and 11.7 percent in East Asia. This is a threat to the sustainable development of the continent as too much pressure on one single location is detrimental to achieve urban economic growth. Evidence shows that in the case where the largest city in a country grows too large compared to other cities, urban development does not favor economic growth (Duranton, 2008). Similarly, negative effects arise when a primate city is above its optimal size and that the excessive urban primacy experienced in Africa has a significant negative impact on economic growth (Overman and Venables, 2005). The demographic pressure in African cities also leads to negative externalities such as congestion and pollution. All these challenges are exacerbated by climate and environmental change.

Little access to employment opportunities, insecure housing, violent environment and limited access to health and education opportunities all result in urban poverty. This is accentuated by the high costs of living in cities that urban incomes, although higher than rural income, cannot compensate for. Housing costs but also the costs of informal service provision that people must turn to are very high. In addition to urban poverty, urban inequalities are present in most cities of Africa. In fact, the region has the highest level of urban inequality in the world (UN-Habitat, 2010). This is because only a few benefits from the urban advantage, while the majority is left behind.

3.3 Seizing the Urban Advantage in Africa

Some African governments tend to consider urbanization as an uncontrollable pathology and have attempted to restrain this process. However, efforts to contain the flow of migrants have not been successful. Urbanization should rather be included in the policy formulation process as it is a cross-cutting subject impacting both social and economic development. The negative effects of urbanization are often overemphasized, although cities represent the best hope for growth opportunities and drivers of economic development. While urban challenges are undeniable, cities are still loci of economic activities that generate economic output as well as employment. In addition, urbanization is associated with rising incomes and living standards. The central role of cities in national economies is more significant in developing countries than in developed countries. The largest cities in Africa account for 36 percent of GDP while only accounting for 16 percent of the total population because of higher labor productivity emanating from agglomeration economies (Godfrey and Zhao, 2014).

Attaining full urban efficiency is extremely difficult to achieve. However, when urbanization is properly managed and planned, African countries could reap the full benefits offered by their cities. The existence of urban inefficiencies only means that cities are less efficient than they could be. Well-designed urban policies could help in counteracting this inefficiency by unlocking the urban potential and generating important gains. Urbanization must be guided through adequate policies designed and implemented at both the national and local levels in order to become a force for ST and development. Not all types of urbanization lead to economic transformation and development. It is sustainable urbanization that contributes to the local and national economies. Sustainable urbanization refers to urban development that impact the economy, the society and the environment in a beneficial manner for the present generation without damaging the living standards and condition of future generations. Sustainable urbanization is enhanced by proper planning, financing and legal mechanisms.

Steered urbanization is essential to prevent challenges, but most importantly, it allows countries to reap gains from urbanization. First, this implies adequate urban governance as well as necessary funding. Local governments should not only receive new responsibilities but should also be given additional financial resources. Political decentralization can only work when accompanied by fiscal decentralization that is a prerequisite for competent management of the urbanization process.

Second, it implies the provision of suitable and enough housing with basic infrastructure. Considerable investments in infrastructure are required to address the influx of people and associated challenges in terms of health, housing, public services, jobs and safety (KPMG, 2012). Improving the quality of infrastructure is essential to provide a business-friendly environment and to enhance the productivity of cities. This includes national networks for telecommunications, electricity and transport in addition to local services for public transport, water and sanitation. Improving the access to serviced land for enterprises is also important for the same purpose. Local governments also need to reform local regulations that impede the operating conditions for enterprises. Legal reforms are indispensable to improve the investment climate of African cities, to enable business creation and expansion, and in turn to generate jobs. Regarding urban primacy, the phenomenon should be attenuated to release the pressure on prime cities. New urban hierarchies must be found while the importance of secondary cities and urban development corridors should be recognized.

All urban dwellers should be able to benefit from the urban advantage. Therefore, cities should be made livable and inclusive. Measures should be taken to prevent insecure tenure and dysfunctional land markets that are affecting the poor. Furthermore, efforts should make the jobs in the informal economy more productive. Targeting informal employment and information settlements in policies would include most urban residents and be a step further toward urban equality.

Furthermore, the large number of youth population in urban areas constitutes a reservoir of labor for transformation and growth and should be seen as an economic asset. Africa is the youngest continent in the world with close to 70 percent of its population aged below 25 (AfDB, 2011). Large shares of these youth constitute the total labor force in Africa. This gives rise to a demographic dividend in African cities, which is promising to promote development.

In a nutshell, urbanization and SC can reinforce each other provided that the required infrastructure and services are supplied, the proper institutions are set up, and adequate planning is specified. Urbanization, industrialization and economic growth are closely interrelated and can mutually reinforce each other when proper policy guidance is applied (UN-Habitat, 2014). This is to bring African cities back to the conventional growth path and to ensure the development of production cities, rather than consumption cities.

3.4 Putting Numbers to the Narrative

3.4.1 Regional Analysis

The regional analyses aim to determine the possible association between urbanization and GDP per capita, on the one hand, and between urbanization and labor productivity, on the other hand. By so doing, we attempt to fill a gap in empirical studies because little effort has been made to determine the relationship between urbanization and ST. Labor productivity is considered an appropriate indicator to measure industrialization. Productivity growth can be brought about by well-guided industrial policies, human capabilities, in addition to optimum allocation of resources that foster technological innovation.

Figure 3.1 shows that the relationship between the level of urbanization and per capita income across African cities is positive (World Bank). It indicates that per capita incomes do not reach more than US$2,000 for majority of

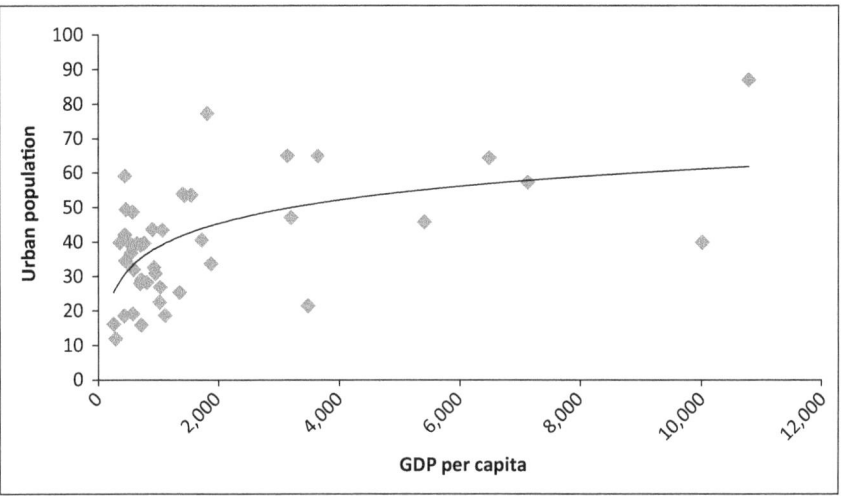

Figure 3.1 Economic growth and urbanization in sub-Saharan Africa
Source: WDI online

African countries and that less than half of the population is urbanized. Very few countries reach per capita income of US$4,000 before being 50 percent urbanized. This suggests that as countries urbanize, they get richer, and they accumulate skills and infrastructural assets to modernize. At the early stages of development, urbanization correlates strongly with GDP growth, but this correlation weakens as countries get wealthier.

On average in 2015, with 37.7 percent of its population residing in urban areas, SSA had a GDP per capita of US$1,571; South Asia with 33 percent of its population residing in urban areas, had a GDP per capita of US$1,528; East Asia and Pacific had 56.6 percent of urban population and a GDP per capita of US$9,337 while Latin America and Caribbean had 79.8 percent urban population and a GDP per capita of US$8,370 (World Bank). The figures show that SSA has not harnessed the potential of its urban population enough to translate to GDP growth.

There are, however, few exceptions. Some countries with higher levels of urbanization—exceeding 50 percent—have low levels of income, implying that urbanization alone is not enough to generate wealth and growth. These countries might not reap the full advantages of agglomerations present within urban areas. It is also possible that urbanization occurs without long-term economic growth. For example, SSA has been characterized by rapid urbanization without the expected economic growth, suggesting that there are other factors contributing to the economic growth. These include appropriate urban planning, and policy and governance, in addition to adequate institutions capable to address the numerous challenges due to rapid urbanization.

This figure indicates that labor productivity is very low in the majority of sub-Saharan countries (World Bank). GDP per person employed, which is our measure of labor productivity, does not exceed US$10,000 in most cases. On average, labor productivity in SSA is low with US$11,486 GDP per person employed. Countries with higher labor productivity tend to have higher urbanization levels leaving a positive association between urbanization and labor productivity. Nevertheless, there are countries with higher urbanization levels but without high productivity. This implies that urbanization alone is not enough to raise productivity levels. Although urbanization helps, its full potential is not realized in some countries to achieve labor productivity growth, which is essential in the process of ST.

3.4.2 Country-Level Analysis

In this section, we analyze for selected countries of SSA the relationship between urbanization (World Bank) and living standards measured as the HDI (UNDP dataEM1_9781785273445.docx - CIT000140), and thereafter turn to the association between urbanization and labor productivity, measured as GDP per person employed (World Bank). We measure living standards by HDI because it is a better indicator of development and prosperity as opposed to income alone. As we have data for the selected countries, we analyze HDI rather than GDP per capita as we did for the regional analysis. HDI is composed of three indices, namely, life expectancy, education and income per capita. While life expectancy is measured as the life expectancy at birth, education is measured as mean years of schooling and expected years of schooling. Income per capita is based on gross national income. HDI data were only available till year 2013 therefore, the analysis is limited to the 2005–13 period.

Before going into the analysis of each country separately, it is considered crucial to present the overall picture of quality of life and urbanization in Africa. The relationship between HDI and DU was quantified using TOBIT analysis and results are presented in Table 3.1. Before subjecting the data to TOBIT analysis, the series were tested for stationarity by using unit root test.

TOBIT is preferred over Ordinary Least Square (OLS) estimates as the dependent variable, that is, HDI is a truncated nonnegative variable with 1 as upper limit. One of the differences between TOBIT and OLS estimates is the iterative procedure followed in TOBIT. Which results in more robust and precise estimates while base results of TOBIT are like that of OLS. It can be

Table 3.1 Degree of Urbanization and Living Standards

Country	Constant Term	Degree of Urbanization			Log Likelihood	Significance level
		Coeff.	t-value	P>|t|		
Botswana	−1.364	0.036	17.26	0.00	35.879	0.00
Ethiopia	−0.256	0.038	10.15	0.00	28.801	0.00
Ghana	0.013	0.011	21.68	0.00	41.389	0.00
Kenya	0.114	0.017	18.59	0.00	40.965	0.00
Nigeria	0.277	0.005	11.89	0.00	40.054	0.00
South Africa	0.270	0.006	3.01	0.015	30.015	0.011
Tanzania	0.074	0.014	32.72	0.00	43.802	0.00
Uganda	0.080	0.027	10.53	0.00	34.280	0.00

Source: Author's calculations

seen from the Table 3.1 that the coefficient of the DU is statistically significant at the 1 percent level (highest level) for all the countries except South Africa where the level of significance is 5 percent.

From Table 3.1, the coefficients of DU are positive for all sample countries suggesting that there is a positive association between HDI and the DU. The magnitude of the coefficients represents the slope of the line of the association. The results show that the slopes of the line are different for all countries. The slope is highest in the case of Ethiopia suggesting that Ethiopia witnessed the highest change in HDI controlling for urbanization. On the other hand, the slope (0.036) of the line for Botswana is the second smallest. Although Ethiopia and Botswana witnessed almost similar urbanization growth, the DU at base year (2000) was different, accounting for 14.74 percent and 53.22 percent, respectively. These findings show that despite a high level of urbanization in Botswana, HDI and urbanization are going hand in hand. This is not the case for South Africa, which is at a comparable level with Botswana.

The slope of the line for Nigeria is smallest (0.005). The association between HDI and urbanization in Nigeria is like that of South Africa. The DU changed from 39.07 percent in 2005 to 46.09 percent in 2013, while HDI changed from 0.47 percent to 0.50 percent. In Nigeria, urbanization is increasing rapidly, but its contribution to the national income is not significant. As evident from SC in Nigeria, the focus was on the agriculture sector where the productivity and the contribution to the national income is low, but the sector provides employment opportunity to a large but relatively poor population living on small farm proceeds.

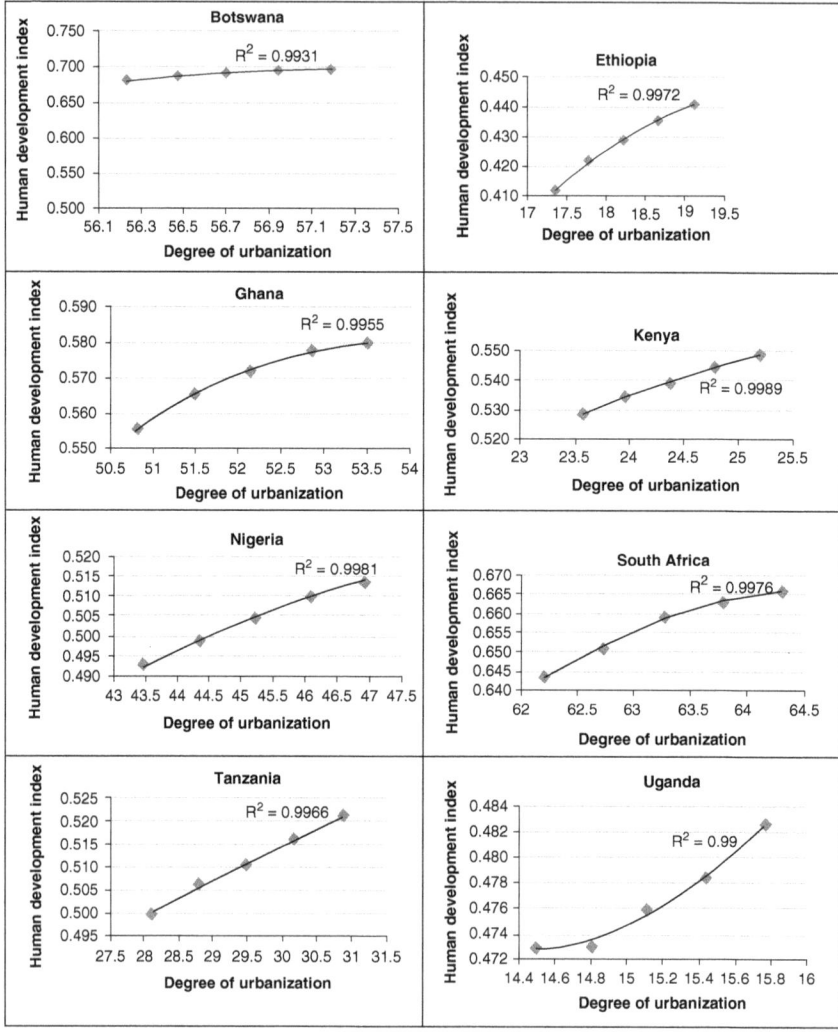

Figure 3.2 Human Development Index and degree of urbanization in African countries

Figure 3.2 presents the association between HDI and urbanization, while the association between labor productivity and urbanization is depicted in Figure 3.3. Tunisia is excluded from the analysis due to lack of data. The R-square values presented in Figure 3.2 are based on single quadratic equation model rather than linear association. The issues of endogenous and exogenous variables are relevant for simultaneous equation models rather than single

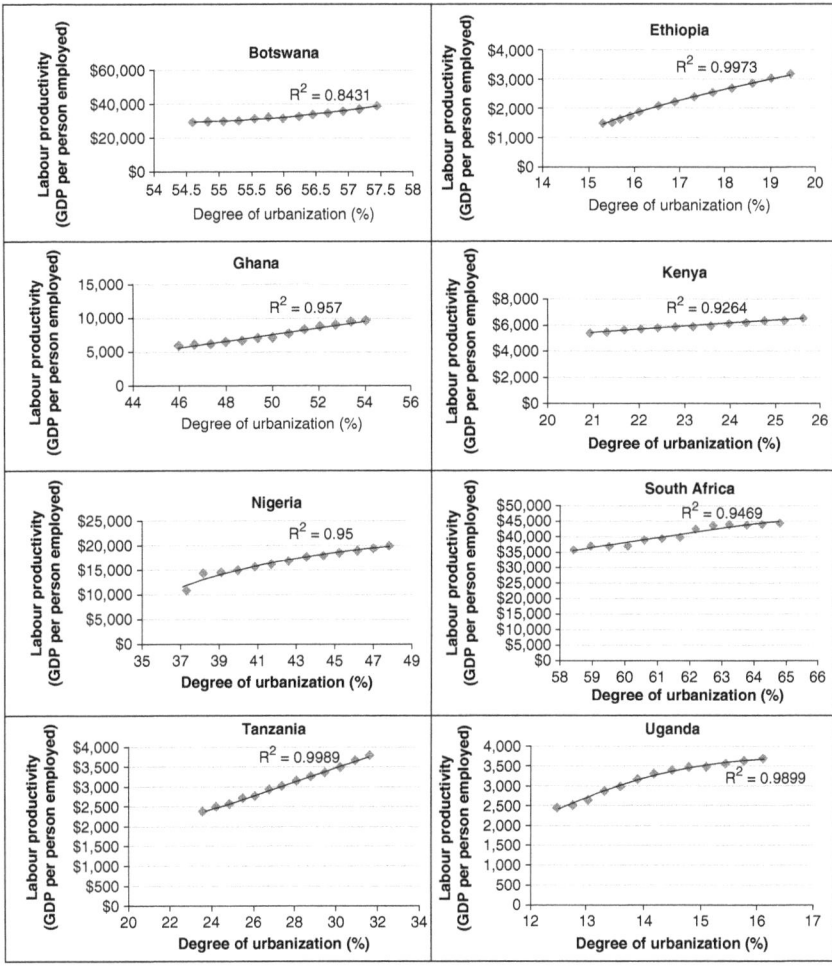

Figure 3.3 Labor productivity and degree of urbanization in African countries

equation. Hence endogeneity issue is not relevant for the results presented in the chapter.

Botswana

Botswana has a very high level of urbanization compared to the regional average. The analysis shows a positive relationship between HDI and urbanization. The very high R-square indicates that this association is strongly significant. As Botswana urbanizes, development metrics improve in the country. However, this relationship appears to weaken over time, as the DU increases. The quadratic relationship means there is a certain level of urbanization (a threshold) at which the relationship weakens. After reaching a level of urbanization of 56.9 percent in 2013 and an HDI of 0.696, the level of development does not seem to change much although urbanization continues to increase.

Other forms of associations such as linear and log-linear, power functions were tried. The functional form that gave the highest R-square has been considered the best fit. This shows that the association between the two is quadratic in nature with a very high R-square. The quadratic form of the association suggests that the rate of change of HDI becomes inelastic to the change in the DU at a certain level of HDI. That level is defined as the threshold level of HDI. The quadratic effect means that the association between urbanization and HDI is not constant but depends on the specific value of urbanization. Beyond a certain value of urbanization, the quadratic model suggests that expected HDI will stabilize.

The relationship between urbanization and labor productivity, measured as the GDP per person employed, was also tested. It shows that productivity growth is in tandem with urbanization. This means that productivity increases as Botswana urbanizes. In addition, the fact that the slope is steeper after 56 percent of urbanization implies that the productivity increases faster from this urbanization level.

Ethiopia

In the case of Ethiopia, the R-square is very high implying that the association between HDI and urbanization is strongly significant. This means that additional DU commensurately contributes to the national economy. As opposed to other countries, the HDI does not seem to reach any threshold in Ethiopia. This is because degrees of urbanization in Ethiopia are still low, less than 20 percent. As Ethiopia urbanizes, it is expected that HDI will stabilize if the country follows the same patterns.

In terms of labor productivity, it is also positively linked with urbanization. This association is statistically significant due to a very high R-square. This means that agglomeration economies found in urban areas resulted in productivity growth. Ethiopia has used the advantages of urbanization to raise labor productivity by establishing industrial zones for light manufacturing based on local raw materials.

Ghana

In Ghana, the relationship between urbanization and HDI is positive and significant. Living standards and development improve as Ghana urbanizes. However, this relationship weakens as urbanization increases. In 2013, Ghana reached a 52.7 percent urbanization level associated with an HDI of 0.577. From this point, urbanization did not contribute much to an increase in HDI. This means that the contribution to economic development by new migrants from the rural areas is comparatively low.

Concerning the linkages between urbanization and labor productivity, the best fit was a linear relationship. It suggests that there is no threshold level of urbanization at which the association weakens.

Kenya

Empirical evidences suggest that urbanization and HDI increased proportionately in Kenya. The pattern of growth of urbanization and HDI in Kenya is much like that of Ethiopia. In both countries, HDI did not reach the threshold level at which it becomes inelastic to urbanization.

Nigeria

In Nigeria, evidence shows a strong quadratic association between the DU and prosperity, which is the result of SC. The nature of the quadratic association is that DU and HDI go hand in hand up to a certain level of urbanization beyond which HDI becomes almost inelastic to DU. However, in the case of Nigeria, it did not reach the HDI threshold level.

South Africa

South Africa has the highest level of urbanization among the selected countries. In fact, it is one of the most urbanized countries in SSA. Similar to other countries of the sample, the association between DU and HDI is positive and strongly significant. However, both DU and HDI did not increase much over the period.

Tanzania

The association between HDI and DU is almost linear. There is no threshold point at which HDI becomes inelastic to DU, because DU is very low in Tanzania. Although the best fit between the two is quadratic in nature, there is no sign of any threshold level of HDI being reached. It implies that the contribution of the newly urbanized population is like that of existing urbanized population.

Uganda

The association between HDI and DU is different from other sample countries. Initially HDI almost remained static with respect to DU but changed proportionately and has not yet reached threshold level of urbanization when HDI becomes inelastic. The association between urbanization and labor productivity is like most of the other sample countries.

3.5 Summing Up

Sustainable urbanization, which translates to safe and resilient human settlements, fosters sustainable growth pathways, reduces inequality, increases productivity and economic opportunities. The linkages between urbanization and economic development suggest that the association between both factors is positive in all countries. The DU also varies between countries from 18.59 percent in Ethiopia to 63.79 percent in South Africa in 2013.

In Africa, Botswana and Ethiopia reached a threshold level of HDI. Beyond this point, the index becomes inelastic to the growth of urban population. The stagnation of HDI at high degrees of urbanization is comprehensible; for this country, the HDI became inelastic to urbanization at the level of 17.74 percent of urban population. The decline in productivity in high-productive sectors, such as industry and manufacturing, has been the major reasons for the stagnation of economic development.

SC results in higher income and better quality of life. Urbanization can breed misery if it is not sustainable as it creates slums, rising congestion, pollution, pressure on natural resources, higher labor and property costs and higher levels of crime and insecurity. This is often in the form of negative externalities or agglomeration diseconomies, which could prevent private investment, reduce urban productivity and hold back growth. Sustainable urbanization and formation of cities can also be harnessed to boost productivity (which increases as workers migrate from agricultural work into urban jobs), demand and investment. If properly harnessed, urbanization and strategic positioning of cities will boost production.

A strategy to promote efficient urbanization should target density level, land market efficiency, connectivity, potential for industrialization and interventions arising from pollution, congestion and concentration of people in vulnerable areas. Efficient governance institutions and effective political leadership are critical to address the interrelated challenges of urbanization and maximize its potentials; the capacity to produce sustainable solutions could also be harnessed. Urban governance is an essential component to effectively manage cities; national, local and regional governments play a strategic roles in guiding economic, social and environmental policy decisions to sustain the quality of urban areas. It is also essential that policies and decision-making are centered on local conditions and viewed within the current economic and social contexts. Overall, economic transformation, which is often known to be associated with the migration of labor out of the rural agricultural sector into the urban industrial sector, has not been strongly experienced in the African context during most of the first five decades of their independence. Driven by urbanization and decades of neglect of agriculture, most countries in the region have seen rapid labor migration out of a stagnating agriculture sector into an informal services sector—with even lower productivity levels. The contribution to overall economic productivity has therefore been negative.

Chapter 4

PATHWAYS TO PRODUCTIVITY GROWTH IN AFRICA

4.1 Introduction

Productivity is the measure of production efficiency, such as labor and capital and how it is being used in an economy to produce a given level of output. It is considered a key source of economic growth and competitiveness, and as such serve as the basis for international comparisons and country-performance assessments (Krugman, 1994). At the industry level, productivity growth is very important as it allows an industry to compete with other sectors of the economy for resources (labor, capital and raw materials) and maintain international competitiveness. There are different measures of productivity and the choice between them depends either on the purpose of the productivity measurement and/or data availability.

Productivity measures include GDP per hour worked and multifactor productivity (MFP), also known as total factor productivity (TFP), which measures the residual growth that cannot be explained by the rate of change in the services of labor, capital and intermediate outputs. MFP is often interpreted as the contribution to economic growth made by factors such as technical and organizational innovation (OECD, 2008). In development economics, labor productivity is one of the major determinants of productivity growth. It measures economic growth and output of a country and has strong implications for economic growth (Heshmati and Rashidghalam, 2016).

Continuous increase in labor productivity is a critical factor for development while ST and skills development are essential for increasing labor productivity. Over time, developed nations have been able to diversify away from low-productivity sectors (agriculture and traditional products) and, as labor and other resources move from agriculture into modern economic activities, overall productivity rises and incomes expand (McMillan et al., 2014). Empirical evidence in this book confirm that productivity increase could be attributed to ST and varying factors at individual level (health, education, skills and experience), at enterprise level (management, investment in plant and equipment, occupational safety and health) and at national level (national macroeconomic and competition policies, economic growth strategies, policies for business environment, level of investment in public infrastructure and education).

In Africa, despite the unprecedented high, sustained economic growth witnessed in the last two decades, African states have been experiencing productivity-reducing SC (Rodrik and McMillan, 2011). On average, a firm in Africa produces about $3,000 of output per worker compared to China, Indonesia, Malaysia and Thailand where firms produces $6,500 of output per worker. This low level of labor productivity in African countries could be attributed to severe impediments to productivity growth such as poor governance, harsh economic policies, poor education and lack of technical skills. Other possible factors include low level of technological advancement, inadequate infrastructural facilities and low level of FDI inflow. These lead to changes in the pattern of allocation of production factors and reduced demand for labor in higher productivity sectors (Taylor, 2003).

Our analyses of African economies over two decades show that labor has in large part been relocated from one low-productivity activity to another low-productivity area, namely, from agricultural to low-end services sector, which is evidenced in terms of the labor productivity share. Over the years, the decline in employment in the manufacturing industry sector has resulted in reallocation of displaced labor into the activities with low productivity such as service and agriculture sectors. This suggests that development policies adopted by African states appear to have fostered an undesirable SC, which led to the movement of labor in the wrong direction.

Expectedly in the region, there are variations among countries regarding the economic structure and levels of labor productivity. Economic activities during the 1970s in African states concentrated more on (Import Substitution Industrialization (ISI)) which gradually shifted toward low-productivity sector (agriculture and services) in the later years of 1990–2000. African economies are dominated by low-productivity firms that offer little contribution to foreign exchange earnings, mostly in non-tradable services such as retail trade. The low-paying jobs that comprise the informal sector are where over 60 percent of labor force in sub-Saharan African economy has been absorbed (UNCTAD, 2011). The main channel through which high-productivity can be achieved is through ST, which reallocates labor force from low-productivity sector (agriculture and services) to a more productive economic activity (manufacturing) (McMillan and Rodrik, 2011).

Since 2000, different countries have experienced and responded differently to SC in terms of labor productivity and employment. Evidence shows that while there is a major gain in the services sector, there has been considerable loss in the industrial and manufacturing sectors. With respect to the levels of labor productivity, there has been a general negative productive SC in most of the countries due to declining share of employment in the manufacturing sector. Against this background, there is a need to foster higher productivity growth in African countries with an emphasis on labor productivity.

For African countries to industrialize and experience productivity growth, dynamic industrial policy and state investments in infrastructure, human capital and energy are required. Such is the catalyst for Ethiopia's pathway to develop a manufacturing sector driven by foreign investment and steered through labor-intensive manufactures bound for export. The regime of high growth that characterizes Asian economies was achieved by shifting labor massively from low-productivity agriculture to higher-productivity manufacturing jobs, see Box 1.

For instance, Ethiopia is taking advantage of the turn in tide and rise in wages for Chinese manufacturers by providing a veritable ground for manufacturing by leveraging on their abundance of cheap labor, low-cost electricity, and cotton-growing potential. This has made it the newest frontier of the global garment trade and a substitute to China, where wages are quickly becoming uncompetitive. In a country where more than three-quarters of the workforce is engaged in small-scale agriculture, opening for manufacturing is a step in the right direction. At present, "Made in Ethiopia" garments are finding their way to the racks of global retailers like H&M, Walmart and Tesco. The US sourcing giant Phillips Van Heusen (PVH) is planning to begin operating from a new 130-hectare industrial park in the southern Ethiopian city of Hawassa. Ten leading textile and apparel firms from India, Sri Lanka, Indonesia, Hong Kong and China will also join PVH. The park is expected to generate 60,000 jobs and $1 billion in export earnings from textiles and garments (nine times the sector's current level) once achieves full capacity in the next few years, if successful, see Box 2.

Asia's rapid rise was in some way done at the expense of Africa's lack of endogenous capabilities to compete; Africa's consumers tend to have abandoned their "used-to-be-thriving" industrial activities in exchange for low-cost Chinese imports. China's industrial productivity and large-scale production have led to deindustrialization in the entire African continent. In addition, the poor performance of African manufacturers is in part the result of severe challenges of basic infrastructure, unfavorable geography, long-neglected energy and transport infrastructure and relatively poor industrial skills. On the bright side, strong growth in the Africa region, rebalancing and rising wages in China, and improvements in the policy and institutional context, provides a unique opportunity that African countries should utilize

> **Box 1**
> **Tales of Ethiopian factory workers (Rosen, 2016)**
>
> Yiman, a 27-year-old mother of one from Addis Ababa, has spent six years working for Ayka-Addis, a Turkish-owned textile and garment factory and the largest firm in Ethiopia's apparel industry. She works for six days a week and earns $68 a month after taxes. Her shift lasts for eight hours and she spends her day churning out cotton for t-shirts, pajamas and bed sheets bound for Europe. Being a relatively senior employee, she's better paid than many of Ayka's 6,000 Ethiopian staff; she admits it would be hard to find a better job with her 10th-grade education, but it's still barely enough. In a country where more than three-quarters of the workforce is engaged in small-scale agriculture, Yimam's job is relatively considered a novelty.
>
> Teshale Yohannes sees life as a daily struggle. A machine operator from southern Ethiopia, he joined Ayka in 2012 because the company offers free lunch and transport; these are incentives unavailable at his previous job in a steel factory. He struggles with the heat at the textiles plant and worries about his exposure to chemicals (an Ayka safety inspector, who listened to Teshale's concerns insisted his job does not involve exposure to anything toxic). Teshale said the pay is simply too low, and his salary leaves him with just $20 after rent to support his wife and child. According to him, the money is never enough, and it's not easy to make it to the end of the month.
>
> Angesom Yohannes, an official with the Industrial Federation of Textile, Garment, Leather, and Shoe Workers Trade Unions, says that fewer than 10 percent of the country's 350,000 workers in these sectors belong to unions. Ayka's 6,000 staff members are an exception. Their active workers' union has succeeded in raising the company's minimum wage to $45 per month, negotiated annual salary increases, and has helped propel more Ethiopian staff into management positions. Ethiopia has no national minimum wage, so the union's presence motivates workers and gives staffs an opportunity to air their grievances but comparatively low efficiency and the low-margin nature of the business limits wage concessions.

to attract investment in higher value-added export-oriented manufacturing (DFID, 2016).

Ethiopia's deliberate plan for economic miracle has triggered plans for eight more government-financed industrial parks across the country.

> **Box 2**
> **Huajian the Chinese Shoemaker (Rosen, 2016)**
>
> Established on the outskirts of Addis Ababa in 2012, Huajian came partly because of Ethiopia's large supply of leather and wage difference with China. Huajian's 4,000 Ethiopian staff, which produces 3 million pairs of shoes per year, mainly for the US market, earns a minimum of $27 per month, one-sixth of the rate at the company's two plants in China. According to Jack Zeng, a company spokesperson, Huajian's Ethiopian staff are only one-third to one-half as productive as their Chinese counterparts, but they are trained to keep order and follow standards. Every morning, Huajian's staff are required to perform marches and calisthenics intended to instill discipline. Affixed to the walls of the factory are banners reminding workers that "late arrival is delay, and quality is life, speed is profit." Huajian's practice in Ethiopia has been positive enough that the company plans to build an entire new industrial zone: a small city shaped like a boot that will accommodate 30,000 to 50,000 jobs in leather processing, shoemaking, garments and textiles.

The development initiative focuses on utilizing government's savings into investments in critical areas for long-term growth such as roads, railways,[1] electricity,[2] agriculture, health care and education. Along with foreign aid, the government has mobilized domestic resources outside of a commodities-driven context at a scale never seen in Africa through improving tax collection, shutting out foreign banks and refusing to privatize telecommunications. Also, 34 public universities and 1,350 post-secondary technical schools were established to enhance vocational training as part of a new German-inspired system. These boosted public investment from 5 percent of GDP in the early 1990s to 19 percent in 2011, which was the third-highest rate in the world. It also powered robust economic growth and improvements in human development and reduced poverty, although foreign investment is being held back due to excessive bureaucracy, which impedes the ease of doing business.

---

[1] A Chinese-built electric railway connecting Addis Ababa to the nearest port in Djibouti is one of several rail lines under construction and is expected to begin operating soon and drastically reduce the shipping costs of exporters.

[2] A sustained investment in hydropower in concert with subsidized tariffs has helped Ethiopia offer electricity at one of the lowest rates in Africa.

On the path to successful industrialization, the Ethiopian government, however, needs to walk over the likely stumbling blocks of shortage of foreign currency, drought and severe food crisis with attendant problems, excessive bureaucracy, lack of genuine participatory process for economic growth and ethnic discontent; these symbolize a threat to the country's hard work toward industrialization. The interest of laborers also needs to be enhanced through the enactment of a national minimum wage in the private sector; this is to ensure employment creation for excess labor does not translate to underemployment, low wages and low living standards, which poses a human rights issue. If successful, the country's passion to industrialize will have a noteworthy impact on the lives of millions of its citizens, with genuine economic growth and development.

Africa is standing on the edge of massive opportunities with considerable possibilities for growth. Yet, the continent has witnessed little ST so far. Economies across the region are booming, FDI has increased, new technologies are being adopted and population is growing, but despite experiencing regional economic growth in recent years, Africa commands a meager 1.5 percent share of the world's total manufacturing output compared to 21.7 percent share for the Asia Pacific region, 17.2 percent for East Asia and 22.4 percent share for North America (BBC Africa, 2014).

African cities can induce higher productivity by drawing from the benefits of agglomeration economies with attendant economic gains and growth by strategic positioning, matching the distinctive requirement of cities for labor, industrial locations and suppliers, improving access to a bigger and improved range of shared services, infrastructure and external connectivity to national and global customers, concentration efficiencies of producers and consumers and information flow, which promotes learning, idea exchange and innovation.

The region also holds a lot of potential for successful manufacturing resulting from relatively low wage,[3] availability of resources,[4] large flows of FDI, growing domestic markets enhanced by the increasing middle class and rising urbanization, which leads to increasing demand for consumer staples. Companies achieve greater economies of scale by spreading their fixed costs over a larger customer base. Urbanization also spurs the construction of more roads, buildings, water systems and similar projects, which will come at cheaper cost if the resources needed are manufactured locally as Africa's annual private infrastructure investments have tripled since year 2000, averaging $19 billion from 2006 to 2008.

---

[3] Taking advantage of the increase in factory wages in Asia.
[4] Mineral and natural, human resources.

Drawing on historical evidence, economic and social progress can be closely linked with urbanization and therefore, African cities, which can be positioned to provide improved quality of life for the continent's increasingly large urban classes through investment in the manufacturing sector. Cities are the most important social invention for productivity growth due to the opportunities they hold as urban population holds potentials for significant economic growth in the modern age. From the start of the industrial revolution, cities have played vital roles in enhancing productivity gains in the process of production of goods. African cities provide potential for productive space for excess labor from the rural sector to earn higher value for their efforts that were cheap in the rural areas; this suggests that productivity of labor is higher in cities and urban areas in general and can be achieved in African cities. Higher labor productivity translates to higher contributions to national products; it increases capacity to provide more employment, better welfare for citizenry and prosperity of the national economy and that of the continent.

4.2 Putting Numbers to the Narrative

Productivity is a vital source of economic growth and competitiveness. It provides basic statistical information for international comparisons and country performance assessments. There are different measures of productivity and the choice between them depends either on the purpose of the productivity measurement or on data availability. Productivity measures include GDP per hour worked and MFP, also known as TFP, which measures the residual growth that cannot be explained by the rate of change in the services of labor, capital and intermediate outputs, and is often interpreted as the contribution to economic growth made by factors such as technical and organizational innovation (OECD, 2008: 11).

Labor productivity is a revealing indicator of several economic indicators as it offers a dynamic measure of economic growth, competitiveness and living standards within an economy. It explains the principal economic foundations that are necessary for both economic growth and social development. Labor productivity can be measured in different ways, although the ratio used in its calculation provides a measure of the efficiency with which inputs are used in an economy to produce goods and services. Labor productivity is equal to the ratio between a volume measure of output (GDP or gross value added (GVA)) and a measure of input use (the total number of hours worked or total employment) (Freeman, 2008: 5).

Labor productivity = volume measure of output / measure of input use

The volume measure of output reflects the goods and services produced by the workforce. Numerator of the ratio of labor productivity, the volume measure of output, is measured either by GDP or GVA. Although these two different measures can both be used as output measures, there is normally a strong correlation between the two (Freeman, 2008). The analysis will be limited to labor productivity and TFP; TFP is included in the analysis due to lack of data.

There are two major sources of change in productivity, namely, technological progress within the sector and productivity gains due to SC. Growth of productivity has also been decomposed into two components using shift share analysis, these being intra-sector changes and changes due to SC. The theoretical concept applied for the decomposition analysis is adopted from van Ark and Timmer (2003) who defined growth of productivity as:

$$\Delta P = \sum_{i=1}^{n}\left(Pi^{T} - Pi^{o}\right)Si^{m} + \sum_{i=1}^{n}\left(Si^{T} - Si^{o}\right)Pi^{m}$$

Where $i \rightarrow$ number of sectors varying from 1 to n
$Pi^{T} \rightarrow$ Productivity in sector i in year T
$Si^{T} \rightarrow$ Share of employment in sector i in year T
$Pi^{m} \rightarrow$ Average of productivity in sector i
$Si^{m} \rightarrow$ Average of employment share in sector i

The first part of the composition equation is the intra-sector productivity changes, while the second part is called "reallocation-effect" also known as "shift-effect" or "structural-change effect." Shift share analysis would reveal the effect of SC on productivity in each sector. The economy was reduced to three sectors; agriculture, industry/manufacturing and services. Sectors such as mining, utilities and constructions have been included in industry while services such as "trade, restaurants and hotels," "transport, storage and communication," "finance, insurance, real estate and business services" and "community, social and personal services" have been merged into the services sector. The analysis of each country is presented in Table 4.1. The number of countries considered in Table 4.1 and the period of the analysis are constrained by the availability of data. The balanced series had to be used for decomposition of productivity.

4.2.1 Botswana

Labor productivity growth shows the efficiency with which factor inputs are utilized in different sectors of the economy. During this period, the average of annual productivity growth in the agriculture sector was 3.06 percent,

Table 4.1 Average Decomposition of Labor Productivity Growth from 1991 to 2013

	Sector	Botswana	Ghana	Kenya	Nigeria	South Africa	Tanzania
Average annual productivity growth	Agriculture	3.06	2.65	0.82	3.46	1.54	1.83
	Industry	5.54	2.10	−3.95	−2.00	2.20	−0.26
	Manufacturing	2.24	1.76	−4.74	1.51	1.99	−1.05
	Services	4.11	1.05	−1.60	6.92	2.56	−0.84
	Total	2.16	2.75	−0.25	2.32	1.83	1.90
Decomposition of productivity growth	Intra-sector productivity growth (percent)	252.13	73.53	−51.36	−100.70	90.63	26.20
	Productivity growth due to structural change (percent)	−152.13	26.47	151.36	210.70	9.37	73.81

Source: Author's calculation

5.54 percent in industry, 2.24 percent in the manufacturing sector and 4.11 percent in the services sector. Table 4.1 shows that labor productivity was lowest in the manufacturing sector and highest in the industrial sector. Also there is overall negative productivity growth and declining trend in intra-sector productivity. For instance, during 1991–95, the contribution of intra-sectoral changes was 182.98 percent and that of SC was –82.98 percent. Such a high differential percentage of contribution is due to intra-sectoral change that contributed to the increase in productivity of all the sectors. At the same time, –82.98 percent contribution of SC was due to a drastic reduction of employment share in industry and manufacturing. In industry, employment share declined from 17.29 percent in 1991 to 12.58 percent in 1995; while in manufacturing, it declined from 6.12 percent to 5.55 percent during the same period. In 2007–11, the employment share of industry dropped from 7.27 percent to 4.98 percent but average labor productivity during the same period was very high (416937.59 BWP) from the sector. This resulted in negative contribution of SC to productivity growth.

4.2.2 Ghana

In Ghana, the average of annual productivity growth for the agriculture sector was 2.65 percent, 2.10 percent for industry, 1.76 percent for manufacturing and 1.05 percent for services. From the table, labor productivity was lowest in the services sector and highest in the agriculture sector both of which are low-productivity sectors. Although the average annual productivity during 1999–2003 was positive in all sectors, employment share in agriculture and industry declined. In the agricultural sector, it declined from 54.10 percent in 1999 to 50.81 percent in 2003 while it declined from 4.77 percent to 4.37 percent in industry during the same period, resulting in lower contributions to productivity due to SC. Also, the intra-sector productivity gains have been much higher than changes in productivity growth due to SC.

4.2.3 Kenya

In Kenya, the average of annual productivity growth in the agriculture sector was 0.82 percent, industry accounted for −3.95 percent, manufacturing − 4.74 percent and services −1.60 percent. In Kenya, contribution of SC to productivity was negative suggesting that the employment share in some key sectors reduced drastically. In fact, the agricultural sector provided employment for 70.35 percent of the labor force in 1991, but its share of employment reduced to 45.68 percent in 2013. On the other hand, the share of employment in other sectors experienced a positive growth rate. In addition, almost all sectors—except agriculture—experienced a decline in productivity during 1991–2003, which marginally increased subsequently.

4.2.4 Nigeria

The average annual productivity growth for the agriculture sector in Nigeria was 3.46 percent, −2.00 percent for industry, 1.51 percent for manufacturing and 6.92 percent for services. From the table, labor productivity was lowest in the industrial and manufacturing sectors and highest in the services sector. It can be observed that the contribution of intra-sector and ST to productivity growth during 1991–95 was −633.81 percent and 733.81 percent, respectively. A share of −633.81 of contribution in productivity suggests a decline in the agricultural sector (average annual productivity growth −2.58 percent). At the same time, a very high contribution of SC (733.81 percent) is due to the substantial productivity gains in the industrial sector, in which the average annual productivity growth was 4.83 percent during the period. Similar arguments hold true for 1995–99 where productivity gains due to intra-sectoral changes and SCs went in the opposite direction with almost similar magnitude.

The situation has changed significantly since then and both components contributed positively, but within 2003–7, the contribution of intra-sectoral changes became negative. This was due to a decline in productivity in the largest employment sector, that is, agriculture; the employment share in agriculture during the period was 62.82 percent. In the subsequent five years, the contribution of intra-sectoral change was positive though marginal (2.09 percent). However, during 2011–13, the contribution of intra-sectoral productivity gains reached 88.38 percent due to productivity gains in agriculture and industry.

4.2.5 South Africa

The average of annual productivity growth in the agriculture sector of South Africa was 1.54 percent, in industry was 2.20 percent, in manufacturing was 1.99 percent and in services was 2.56 percent. From the summary table, labor productivity was very low in subsector of South Africa's economy, and it is the lowest in agriculture and manufacturing. The table also shows contribution of ST in productivity growth during 1991–95, 2003–7 and 2011–13, which was positive. On the other hand, the contribution of intra-sectoral changes during 1995–99 was –99.89 percent. This contributed to a decline in productivity in the agricultural and services sectors and a decline in agricultural employment. The share of employment in agriculture declined from 20.23 percent in 1995 to 19.02 percent in 1999 while it declined from 13.94 percent to 9.50 percent in industry during the same period. Hence the contribution of intra-sectoral changes in productivity growth was negative.

In the subsequent five years, productivity rebounded in agriculture, which resulted in reversing the contribution of both factors to productivity growth. In fact, the intra-sectoral contribution became positive, while the contribution of the SC became negative. This negative contribution could be attributed to a decline in productivity in the manufacturing sector. The scenario remained similar in the succeeding five years, but during 2003–7, the contribution due to SC became positive. This was attributed to an increase in productivity during the period when annual average productivity growth in agriculture became 8.23 percent. During the ensuing five years, labor productivity in the sector declined resulting in negative contributions (–119.68 percent) of SC.

4.2.6 Tanzania

From 1991 to 2013, the average of annual productivity growth in agriculture sector was 1.83 percent, industry was –0.26 percent, manufacturing was –1.05 percent and service was –0.84 percent. From 1991 to 1995, the total productivity growth was negative. Looking at the sectoral productivity growth, the industrial and services sectors' growth was negative, both components contributing to the downfall in productivity. The contribution of intra-sectoral changes was almost double to that of SC (35.06 percent). The contribution of the first component was higher because, although employment in industry was smaller (1.27 percent) compared to services (8.17 percent), the average labor productivity was much higher in industry compared to services.

It is worth noting that overall productivity of the Tanzanian economy declined during 1999–2003. Also, the employment share in agriculture declined from 80.39 percent in 2003 to 74.65 percent in 2007 and the average annual productivity growth in other sectors were –0.35 percent, –4.30 percent and –0.06 percent, respectively. This kind of SC was very detrimental to the Tanzanian economy as it created unemployment in the agricultural sector and was unable to provide displaced labor in high-value-added activities in other sectors. Surplus labor from agriculture was absorbed in low-value-added activities of other sectors resulting in low productivity of the sectors.

From the case study on countries' experience, it is evident that some African countries have experienced improved productivity while some had negative productivity in all sectors. Despite the significant role that productivity plays in promoting competitiveness and economic growth, its impact has not been mainstreamed in the industrial and manufacturing sectors of most African states. This developmental problem emerged as a result of weak productivity governance, poor productivity infrastructure, weak broad-based productivity-driven research and development, lack of skilled manpower and low level of technological advancement, thus making Africa lag behind in developmental process. To address this developmental challenge, African states must embrace industrialization as a way to a high-productivity pathway.

4.3 Summing Up

The overall productivity growth in African economies was positive in Botswana, Ethiopia and Ghana during the period under consideration, although it was negative in the initial period in other countries. Productivity growth followed an increasing trend during the concluding period. Productivity growth in Ethiopia was the highest, followed by Nigeria. The highest productivity growth (5.72 percent) in Ethiopia was recorded between 2007 and 2011, while it was 3.75 percent during 2003–7 in Nigeria.

The contribution of SC to productivity growth was always positive in Ghana, Nigeria and Tanzania. Increase in productivity in sectors other than agriculture could be attributed to this phenomenon, but Nigeria remains the only country where the productivity and employment share increased during the study period. The labor productivity analysis suggests that in many countries, it increased due to ST while in others it was due to intra-sectoral changes.

For instance, in Botswana, the productivity growth was due to intra-sectoral changes rather than ST in all periods, notably, SC contributed negatively to productivity growth. In Ghana, the growth in productivity was due to ST as well as intra-sectoral change. In all periods, the contribution of ST to productivity growth was higher than intra-sectoral change. This may be treated as the best example of ST going in the right direction. On the other hand, in Kenya, the contribution of ST was 29.36 percent in 2003–7 while it was 96.36 percent in 2007–11. ST contributed significantly in 2011–13 but overall it contributed negatively in other years.

In Nigeria, the contribution of ST towards productivity growth was positive for all the years and was higher than intra-sectoral change. However, in South Africa, ST contributed positively in 1991–95, 2003–7 and 2011–13, but the contribution was smaller than intra-sectoral change most of the time. Tanzania moved in the right direction of ST, resulting in its positive contribution to productivity growth. It may also be noted that the contribution of ST was higher in the entire period except 1991–95 (35.06 percent). In Ethiopia, the contribution of ST to productivity growth was positive except in 1995–99, and in most of the years it was higher than the contribution of intra-sectoral change.

It is clear from empirical evidence that African states need to embrace industrialization that fosters a high-productivity pathway.

Industrialization is an integral and fundamental part of ST, a prerequisite for economic growth and increasing GDP per capita leading to improvement of living standard. As clearly shown in this book, hardly has any country grown without industrialization. The role of industrialization is centered on leveraging manufacturing as an engine of growth and reallocating labor from low-productivity sectors to high-productivity sectors, reducing unemployment. Several policies and reforms have been adopted by different African states, yet sectoral contribution of the industrial and manufacturing sectors to the GDP remains very low and insignificant. The industrial sector in Africa has experienced decades of low productivity with resultant reduction in its share of industrial employment and manufacturing contribution to GDP. To achieve dynamic and sustainable industrialization in Africa, there is a need for productivity improvement. Productivity improvement is an act of increasing output from available resources such as capital and equipment, labor, natural capital and mineral resources, management capacities and finances (UNECA, 2013). It always comes in the form of cost reduction, maximization of output, system optimization, elimination of ineffective system, reduction of variation and improvement of quality. These can only be achieved through a variety of measures including innovation and technological advancement, FDI, investment in human capital, physical capital and infrastructural development and establishment of relevant institutional framework.

4.3.1 Improve Productivity through Innovation and Development of New Technologies

Ever since the dawn of the Industrial Revolution, innovation and technological advances have been the major drivers of long-term economic growth and increases in productivity. Technological Innovation is a creative–destructive process. It destroys jobs in low-productivity sectors and enhances growth and competitiveness through creation of jobs in different industries that require different skills. In Africa, innovation and technology foster firm-level productivity, and indirectly raise economy-wide productivity through diffusion and adoption. As innovation and technology become pervasive, the potential for economy-wide productivity gains in Africa will shifts from low-productivity sector to high-productivity sector and from high-productivity sector to high-tech manufacturing, and also expanding the service sector.

Policy framework on science and technology, and productivity and incomes should be formulated for various actors in the economy, to engage in R&D activities to take advantage of international sources of technology, and also to encompass direct policy initiatives providing services to firms aimed at increasing their capacity to absorb new technologies, as well as to engage in collaborative research with other firms. Also policy reforms must be put in place to support technological innovation and productivity outcomes. Enhancing the business environment for technological innovation is especially important, as business is the main driver of innovation. Furthermore, the services sector should be liberalized in order to foster stronger innovation in the manufacturing sector (high-productivity sector). More innovation-friendly regulation, combined with lower barriers to trade and FDI, would enhance competition and would foster the flow of technology and knowledge across Africa as a continent. Reform of labor markets, notably through well-designed employment protection legislation, would help firms to adjust and allow them to draw greater benefits from their investment in innovation and technology.

4.3.2 Harnessing Foreign Direct Investment for Industrialization

The recent productivity increases experienced in Africa after 2000 happened without significant ST that shifts resources and labor from low-productivity sector to high-productivity sectors. Also the wave of trade globalization and FDI in manufacturing is largely missing in Africa. While most developing countries are contributing increasingly larger share to global manufactured exports, Africa's manufacturing sector is still stagnated in the low single digits. This has led to stagnation in growth potential and job creation in the high value-added sectors. To raise productivity in Africa's manufacturing sector and expansion of value-added services, African governments should create an enabling environment for foreign firms to invest in Africa's manufacturing and high-value-added services. To exploit these opportunities and attract FDI, appropriate policies must be put in place to address poor quality of institutions, inadequate infrastructure, and policy-distorting price incentives. FDI is an important mechanism to catalyze industrialization and ST as it is capable of increasing firm productive capacity and generating productivity spillovers through technology and know-how transfers. It will also help to engineer a structural shift to higher productivity jobs and high-value-added industry niches.

To attract FDI in Africa, infrastructure, institutions and incentives must be well addressed. Although Africa's infrastructure is improving, it is starting from a low base. Lack of efficient basic infrastructure such as transportation, electricity, water and ICT is a major cause of low productivity and competitiveness in the manufacturing sector of Africa, along with low numbers of exporters and limited intra-regional trade. In Africa, electric power supply remains the greatest infrastructure constraint to investment in the manufacturing sector. Access to power supply, reliability and high cost are key issues with electricity in Africa. The report of World Bank Enterprise Survey in 2013 affirmed that 37 percent of foreign manufacturing firms identified electricity as a major constraint for doing business in Africa. Reliability of electricity supply is another major problem. African manufacturing enterprises experience power outages 56 days per year, on average, resulting in a loss amounting to 6 percent of annual sales.

Transport infrastructure is one constraint to foreign investment in Africa's manufacturing sector. The poor state of infrastructure increases the cost of inputs to manufacturing and other activities, especially in landlocked countries. In Rwanda, it was reported that transport costs from coastal ports to Kigali add roughly 50 percent to the cost of landed inputs. Another instrument for attracting FDI to Africa's manufacturing sector is strengthening institutions like investment agencies and customs authorities. All these must be accompanied by policies to increase FDI spillovers and backward linkages to support ST and industrial growth. The combination of long-term investment with policy control will facilitate the transfer of capability (technology and management know-how), and provide access to regional and global value chains to Africa's manufacturing sector. To attract FDI to Africa's manufacturing sector, policies must be put in place to address constraints in three key areas: infrastructure, institutions and incentives.

- On infrastructure: Policies should focus on improving access to and reliability of competitively priced electric power, and upgrading the transportation system and ports, as well as improving policies to promote the efficient use of existing infrastructure.
- On institutions: Policies should focus on improving investment promotion agencies, export promotion agencies, standards bodies, border control authorities and customs.

- On incentives: Policies should focus on reducing anti-export bias in tariffs and nontariff barriers, on maintaining competitive real exchange rates and on the potential role for special economic zones.

If all these can be achieved, FDI will facilitate productivity increases, not only in the manufacturing sector, but also in other sectors as well by increasing within-sector competition, increasing domestic firms' efficiency and driving out the least efficient firms.

4.3.3 Investment in Human Capital

During the early period of independence, most African countries had strength in manufacturing and industrial development. Asian countries that were unable to compete with African states in both manufacturing and economic arenas before are now competing with industrialized giants like United States, Germany, Spain and Australia through the ways they develop and produce goods. Through industrial modernization, development of highly skilled labor force that develops and uses technology, these countries had been able to increase their productivity through sustained industrialization. Human capital plays a crucial role in industry's ability to produce products that will stimulate productivity and economic growth. Empirical findings reveal that countries/regions that failed to develop and effectively utilize its human capital in the national/regional economy will continue to experience failure in economic development and international competitiveness at the global marketplace.

Presently, most African countries have a dearth of skilled labor force particularly in the manufacturing sector, and this has over time led to low productivity and inability to effectively compete in the global market. The role of human capital in Africa's growth is complex. In Africa, inadequate investment in education and health has made labor to be less economically productive. Also government and companies are not pooling resources to improve labor force skills. This problem becomes evident as many African high school and University graduates lack employability skills. Even if African states should invest in developing infrastructures, capital expenditures for manufacturing, improvement in productivity will only be a mirage unless the human capital has the educational training and skills needed to handle the advanced technologies. Another problem facing human capital that is always taken for granted is health. Ill health always affects workers' productivity due to loss of man-hours through absenteeism, recuperation and attending the sick.

For productivity to be improved, African governments need to invest heavily on labor force to be multi-skilled through constant training, retraining, skilling and reskilling because manufacturing deals with high technical equipment and machinery. Investing in human capital will lead to higher productivity and will also generate a positive spillover effect that benefits firms and competitors. Improving the quality of human capital will enhance productivity and absorptive capacity in the wide range of technological advancement in the manufacturing sector. Government, companies and individuals should collaborate with the view of improving the skills level of the labor force. Also there should be an appropriate policy that will drive improved access to quality health care to reduce sickness and absence which should increase output per worker.

4.3.4 Improving Productivity through Infrastructure Development

Over the last three decades, African countries have been losing competitiveness at global marketplace due in large part to lack of infrastructure. The resultant effect of poorly developed infrastructure is low productivity, high transaction costs of goods and uncompetitive products. Infrastructure (transport, energy, water and communications) plays a critical role in promoting and sustaining industrialization. Without efficient and proper systems that support movement of inputs and output, energy to run factories as well as shipping and communication networks that support trade and create markets, no country can industrialize or effectively participate in trade. To accelerate industrial productivity in Africa, there is a need for heavy investment in infrastructure, including energy. Infrastructure development should be made a priority at continental, regional and national levels. The development of infrastructure through regional cooperation will thus reduce production and transaction costs, improve regional markets and make production and exports more competitive. Regional integration would also contribute to reducing the regulatory burden facing African industries through harmonizing policies and restraining unfavorable domestic policies. Furthermore, it would boost inter- and intra-African trade thereby accelerating industrialization in Africa.

4.3.5 Improving Productivity through Financing and Resource Mobilization

Access to finance is one of the key instruments for industrial development. It enhances the smooth running and management of other factors of production. Despite existing policies on financial support for small, medium and large industrial establishments at regional and global levels, access to investment finance remains one of the significant challenges to industrial development in the African region with resultant negative effect on economic growth, employment and shared prosperity. Difficulty in access to finance in Africa could be attributed to restrictive borrowing conditions such as availability of fixed assets, collateral and guaranteed higher borrowing interest rates of up to 20 percent, limited availability of long-term capital and lack of credit bureau, which makes access to finance challenging with higher borrowing rates. In the last two decades, there has been an improvement in Africa's financial systems; however, it still lags behind other developing economies thus impeding the positive effects of financial inflows.

Lack of access to affordable financing impedes the employment of skilled labor and acquisition of new technology and machinery thus reducing the growth, competitiveness and productivity of the manufacturing sector in Africa. Presently, there is not enough institution capacity to steer and support the development of the manufacturing sector in Africa. Financial institutions in Africa operate short- to medium-term financial services through commercial banks. Additionally, existing financial institutions including development banks, commercial banks, mobile financial services, microfinance institutions, credit bureaus, micro insurance and collateral registries need to be strengthened with appropriate policies with the aim to support industrial development and to promote inclusive economic growth. Creation of security and local capital markets will facilitate access to finance for industrial development.

Chapter 5

PATHWAY TO EMPLOYMENT CREATION

5.1 Introduction

The previous chapters articulate in detail the principles of ST and the implications for urbanization, industrialization and quality of life. This chapter sets out to describe the pathways to employment and the relationships between structural economic transformation and employment. Equally, the chapter demonstrates how this crucial relationship impacts development and growth for African economies. Employment is understood technically as a contractual relationship between two parties where one party works while the other pays for this work, resulting in opportunities for people to earn a living. In the grand scheme of things, employment results in economic development as it allocates the work force into sectors with the highest growth potential and productivity. Other than this, employment also creates the environment for social welfare to flourish; it enables a rise in the living standards and minimum-wage employments, among others. Studying this relationship between ST and employments enables better understanding of the true long- and short-term causes of rural and urban unemployment.

Global unemployment has continued to rise particularly since the financial crisis, but the situation in Africa is of particular concern given its large percentage of youth. From AfDB (2016) data, one-third of the African youth are unemployed and discouraged, another third are vulnerably employed and only one in six are in wage employment. Africa has the fastest growing and most youthful population—with nearly 420 million people in Africa between 15 and 35 years of age; the youth face roughly double the unemployment rate of adults, with significant variation by country. This proportion of the region's population constitutes a significant asset if properly managed but a ticking socioeconomic time bomb if left undeveloped and unemployed in productive work.

Currently, unemployment constitutes a major socioeconomic challenge to the region. For instance, unemployment rate in South Africa rose to

27.6 percent in the first quarter of 2019 from 27.1 percent in the previous period. Nigeria also experienced an increasing rate of unemployment from 22.70 percent in the second quarter of 2018 to 23.10 percent by the end of the third quarter (Trading Economics, 2019b).

There is a clear connection between employment and economic growth although the growth-employment nexus varies considerably with economic structures and levels of development. For instance, while informal employment is strikingly extensive and widespread in many Asian and African cities, formal employment is more prevalent in advanced industrial economies. For much of the past few decades, informal employment in most cases has been growing at the expense of formal employment, and is generally not considered to be productive or decent work. The informal economy is able to generate millions of jobs and incomes for poor urban residents and this is partly because working conditions and labor standards are low. These are flexible, labor-intensive operations with simple organizational and production structures and low levels of investment and technology.

There are a variety of employment dynamics including youth and gender employment, which has taken on the form of a special challenge in cities around the world. The peculiar trajectory of the African economy has exposed the vulnerability of young people in the country's labor market. Due to several interrelated reasons, a large swathe of the youth do not get integrated into the world of work after leaving school and tend to risk long-term exclusion. This population represents a wasted asset for the nations, and in the long run a burden on the state. Young people are also more likely than adults to be among the working poor in informal jobs. Being forced into precarious livelihoods by intense poverty and lack of social protection is a lost opportunity since they might otherwise attend school or college and acquire skills and competences that could raise their future productivity and earnings.

Additionally, in this chapter, we demonstrate that employment and structural economic transformation are two interconnected phenomena determining current growth and development patterns in Nigeria. At the micro level, employment creation provides opportunities for earnings and underpins increases in household expenditures and secure livelihoods. At the macro level, development occurs through the reallocation of labor toward sectors with the greatest growth potential and the highest productivity. Jobs also facilitate social (e.g., female wage employment) and political (seeking identity) transformations. In understanding the root cause of jobless growth in Africa, we will examine the historical evolutionary roots of long-term unemployment through an empirical analysis of urbanization and, more importantly, ST across the region; it is in doing this that we can unearth the remote as well as the immediate causes of urban unemployment.

Employment creation is the most common feature in both global and national development plans and schemes due to its many direct and indirect benefits to economic growth, investments, international relations and trade. On the global scale, unemployment rates increased by 1 million over a year soaring at 197.1 million in 2015 as compared to 2014, which is deemed as 27 million higher than precrisis level (International Labor Organization (ILO), 2016b; IMF, 2015). Global unemployment rate has reportedly dropped to 5 percent, the lowest level since the global economic crisis in 2008 (ILO, 2019). However, ILO reports that the jobs being created are poor quality jobs that keep most of the world's workers mired in poverty. Unemployment has various forms, but youth unemployment and gender-based unemployment are two of the most prominent. Notably, 75 million out of the 202 million unemployed in 2012 were youth made up of the huge numbers of poorly educated individuals entering the job market that is devoid of worthy opportunities.

For African economies to achieve the targets set out under Sustainable Development Goal 8 (SDG 8), sustainable ST is the pathway that needs to be promoted by every country to resolve unemployment and underemployment. SDG 8 aims to promote sustained, inclusive and sustainable economic growth, full and productive employment and decent work for all. These objectives as described throughout this book are potentially achievable through the process of ST. Along with achieving targets set by SDG 8, there is a need to create 470 million jobs across the globe for new market entrants' projected surplus between 2016 and 2030.

5.2 Unemployment and Underemployment in Africa

Africa is growing at an average growth rate of 5 percent per year making it one of the fastest growing regions of the world (UNECA, 2015). African countries provide a paradoxical spectacle of economic growth because they are seen to be growing despite their struggles with civil wars, political instabilities, myriad endemic diseases and refugee crisis. SSA experienced a declining economic growth rate from 2.5 percent in 2017 to an estimated 2.3 percent for 2018 (World Bank, 2017); with an increasing unemployment rate of 7.2 percent in 2017. North Africa witnessed economic growth but at the cost of social progress, specifically in youth employment where 30 percent of North African youth are currently unemployed with 45 percent of them being female (ILO, 2016b).

Industry, especially manufacturing, accounts for about 23.2 percent of global employment. However, several countries have witnessed a decline in the manufacturing share of GDP. The rise of skill-intensive and highly efficient workforce along with the latest technical advancements means joblessness is an unavoidable outcome for the less skilled. Manufacturing jobs suffer the most as globalization and labor-efficient technology replace laborers leading to premature deindustrialization as is the case in SSA (UNDP, 2015).

5.2.1 Youth Employment

Data collected on global employment status suggest improvements over the past few years in youth employment rates; however, the youth remains a large proportion of the global unemployed population (ILO, 2015b). A study on the urban youth employment situation in Burkina Faso and how it has changed over a 20-year period was carried out in the year 2000 with a specific focus on young women and educated youth. The result showed a clear trend of increase in Burkina Faso's youth unemployment but an increase in the proportion of youth employed in the informal sector. This did not only suggest that there is a mismatch between the education given to the youth and what is required by Burkina Faso's labor market, but also that the informal sector is absorbing youth in larger numbers than before (Calvès and Schoumaker, 2004).

Another study in Egypt confirms the rise in the trend of educated youth moving to the informal sector to seek unstable employment. Job stability and social security are of great importance to Egyptian youth, and they often relate these two fundamental characteristics only with government jobs. For this reason, working in the informal sector may be perceived as even more unfortunate for the educated youth of Egypt. Ghana is an example of a country where despite the country's high investment in extractive industry, the youth have not benefited from an increased number of job opportunities as would be expected of this resource-rich country. This has only increased the youth unemployment crisis for Ghana and brought to the forefront the common increasing trend in youth unemployment in most of Africa (Ackah-Baidoo, 2016).

The global economy faces several challenges, among which increasing unemployment and inequality tend to be widespread and endemic in poor countries. A study on the impact of financial literacy on youth entrepreneurship in South Africa's Vhembe district revealed that it is a key factor in the success of the district's entrepreneurs and contributes greatly toward the skill set they require for making their livelihood (Oseifuah, 2010). In Swaziland, the lack of entrepreneurial skills and knowledge experienced by youth entrepreneurs constitute barriers to effective start-up success (Brixiová et al., 2015).

In Africa, despite high youth unemployment rate, African enterprises are unable to fill large numbers of their job openings. South Africa and Egypt are good examples where this phenomenon persists. In 2012, 600,000 of South Africa's young graduates were unemployed and approximately 3 million young people were not in employment, education or training. Meanwhile, the country had 800,000 open vacancies that were not filled. In Egypt, the private sector struggled to fill its 600,000 open positions while 1.5 million of the country's youth were unemployed (*The Economist*, 2012; ILO, 2011). This clearly suggests that the supply of job opportunities is not the only issue but instead a mismatch exists between the training of the unemployed required by employers. Also, lack of information about the vacancies to the job seekers may be among the reasons for this statistic. The mismatch in training completed and that required by the labor market is confirmed as a major challenge feeding Africa's unemployment scenario by a survey conducted in 36 African countries in which 54 percent of the experts identified it as a main cause of unemployment; 41 percent of the experts opined that a general lack of skill tend to explain this high rate of unemployment (AEO, 2012).

This suggests that skill development needs to be a priority of national governments. Focus needs to be placed on training their national youth via formal education, skills and vocational training to better fit the requirement of the labor market. Governments also need to focus their efforts on strengthening education and training policies to match specific sector needs (Asian Development Bank (ADB), 2012).

5.2.2 Gender Employment

In Africa, only 39.2 percent of the women are in employment compared to 69.2 percent of its employed male population (ILO, 2008).. At least 60 percent of Africa's working women are engaged in the agriculture sector in what are often unpaid jobs or very poorly remunerated ones, while 34.9 percent women are usually working as contributing family workers. Also, the majority of these women work in labor- and time-intensive activities of the agriculture sector and not the skill-intensive ones (ILO, 2016). Women in Africa continue to struggle to find and retain reliable-income jobs (ILO, 2016).

Although gender equality in Africa is gradually being addressed, an increase from 70 percent to 76 percent (Anyawu and Augustine, 2012) showed more women than men to work in the informal sector with a gender gap of 13 percent in the nonagricultural context (ILO, 2016a). The gender gap persists in unpaid household work where women in the developing countries of Africa carry out at least 73 minutes more unpaid household and care work compared to men; whereas, it is 33 minutes in the developed parts of Africa. Northern Africa suffers the greatest gender gap when it comes to unemployment where female youth unemployment rate is almost double that of male unemployment with the gap being as high as 44.3 percent. The report also shows that 63.2 percent of sub-Saharan African women in wage employment do not enjoy social protection, which is much higher than the global average of 40 percent.

"Getting to Equal by 2030: The Future is Now" was the ILO's theme for International Women's Day in 2016 suggesting that filling the gender gap is now a priority in order to achieve the 2030 Sustainable Development Agenda. The ILO aims to close the long-existing gender wage gap via promotion of the equal opportunities principle. Support for women entrepreneurs and reorganizing structure of unpaid care work by promoting paid jobs in the care economy will further ensure closing of the gender gap. It is essential for regions, countries and organizations to adopt gender equalizing policies and begin dialogue to facilitate the same if Africa intends to grow economically in a sustainable manner.

5.2.3 The Skills Root of Development and Employment

Supply Side of Skills: The role of skills in the performance of urban markets has been an issue of longstanding debate in policy circles. One view holds that workforce skills and the quality of labor supply are fundamental determinants of the level of employment. Weak or obsolete skills, sometimes in combination with poor motivation to work, are deemed responsible for people's inability to secure employment and employers' reluctance to hire extra staff. There may be a particular problem for migrants from rural areas, who may lack the range of competencies and personal contacts required to compete for formal employment in cities. These supply-side arguments imply that a policy priority is required to improve education and training in order to equip people to be more employable and productive.

Demand Side of Skills: The opposite view is that the demand for labor is more important than attributes of labor supply in determining the level of employment. Urban unemployment is mainly a function of the lack of labor demand in the city, in turn a reflection of localized industrial decline or the fact that population growth is outpacing local job growth. It may also reflect deficient aggregate demand for goods and services resulting from a national economic recession or restrictive macroeconomic policies. The policy priority is to expand economic activity and increase the job opportunities available by stimulating demand and boosting private investment, as this is the only way to absorb the growing number of people seeking work. Attributing urban unemployment to low skills and motivation implies a focus on the symptoms of economic weakness and a diversion from the underlying problem.

Structural unemployment is a more specific form of lack of demand. It focuses on deep-seated obstacles or inefficiencies in urban labor markets; for example, a mismatch between the characteristics of labor demand and supply in terms of necessary skill sets. It may result from shifts in the composition of urban economies from industry to services, or from low-skilled to highly skilled occupations, and may require a combination of demand- and supply-side policy responses.

5.2.4 Informal-Sector Unemployment

Informal employment is very extensive, even though it is difficult to observe and measure because it is not directly taxed or regulated. In Africa, 85.8 percent of employment is informal. The proportion is 68.2 percent in Asia and the Pacific, 68.6 percent in the Arab States, 40.0 percent in the Americas and 25.1 percent in Europe and Central Asia (ILO, 2018).

The traditional definition of the informal sector was based on enterprises rather than employment. It covered all unregistered enterprises below a certain size including (i) microenterprises owned by informal employers who hire one or more employees on a continuing basis and (ii) own-account operations owned by individuals who may employ contributing family workers and employees on an occasional basis (ILO, 2000).

There are different explanations for the growth and survival of the informal sector. It comprises low value, marginally productive activities that allow large numbers of people to escape extreme poverty and to earn a basic livelihood. Informal workers are forced to create their own jobs and employ family members because there are insufficient jobs in the modern sector of the economy. There is a high level of underemployment, low and erratic incomes and long working hours, among informal workers. There are low barriers to entry, and growth takes an extensive character (proliferation of more of the same small units lacking capital, skills and technology), rather than higher productivity. There is a spatial dimension to the problem, where informal enterprises are confined to marginal locations on the periphery of cities where consumers are poor and competition is intense.

5.2.5 Structural Unemployment

Economists generally distinguish between three different types of unemployment. Frictional unemployment exists when a lack of information prevents workers and employers from becoming aware of one another. It is usually a side effect of the job-search process, and may increase when unemployment benefits are attractive. Structural unemployment occurs when changing markets or new technologies make the skills of certain workers obsolete. And finally, cyclical unemployment is a result of the cyclical nature of the economy and occurs whenever there is a general downturn in business activity.

Structural unemployment can create a higher unemployment rate long after a recession is over. If ignored by policy makers, it can even lead to a higher natural employment rate.

Broadly, structural unemployment may originate from several sources. First, it could result, for instance, when farming skills move from rural to urban areas with low or no other skills to be engaged in the modern sector, particularly in industry. The second source is a situation whereby graduates are trained in the theory but lack the practical skills and experiences to operate modern industrial machinery and plant. To compound the conundrum, a significant number of university graduates and other tertiary-level institutions enter into the employment market that is already crowded with the unemployed and unskilled youth yearly.

The third source could be where a person has been trained but the skills acquired have become obsolete due to technological advancement in an industry as has often been the case in manufacturing where poorly skilled are becoming unskilled workers. This is the case in ICT-based operations where workers, in order to meet new skill specifications, must now get training in computer operations to manage new relatively sophisticated technology to get jobs in the same factories they worked in before.

The fourth source of structural unemployment seems to be the most dominant; a condition whereby thousands of graduates are being produced by universities and moving on into an economy where industry simply has gradually disappeared, and new industries and enterprises are not being created in enough numbers to accommodate them.

5.3 Putting Numbers to the Narrative

To examine the effect of ST on employment, the analysis of the trajectory of wealth creation in Africa using the GDP per capita in USD (Constant 2010) of a sample of nine African countries (Botswana, Ethiopia, Ghana, Kenya, Nigeria, South Africa, Tanzania, Tunisia and Uganda), from 1991 to 2017, was taken into consideration. Results are summarized in Figures 5.1 and 5.2. Accommodating all the countries was impossible due to huge variation of GDP per capita among the sample countries.

The sample can be divided into two subgroups with the GDP performance of the sample countries over the period being the discriminator. Botswana, Nigeria, South Africa and Tunisia constitute the first category, and they show higher values of GDP per capita than the rest of the sample. Considering the base-year income and CAGR of the sample countries, Kenya and Ethiopia experienced the lowest and highest growth of 1.09 percent and 4.65 percent, respectively. Nigeria has a growth rate of 2.90 percent, with South Africa and

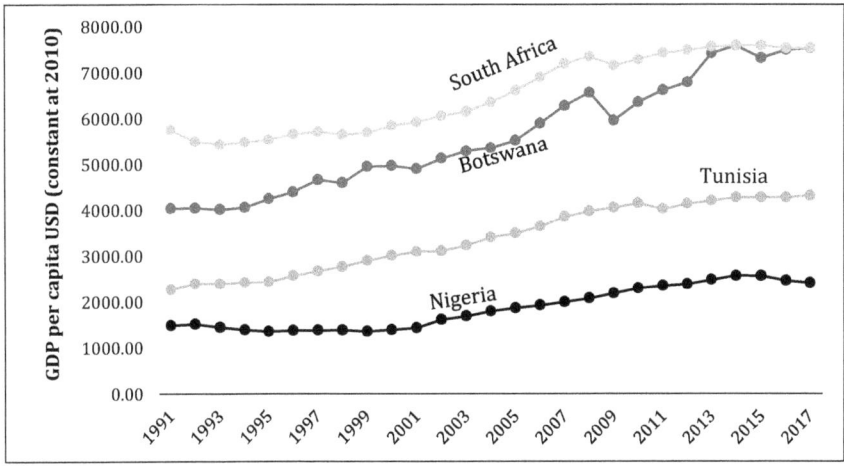

Figure 5.1 Wealth growth in sample countries (set 1)

Source: WDI online

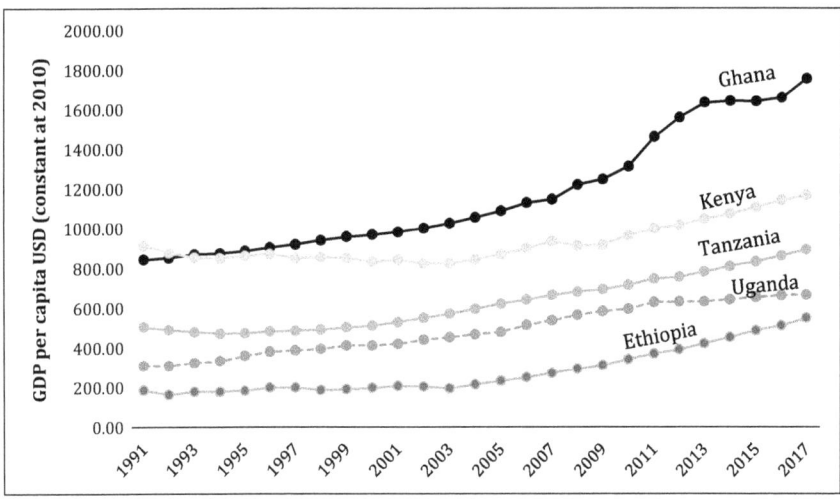

Figure 5.2 Wealth growth in sample countries (set 2)

Source: WDI online

Botswana having 1.58 percent and 2.75 percent, respectively. The CAGRs of Tanzania, Ghana, Tunisia and Uganda were 2.65 percent, 3.03 percent, 2.80 percent and 3.27 percent, respectively.

We further examined the impact of SC, the shares of value-added core sectors, that is, agriculture, manufacturing and services in the sample of

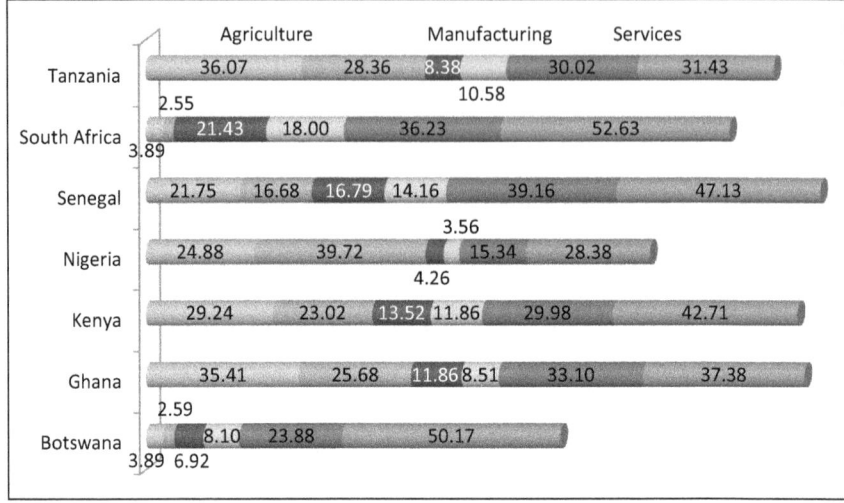

Figure 5.3 Shifts of shares for main economic sectors
Source: Figure is based on GGDC Structural Transformation Data

African economies between 1991 and 2013. The results of the study are hereafter summarized in Figure 5.3. The analysis is constrained by the availability of data.

What stands out in the figures for Botswana is the decline in share of agriculture—from 3.89 percent to 2.59 percent within the 22-year time frame. However, the share of the services sector grew at the rate of 2.66 percent per year for the country, reaching a 50.17 percent in 2013. As the sum of the contribution of agriculture and manufacturing can be considered as negligible for the economy of a country heavily relying on gold and diamond mining, the SC of Botswana follows the typical trend of developing world countries, with the services sector having grown faster than the other two.

The share of services constituting the Ghanaian economy follows the same trend as Botswana, although at the rate of 0.73 percent per year, reaching 37.78 percent in 2013. Despite constantly decreasing, agriculture represents one-quarter of Ghanaian economy as of 2013. The share of manufacturing sector declined from 11.86 percent to 8.51 percent during the period object of analysis, with the possible root causes of this decline being the availability of cheap Chinese products imported in the country or the abolition of quota system in 2005 by WTO in garments manufacturing.

The structure of the Kenyan economy followed analogous structural shifts, with the agriculture sector starting at 29.24 percent in 1991, declining at the rate of 0.66 percent, and the services sector share growing at 1.39 percent per year and reaching 42.71 percent in 2013. Still following the same pattern as the Ghanaian economy, the share of the manufacturing sector dropped from 13.52 percent to 11.86 percent with the abolition of quota system in apparel manufacturing being a possible root cause of the downturn.

The Nigerian economy presents a unique economic structure, being the only country in the sample for which the share of agriculture recorded an increment, moving from 24.88 percent to 39.72 percent. The services sector grew at a similar rate (2.59 percent per year), closing the period of observation with a share of 28.38 percent. The manufacturing sector share fell from 4.26 percent to 3.56 percent. These features are a reflection of Nigeria's focus on agriculture over manufacturing, with the country mainly relying on imports and making the former a source of employment and food security for Nigerians. Inevitably, the country equally imports significant agricultural products including processed tomatoes.

Both the agricultural and the manufacturing contribution to South African economy followed a negative trend within the 22-year interval, with the first one not being noteworthy and the second one shifting from 21.43 percent to 18.00 percent. Conversely, services sector grew at the rate of 1.95 percent per year, reaching a share of 52.63 percent in 2013.

The main contributions to the Tanzanian economy derive from agriculture and services sector, both moving down from 36.07 percent to 28.36 percent and from 30.02 percent to 31.43 percent, at a negative yearly rate of 1.36 percent and 0.18 percent, respectively. The share of services overtook that of agriculture showing that Tanzania shares this pattern of growth with Botswana and South Africa. Tanzanian manufacturing moved from a share of 8.38 percent to that of 10.58 percent.

A further analysis of shifts of value-added share was conducted for the mining, utilities and construction sectors for the African sample economies with data in the period between 1991 and 2013. The findings are presented in Table 5.1. Analysis is constrained by the availability of data.

The results of the analysis highlight two major STs. The first for Botswana, which moved from mining to services sector, is evidenced by the drop in the share of mining (from 41.57 percent to 17.16 percent) and the simultaneous growth of the services sector at a comparable rate (2.66 percent per year, reaching 50.17 percent in 2013).

The second notable transformation is with Nigeria where the share of mining declined at a rate of 3.14 percent per year down to a 28.17 percent share in 2013, positively spilling over agriculture and services sector.

The shift in employment between years 1991 and 2013 in the economic sectors (see Figure 5.4) completes the analysis of SC impact for the six African

Table 5.1 Shift of Value-Added Share in Mining, Utilities and Construction

Country	MIN_91	MIN_13	UTI_91	UTI_13	CON_91	CON_13
Botswana	41.57	17.16	1.28	1.29	8.88	7.59
Ghana	2.90	8.06	1.90	1.74	5.34	9.61
Kenya	0.64	0.58	2.64	2.08	5.10	5.41
Nigeria	52.61	28.17	0.13	0.14	1.53	2.30
South Africa	11.44	5.86	2.63	2.14	3.15	3.78
Tanzania	0.83	3.70	2.44	2.40	9.15	11.03

Source: Author's analysis

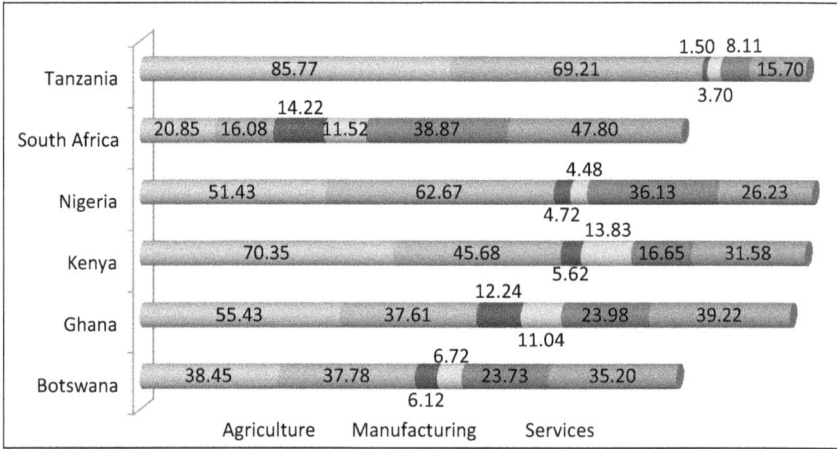

Figure 5.4 Shifts in agriculture, manufacturing and services employment

Source: Figure is based on GGDC Structural Transformation Data

countries constituting the sample. The data are available up to 2013 only and unavailable for other sample countries.

The trend for employment in Botswana's agriculture sector was traced by its value added, although declining at a considerably lower rate (−0.27 percent versus −2.95 percent yearly) and yet maintaining the largest share in terms of total employment. Parallel trends between employment and value added are to be found also for the services sector, with this last reaching an employment share of 35.2 percent in 2013. With regard to manufacturing, employment in the sector grew considerably faster than the value added.

During the 22 years observed, Ghana's services sector became its main source of employments (39.22 percent share), taking over from agriculture for which there was a dramatic decrease in employment reaching 37.22 percent from 55.43 percent in 1991. Among services in Ghana, employment in "finance, insurance, real estate and business services" was the one that grew the most (8.48 percent), then "trade, restaurants and hotels services" (5.10 percent).

Similar to Botswana, Kenyan agriculture sector with 45.68 percent share remained the main source of employment for Kenyans in 2013, despite having followed a negative trend (1.92 percent per year) within the period of observation. Numbers of employees for the other two sectors grew steadily, with manufacturing tripling its value and services growing at a rate of 2.78 percent per year. Within the latter sector, "employment in trade, restaurants and hotels" and "transport, storage and communication services" presented comparable growth rate of 6.92 percent and 6.90 percent, respectively. The growth of employment in "finance, insurance, real estate and business services" followed a more moderate path of 3.26 percent growth per year.

Unlike any other country included in the sample, Nigeria witnessed an increase in the share of both value added and employment in agriculture at a rate of 2.66 percent and 0.72 percent per year, respectively. It is also worth highlighting that the other two sectors recorded a decline in their shares of employment (with Nigerian services sector being the only one in the sample to lose shares of employment), the value-added share of services grew positively: this discrepancy regarding the services sector may imply that although productivity in both agriculture and services increased, the latter had a faster change.

On the same trajectory, South African manufacturing share in employment witnessed a negative growth rate (−0.43 percent) during the study period, together with the one of agriculture (reaching 16.08 percent in 2013 from 20.85 percent in 1991). A positive trend characterized the employment share of services sector, which grew from 38.87 percent to 47.80 percent at an annual rate of 1.05 percent. Within this sector, the highest growth rate was realized by "finance, insurance, real estate and business services" (5.22 percent), whereas "trade, restaurants and hotels services" grew at an annual rate of 2.19 percent.

Growth in employment share was recorded for Tanzanian manufacturing and services sector, growing averagely at 4.97 percent and 3.28 percent per year, although the latter remained a minor source of employment (15.7 percent). Despite being the largest source of employment for Tanzanians as of 2013, the agriculture sector saw its share falling from 85.77 percent to 69.21 percent. Similar to other African economies, "finance, insurance, real estate and business services" were the type of services growing faster (10.56 percent growth rate), followed by "transport, storage and communication" (8.98 percent) and "trade, restaurants and hotels" (6.27 percent).

To complete the picture, a similar analysis was carried out for value added; the share of employment in mining, utilities and construction sectors was the

Table 5.2 Change in Employment Share: Mining, Utilities and Construction

Country	MIN_91	MIN_13	UTI_91	UTI_13	CON_91	CON_13
Botswana	2.96	1.81	1.43	0.51	12.90	2.20
Ghana	0.99	2.89	0.39	0.36	1.65	3.30
Kenya	0.09	0.71	0.32	0.18	1.46	3.17
Nigeria	0.29	0.28	0.42	0.26	1.03	1.95
South Africa	8.44	1.76	1.03	0.52	5.28	7.12
Tanzania	0.52	0.74	0.10	0.56	0.67	1.64

Source: Based on GGDC structural transformation data

subject of observation and terms of comparison. Results of this study are summarized in Table 5.2.

Comparing value-added shares with the ones in employment, there is evident discrepancy between the significant contribution in value added for the mining sector in Botswana and Nigeria and a relatively small share in employment. A possible explanation for the phenomenon in Nigeria is the capital intensiveness of activities such as oil exploration, which do not contribute significantly to employment.

Clearly, when comparing the value-added share by various sectors in Africa, a common trend between countries seems impossible to find for long-term trend similarities.

The share of agriculture in added value declined in all the countries constituting the sample except for Nigeria. For this last, share of the sector is significantly big (39.72 percent), opposed to the relatively small values of Botswana and South Africa.

Similarly, at lower rates, manufacturing sector witnessed declines in Ghana (−1.40), Kenya (−0.71), Nigeria (−0.68) and South Africa (−0.70), with the remaining two countries growing their respective shares in manufacturing at comparable rates.

Shares of services sector grew for all six countries, with Botswana reaching a higher than 50 percent share in 2013, with the highest growth rate (2.66 percent). Shares of employment in mining, utilities and construction are not significantly large and did not undergo major changes during the observation period. Shares of mining in Botswana and Nigeria, in particular, went from being large in 1991 to declining sharply in 2013.

Moving from a comparison within countries to one involving the shares in question, although shares of employment do not seem to be proportionate with value-added shares; they do seem to follow the same trend. It is nonetheless important to highlight how value-added share in agriculture in Botswana and South Africa registers low percentages (2.58 percent and 2.55 percent, respectively). For the same sector, shares of employment are of 37.78 percent and 16.08 percent for the two countries, respectively. Conversely, in other countries, share of employment for the same sector, being significantly higher than the share of value added, signals the fact that completely neglecting the sector would mean shutting down a source of substantial employment.

With regard to employment share of agriculture, the only negative growth was registered in Nigeria (−1.18 percent rate), while South Africa (1.05 percent), Botswana (1.83 percent), Ghana (2.45 percent), Kenya (2.78 percent), and Tanzania (3.28 percent) all had positive trends.

5.4 Summing Up

The chapter confirms earlier analyses whereby the services sector registered far greater and significant growths in all the African economies. Although its productivity is far lower, it is a potential source of youth employment, albeit at the expense of the far more employment-inducing manufacturing sector. Kenya was the only exception where the limited growth and presence of the manufacturing sector constrained the share of employment, which remained approximately static during the period under analyses.

Clearly, Africa has experienced significant structural unemployment due to the absence of positive ST. The various analyses highlight, globally, well-rooted obstacles or inefficiencies in the urban labor market of the region, such as the gap between the characteristics of labor demand and supply, in terms of the set of skills required. As the features of the study suggest, this may be a result of the shift from industries to services, or from low-skill jobs to high-skill ones, of urban economies, and may therefore necessitate a mixture of demand- and supply-side policies in response.

SC has contributed to wealth creation significantly, and the relationship between the two is linearly positive; however, as for employment, the association with SC is not straightforward. For instance, SC (1.48 percent) in Tanzania was lowest while employment has recorded second-highest growth rate (3.01 percent). On the other hand, Kenya witnessed highest employment growth (3.50 percent) but experienced second-lowest SC. In other economies, the employment growth was around 2.5 percent except in South Africa, which experienced lowest employment growth of 1.33 percent. In sum, we find that while SC contributes to wealth creation, it does not necessarily guarantee employment creation.

Chapter 6

PATHWAYS OF URBAN LIVING STANDARDS

6.1 Introduction

Poverty reduction continues to be the central goal of the international development Agenda because poverty and inequality are not just manifestations of economic and industrial backwardness; they are sources of social tension and powerful sources of societal conflict and widespread mistrust between different groups. According to Adam Smith (2007), "No society can surely be flourishing and happy, of which the far greater part of the members are poor and miserable. It is but equity, that they who feed, clothe, and lodge the whole body of the people, should have such a share of the produce of their own labor as to be themselves tolerably well fed, clothed, and lodged." Therefore, poverty elimination was prioritized at the Millennium Summit debate as a key social development goal, it is also the capstone objective of the SDGs. Despite a significant reduction in the general poverty levels worldwide, about one billion of the world population lives under extreme poverty. The international target originally widely adopted in 2000 was to reduce by half the proportion of people living in extreme poverty by 2015. Despite concerted efforts at the highest level, the goal was met in some countries but remained a difficult challenge for many other countries. A new 2030 date has now been set arising from the post-2015 Agenda debate (United Nations, 2013).

A study for the United Nations University World Institute for Development Economics Research (UNU-WIDER) (2006) concluded that "high levels of inequality (above a Gini coefficient of 0.40) negatively impacts growth, due to "incentive traps, erosion of social cohesion, social conflicts, (and) uncertain property rights." Poverty has wide-ranging negative effects in all societies especially developing countries because, by their very nature of being less industrialized, African countries are characterized by laterally unintegrated production structures and fragmented markets that are weak relative to advanced industrial nations. Equally, governments in these countries are less effective in compensating through public policy for these weaknesses because the state itself lacks financial capacity. In other words, regardless of the level of development, poverty has a large *destructive* component associated with unequal opportunities, and this destructive inequality contributes to lower growth (Birdsall, 2006).

According to the World Bank (2000), "poverty is pronounced deprivation in well-being," where well-being can be measured by an individual's possession of income, health, nutrition, education, assets, housing and certain rights in a society, such as freedom of speech. Poverty is also viewed as a lack of opportunities, powerlessness and vulnerability. This definition broadens the definition of poverty to include hunger, lack of shelter, being sick and not being able to see a doctor, not being able to go to school and not knowing how to read, not having job, fear for the future, living one day at a time and losing a child to illness brought by unclean water. Poverty further entails lack of representation and freedom.

This chapter discusses industrial origins of rising living standards (LS) and the pathway for generating wealth and as mechanisms for getting Africa out of poverty. We examine the link between manufacturing, sustainable urbanization and LS, and their relationship to poverty in Africa. In so doing, we study the nexus of skill of workforce and poverty, and productivity growth, as a driver of employment in the process of ST. As countries industrialize, workers are pulled out of low-productivity agriculture to manufacturing, leading to both a rise in economy-wide productivity as well as an increase in the total proportion of workers with higher skills and competences migrating to higher-income wages in manufacturing. When compared to the subsistence income that these workers earn in agriculture, the wage gains that attend the process of industrialization represent a very significant step in changing the material conditions of large numbers of people previously mired in mass poverty. The channel for transmitting this specific competence-based mechanism includes education and training. This is because in a typical low-income African country, individual labor is by far the most critical asset possessed by the poor. In addition to these direct effects, industrialization can also be crucial in reducing poverty indirectly through the economy-wide positive employment effect on economic growth. The corresponding rise in income because of increased levels of employment stimulates spending thereby creating further demand and investments. Clearly, structural shift from agriculture to industry is therefore a well-known pathway out of poverty because it creates diverse avenues for wage employment.

At the early stage of transition from an agrarian economy to a modern economy, the manufacturing sector in an industrializing context possesses considerable potential in terms of labor absorption in contrast to the services sector. The services sectors of poorer countries are characterized by low-productivity activities largely in the informal services. Additionally, the high-productivity services sector is knowledge-based and skills-driven, and for this reason, unskilled workers migrating from agriculture do not find a fit for their level of training and knowledge. These include formal services sectors such as banking, insurance, finance, communications and information technology that are characterized by idiosyncratic knowledge sets. They are relatively low employment elastic and often require far more than the average farm worker possesses. The lower-level informal service sectors provide the employment basket for unskilled workers including retail trade and distribution, passenger transport and construction where wages and productivity are often low.

In other words, a very important channel for redistributive growth is employment, but large swathes of the population, particularly the youth and the middle class, have suffered greatly in the prevailing African employment market. This characteristic of the market, where we have growth without attendant employment opportunities strikes at the heart of the notion of human development as the agent of prosperity. Opportunity deprivation including that of jobs with decent wages robs society of its asset—its people, who are not engaged in productive activities. In this chapter, we argue for the central role of the human asset as an important prerequisite for dynamic industrialization, and for this reason, the systematic underinvestment in skills and education (including technical and vocational) might be one of the reasons why the African environment tend to sometimes circumscribe social and technological innovations common in dynamic Asian economies. Widespread unemployment in the absence of industrialization tend to widen inequality that is in turn closely associated with poor human capital formation (education, experience, apprenticeship) while lower level of human capital is associated with slower economic growth.

Following the above, a dynamic manufacturing sector operating in a sustainable urban milieu could be instrumental in fostering sustainable development through its capacity to generate wealth, create employment opportunities and produce a variety of goods and services, among other benefits. All of which improve quality of life and contribute to poverty reduction. As discussed in earlier chapters, the faster the growth rate of manufacturing output, the faster the growth rate of the GDP, which correlates highly with rising income, manufacturing labor productivity due to increasing returns, high skills and specialization, direct and indirect employment, job creation and lower prospects of structural unemployment (Kaldor, 1966, 1967). Moreover, linkage and spillover effects are stronger in manufacturing than other sectors. The evidence from several past studies of countries undergoing rapid growth confirms the centrality of manufacturing as an important engine of growth and, by implication, generation of employment in developing countries (Fagerberg and Verspagen, 2002; Kathuria and Raj, 2010; Szirmai, 2009).

Specifically, manufacturing contributes to growth in various ways. First, manufacturing productivity commands higher wages and remunerations than that associated with the agricultural sector, thus contributing more to improved LS. Second, the contribution of manufacturing to improved livelihoods is indirect via forward and backward linkages. According to some estimates, for every job created in manufacturing there is a multiplier effect of between five and twenty indirect jobs (UNIDO, 2012).

The environment of work, level of education and the work experience of an individual as well tend to affect LS, health and even the psychological state of individuals' and households' well-being. Most prominent among the measures of well-being is the income of the individual or of households; a variable considered the main indicator of economic development. Though the economic development of a nation is usually measured by income per capita, this approach has been questioned by scholars as the distribution of wealth among certain portion of the population is never fully captured by per capita income. For instance, income generated within the informal economy is often not aptly accounted for, while actual substandard living conditions are hidden in national income per capita statistics.

In addition to these factors, increase in informal sector employment, inequity in income, as seen in differing income levels between many in the informal versus formal sectors could also be due to inequity in opportunities or inequities in circumstances in which people were born and in which they live. This inequity does consider the known concept that individual effort levels could lead to differentiated income levels, whereby hard workers receive the biggest pay. However, this factor highlights the fact that lack of opportunity and differences in economic, educational and social background lead to the perpetuation of informal economic activities.

If the income of an individual or of households is considered the main indicator of their well-being, then the uncertainty and the relatively low earnings from much of the work in the informal small- or less-productive firms means that these workers earn less—in monetary terms, they have less eligibility for financial loans, and housing mortgage. As the working place or conditions of an individual determine more than the income they receive, poor working environment conditions may, therefore, translate to a lock-in into low quality of life. Furthermore, as poorly earning workers tend to live in informal settings and slums, they are forced to pay high prices for poor levels of goods and services, with little hope of remedial action taken by the state to meet the basic needs (Oyelaran-Oyeyinka, 2014).

6.1.1 *Living Standards and Employment*

Economic conditions, gender, education and family circumstances all contribute to the nature of employment, which in turn affects the quality of life and type of access to shelter. Institutions[1] and the rules that regulate the way things are organized within any society, whether economically, politically, culturally or legally, also affect the nature of employment. In turn, these same institutions would necessarily be part of any solution to the alleviation of workings conditions.

Industrial employment contributes to the LS of citizens in various ways and at different levels. At the level of the individual, paid employment provides income and therefore offers a route out of poverty. Because this income comes from productive activity, rather than a tax on such activity, it is often regarded as a 'sustainable' route out of poverty. At the household level, employment can raise LS and improve family stability.

At the city level, more people in work means higher aggregate incomes and consumer-spending power, which in turn stimulates overall economic activity and growth through a multiplier effect. It also means more people paying council rates and service charges, which improve the city council's financial position and its ability to borrow for additional investment in infrastructure and services. This can both respond to people's rising expectations of service quality and improved amenities, and the demand for additional services for households and firms moving to the city from elsewhere. The result can be a virtuous circle of self-reinforcing growth and improvements in the quality of life and subjective well-being of ordinary people.

6.2 Putting Numbers to the Narrative

By 2050, a projected two-thirds of the world's population will live in urban settlements and only one-third in rural areas.[2] The ST of Africa is evolving, but the nature and scale of a future urban Africa will be shaped by how well

---

[1] "High business costs and widespread informal sector activity are mainly caused by: ill-designed and unstable rules and regulations; a lack of well-defined and secure property rights; poor quality and nonexistent infrastructure and public services; deficient capacities and resources of government agencies to administer and enforce laws and regulations; a lack of transparency, accountability and political autonomy of governmental institutions; as well as a high degree of macroeconomic instability, unemployment and corruption" (Eggenberger-Argote, 2005: 12).

[2] Unless otherwise referenced, all population data in this chapter comes from United Nations Department of Economic and Social Affairs, Population Division (2014): 2014 Revision of the World Urbanization Prospects, CD-ROM Edition and World Urbanization Prospects: The 2014 Revision, Highlights (ST/ESA/SER.A/352).

African cities are planned and governed. Clearly, urban growth is inevitable; in 1950, 0.7 billion people lived in urban areas; this had increased to 2.6 billion by 1995 and to 4.0 billion by 2015. Over the next 30 years to 2050, it is projected an additional 2.4 billion people will live in urban areas while rural population will slowly decline from 2020, reaching around 3.2 billion in 2050, the urban population will increase to 6.3 billion.

In the main, urban growth transforms cities and citizens due to progressive productivity growth that result in improved standards of living. Between 1990 and 2013, the United Nations Development Programme's HDI for the world increased by almost 18 percent (UNDP, 2014). The world has experienced massive reduction in the number of people living in extreme poverty although averages hide the skewed country-specific and regional distribution of the changes. The World Bank estimates that the number of people living in poverty (on less than $1.25 a day (purchasing power parity (PPP)) declined from 1.93 million in 1990 (36.4 percent of the total global population) to 1.01 million in 2011 (14.5 percent of the global population) (World Bank, 2014). Economic transformation with the growth of cities has resulted in the greatest improvement in standards of living and reductions in poverty in history.

6.2.1 Methodology and Data

Drawing on the broad objectives of the book, we propose to quantify the association between DU (urbanization rate) and ST, along with other socioeconomic variables, specifically, LS. We applied econometric techniques to the analysis of selected countries representative of all the regions of Africa over a reasonable period to ensure that the association of urbanization and other indicators are well captured within a country. The analysis of these countries would enable us capture the role of country-specific characteristics in the urbanization process and ST. The selection of countries is representative of low- and high-income countries and as well, natural resource/manufactured-product exporters.

The analysis of five countries, namely, Ghana, Senegal, Morocco, Ethiopia, and Zambia, are presented in this chapter. In addition to basic statistical techniques, we used appropriate econometric techniques to quantify relationships between urbanization and LS indicators. The dependent variable being a censored one (percentage of urban population), the use of OLS method was inappropriate. Therefore, Censored Regression technique was utilized for the econometric analysis. The parameter coefficients enabled the sensitivity analysis as well. Such analysis not only quantifies the linkage between urbanization and other indicators of LS but also helps in drawing conclusions and recommendations related to policies, which is one of the main objectives. Individual-country analysis enables us to compare the impact of various indicators on urbanization in each country, which may vary from one country to another.

The definitions of the indicators used in the report are as follows: Mortality rate is taken as deaths under 5 per 100 live births, while fertility rate is number of births per women. The water and sanitation coverage are the percentage of population having access to improved water sources and sanitation facilities. The analysis is limited to 2013 because the data for LS variables are not available beyond this period. The FDI is the net flow of FDI as a percentage of GDP.

The econometric model specification is as follows:

Urbanization rate = f (VA_AGR, VA_IND, VA_MAN, VA_SER, GDP),

where

VA_AGR → Value added share by agriculture
VA_IND → Value added share by industry
VA_MAN → Value added share by manufacturing
VA_SER → Value added share by services
GDP → GDP per capita in USD (constant at 2005)

In addition, to the econometric model, the unidirectional association of the LS indicators with ST are identified. These are value-added share (agriculture, industry, manufacturing and services), child mortality rate, fertility rate, FDI and urban basic services (water and sanitation). The results are presented in Table 6.6. The most sensitive sector was used for relating ST to LS indicators in all the countries except Ethiopia. The most sensitive sector was identified by sensitivity analysis of coefficients of explanatory variables presented in Tables 6.1–6.5. Although the most sensitive sector in Ethiopia was industry, services sector (second most sensitive) was taken into consideration for relating ST with LS. This is because the value-added share of services is very high compared to industry.

6.3 Statistical and Econometric Analysis

To understand country-specific factors that influence urbanization and ST, we analyzed each country separately. As indicated earlier, the censored regression technique is used to quantify the relationship between urbanization and other indicators. The likelihood ratio (LR) Chi-square test is considered a better test for assessing the goodness of fit of the model rather than R-square statistics. An LR Chi-square test is a statistical test used to compare the goodness of fit of two models, one of which (the null model) is a special case of the other (the

Table 6.1 Urbanization and Structural Transformation in Ethiopia

Variables	Dependent variable: Degree of urbanization		Min.	Max.	Remarks
	Model 1	Model 2			
Constant	34.101	6.888			
AGR	−0.276*** (−5.23)		40.12	65.97	Value-added share of agriculture
IND	−0.449** (−2.59)		6.30	13.88	Value-added share of industry
MAN		0.166*** (3.07)	3.22	7.80	Value-added share of manufacturing
SER		0.080*** (6.60)	27.73	46.00	Value-added share of services
GDP		0.027*** (17.75)	113.71	293.60	GDP per capita in USD (constant 2005)
LR Chi-square	20.42***	86.49***			

Source: Author's calculation
Note: Figures in parentheses are T-statistics; Level of significance: ***→1 percent, **→ 5 percent, and *→10 percent.

Table 6.2 Urbanization and Structural Transformation in Ghana

Variables	Dependent variable: Degree of urbanization				Min.	Max.
	Model 1	Model 2	Model 3	Model 4		
Constant	67.536	69.211	27.606	22.109		
AGR	−0.680*** (−9.00)				23.15	45.56
IND	0.111 (0.91)				16.98	28.94
MAN		−2.633*** (−5.08)			5.4	10.51
SER			0.466*** (5.09)		29.56	49.36
GDP				0.047*** (11.32)	385.56	752.13
LR Chi-square	37.44***	18.51***	17.17***	47.04***		

Source: Author's calculation
Note: Figures in parentheses are T-statistics; Level of significance: ***→1 percent, **→ 5 percent, and *→10 percent.

Table 6.3 Urbanization and Structural Transformation in Morocco

Variables	Dependent variable: Degree of urbanization				Min.	Max.
	Model 1	**Model 2**	**Model 3**	**Model 4**		
Constant	99.342	91.710	4.548	40.161		
AGR	−0.890*** (−6.60)				12.20	22.25
IND	−1.061** (−2.45)				27.15	29.79
MAN		−2.119*** (−5.28)			15.93	19.65
SER			0.904*** (6.63)		49.18	60.10
GDP				0.008*** (17.60)	1373.12	2521.60
LR Chi-square	25.47***	17.95***	25.33***	60.51***		

Source: Author's calculation
Note: Figures in parentheses are T-statistics; Level of significance: ***→1 percent, **→ 5 percent, and *→10 percent.

Table 6.4 Urbanization and Structural Transformation in Senegal

Variables	Dependent variable: Degree of urbanization				Min.	Max.
	Model 1	**Model 2**	**Model 3**	**Model 4**		
Constant	55.208	53.593	11.619	27.142		
AGR	−0.493** (−5.17)				13.77	21.01
IND	−0.238 (−0.85)				22.21	25.47
MAN		−0.830*** (−5.14)			13.71	17.24
SER			0.499*** (5.17)		55.21	62.21
GDP				0.019*** (11.62)	635.06	801.50
LR Chi-square	18.5***	17.44***	17.59***	42.67***		

Source: Author's calculation
Note: Figures in parentheses are T-statistics; Level of significance: ***→1 percent, **→ 5 percent, and *→10 percent.

Table 6.5 Urbanization and Structural Transformation in Zambia

Variables	Dependent variable: Degree of urbanization				Min.	Max.
	Model 1	Model 2	Model 3	Model 4		
Constant	44.914	23.404	41.030	28.063		
AGR	−0.542*** (−15.73)				9.64	18.28
IND		0.442*** (6.71)			26.31	35.40
MAN			−1.382*** (−7.03)		8.11	11.34
SER			−0.060 (−0.36)		51.88	56.50
GDP				0.012*** (28.44)	582.62	1004.71
LR Chi-square	39.43***	19.85***	20.79***	54.79***		

Source: Author's calculation
Note: Figures in parentheses are T-statistics; Level of significance: ***→1 percent, **→ 5 percent, and *→10 percent.

alternative model). The results for each country are presented and discussed separately in the following subsections.

6.3.1 Urbanization and Productivity Country Analyses

Ethiopia

The parameter estimates along with test statistics of the econometric model for Ethiopia is presented in Table 6.1. It is seen from the table that there are two models with different specifications. It was not possible to include all the explanatory variables in a single model due to multicollinearity problem. Hence a two-model specification was used. The results show that value-added share of agriculture and industry is negatively associated with DU suggesting that the share of these two sectors have declined with increasing DU in Ethiopia. The coefficient of industry is significant at 5 percent while that of agriculture is at 1 percent (highest level of significance). On the one hand, the share of agriculture continuously declined since 1991 while that of industry increased from 7.61 percent in 1991 to 13.88 percent in 2003 and then dropped to 11.92 percent in 2013.

On the other hand, the parameters of manufacturing and services are positively significant at the highest level; value-added share of manufacturing and services have increased with increasing DU. Although the sign of association of manufacturing sector with urbanization was positive, its share was fluctuating. It was 3.37 percent in 1991, reached 7.80 percent in 1997 and declined subsequently to 4.03 percent in 2013. Like the industry and manufacturing sector, the share of services attained its peak in 2003 (46.00 percent) and has been fluctuating since then. The share of services varies from 31.03 percent in 1991 to 43.19 percent in 2013.

Ghana

The quantified association of urbanization with ST is presented in Table 6.2. Four econometric specifications were used to get rid of multicollinearity. The table shows that association between urbanization is negatively associated with the agriculture value-added share at the highest level of significance. The highest level of significance suggests that the association is robust. Model 2 shows that coefficient of MVA share is negative but highly significant. The negative association between urbanization and loss of value added in manufacturing should be a concern for the Ghanaian government. The results of Models 2 and 3 suggest that the value-added share of services and GDP per capita are positively and significantly related to the DU. The table also shows that econometric validity of all the models is substantiated by highest level of significance of LR Chi-square statistics.

The decline in the share of agriculture is on the expected lines of ST. Its share declined from 45.56 percent in 1991 to 23.15 percent in 2013 and was continuously declining. On the other hand, the industry share although increased from 16.98 percent in 1991 to 28.74 percent in 2013, it was fluctuating leading to positive but insignificant association with SC. The manufacturing share has also been fluctuating; it reached its peak of 10.51 percent in 1993 and declined to 4.59 percent in 2013. The services sector share dipped in the mid-1990s and regained from 30.36 percent in 1994 to 48.11 percent in 2013. The declining share of manufacturing and unstable share of industry needs to be the concern of the government.

The driving force behind the positive SC is the decline in productivity in low-productive sectors and increase in productivity in high-value-added sectors. It is expected that productivity in highly urbanized societies will be high. Figure 6.1 depicts the trend in productivity with the changing urban population in Ghana. It is evident from the figure that productivity in the industrial sector continued to decline until 2000 with an urbanization rate of

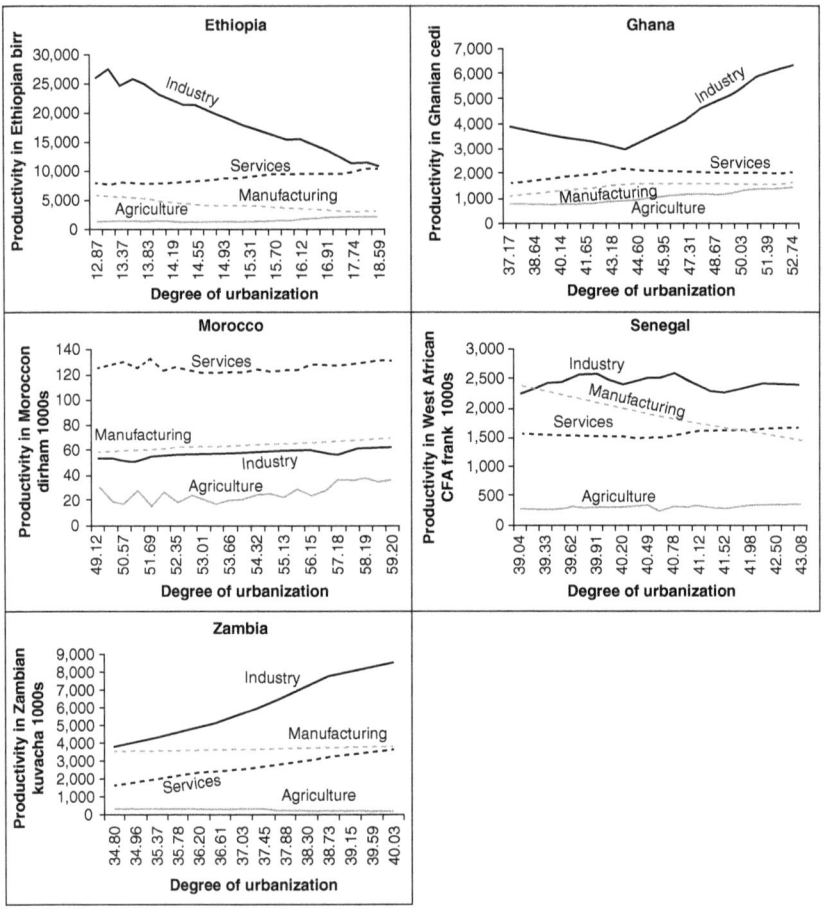

Figure 6.1 Labor productivity and urbanization

43.93 percent. However, industrial productivity has recorded a positive trend since then; it reached 6,311.12 Ghanaian Cedis in 2013. Productivity in all other sectors and urbanization have gone hand in hand, registering a positive growth. The findings suggest that the ST taking place in Ghana is, to some extent, positive. That being said, as with other African countries, the expected industrial growth was less than envisaged.

Morocco

The parameter estimates of the association between urbanization and ST in Morocco is presented in Table 6.3. Like Ethiopia, the association of urbanization with value-added share of agriculture and industry is negative but significant. These highly significant coefficients suggest that with increasing DU, the value-added share of these sectors decline consistently. Urbanization in Morocco increased from 49.12 percent in 1991 to 59.20 percent in 2013. The decline of value-added share of agriculture sector was from 22.25 percent in 1991 to 14.75 percent in 2013, while that of industry was fluctuating around 29 percent during the study period.

The result presented also shows that manufacturing share is also negatively but significantly associated with urbanization. The value-added share of manufacturing declined from 18.53 percent in 1991 to 17.03 percent in 2013. There was a net decline in manufacturing share fluctuating between 16 and 18 percent. The association between urbanization with value-added share of services and GDP per capita is like that of other countries. It is not only positive, but also highly significant. The decline in value-added share of industry and manufacturing is against the true spirit of ST. The changes in productivity might help in explaining the phenomenon. The association of urbanization and productivity is depicted in Figure 6.1.

From the figure, relative productivity levels in all the sectors did not change much. With comparatively high levels of urbanization of 59.20 percent urban population in 2013, the Moroccan economy is gradually tending toward a mono-sector economy, that is, services. The country is experiencing a shift in productivity through intra-sectoral changes; the workforce is moving away from a high-value-added sector: manufacturing. This is substantiated by the decline of employment share in manufacturing. It reduced from 15.20 percent in 1991 to 12.87 percent in 2013. Clearly, the services sector has grown relatively faster, as with other African countries pulling more people toward the sector. This is substantiated by the employment share of the sector, which increased from 19.20 percent in 1991 to 26.09 percent in 2013.

Senegal

The quantified association between urbanization and ST in Senegal is presented in Table 6.4. It shows that the association follows the pattern of other sample countries. The DU is not only negatively associated with value-added share of agriculture, industry and manufacturing sectors but it is highly significant in case of agriculture and manufacturing.

The urban population in Senegal increased from 39.04 percent in 1991 to 43.08 percent in 2013 while the share of agriculture declined from 20.28 percent in 1991 to 15.62 percent in 2013. The share of the sector was continuously decreasing except in 1993 (increased marginally to 20.58 percent and 21.01 percent in 1993 and 1995, respectively). The share of industry was

22.21 percent at the beginning of the study, fluctuating between 22.21 percent and 23.82 percent during 1991–2013, but was highest in 2002 (25.47 percent). The share of manufacturing was lowest among all the sectors in 1991 (15.43 percent) and reached to 17.24 percent in 2002. The share has been declining since then, reaching 13.71 percent in 2013 and resulting in negative and significant association with the DU.

On the other hand, the share of services was 57.52 percent in 1991 and declined until 1993 to 55.93 percent; it then increased to 60.57 percent in 2013. It is obvious that the value-added share of services is positively and significantly associated with urbanization. The results also suggest that as the GDP per capita increased, the percentage of urban population also increased.

It is evident from the figure that labor productivity in the manufacturing sector drastically declined with increasing DU while in the agriculture and services sectors it registered a positive trend. The decrease in employment share of agriculture suggests that the workforce is moving away to other sectors. Productivity in industrial sector has been fluctuating resulting in overall decline in productivity growth (CAGR: −0.10). The increase in labor productivity may be due to intra-sectoral changes in the industrial sector in the form of mechanization.

Although value-added share and productivity of industry saw a decline from 1991 to 2013, the share of employment increased from 2.31 percent in 1991 to 4.52 percent in 2013. It may be inferred that additional workforce is absorbed in low-value-added activities of the sector, giving rise to low-skilled employment and declining productivity. The manufacturing sector follows a similar trend to that of industry. The services sector is the only sector where labor productivity and employment share increased with increasing DU.

Zambia

Table 6.5 presents the association of DU[3] with ST and economic growth. From the table the coefficients of value-added share of agriculture and manufacturing are negatively associated with urbanization at the highest level of significance (1 percent), while the coefficient of industrial sector is positively associated with significance at the same level.

The value-added share of agriculture has been steadily declining since 2000. It dropped from 18.28 percent in 2000 to 9.64 percent in 2013 while urban population changed from 38.40 percent to 40.03 percent during the same period. Therefore, the relationship between urbanization and SC with respect to share of agriculture is understandable. The share of manufacturing follows a similar trend to that of agriculture. Its share declined from

---

[3] Zambia is the only country where urban population decreased from 38.99 percent in 1991 to 35.26 percent in 1999 and since then it has been increasing.

10.70 percent to 8.13 percent during 2000–13. On the other hand, the share of industrial sector increased from 26.31 percent in 2000 to 33.85 percent in 2013 leading to highly significant association.

The associations between value-added shares of these sectors with urbanization are not surprising as this is the case in many of the sample countries. What is surprising is the association between DU and value-added share of services sector. The share declined during 2000–7 from 55.41 percent to 51.83 percent and has been increasing marginally since then. The share reached the value of just 56.50 percent in 2013. The results show that services sector is not performing well in Zambia rather it is the industrial sector that increased its value-added share. The productivity analysis presented in Figure 6.1 would unlock the mystery of SC in Zambia.

The results depicted suggests that productivity in agriculture sector declined from 2,892,130 to 1,817,150 Zambian kwacha during 2000–13, a phenomenon unique to Zambia compared to other sample countries. Labor productivity in other sectors registered a positive growth, the highest being in industrial sector (CAGR: 6.86 percent) followed by services sector (CAGR: 6.19 percent). The noticeable fact is that although productivity in services sector increased, value-added share remained stagnant which may be due to decrease in employment. This is substantiated by the fact that the share of employment in services sector declined from 22.64 percent to 20.77 percent. It may be inferred that productivity gain in the sector is due to layoff of the workforce. The positive aspect of the ST is the increase in productivity and value-added share of the industrial sector.

The industrial sector is the only one that has experienced growth of productivity as well as share of employment and value added. Productivity increased from 37,950,060 to 85,165,440 Zambian kwacha while the share of employment increased from 3.00 percent to 4.18 percent. The increase in productivity and share of employment contributed to increase in value-added share of the sector. The manufacturing sector did not experience much change in labor productivity as well as share of employment. Although the employment share in the sector grew at the rate of 1.35 percent annually, its magnitude is very small (3.34 percent in 2013) compared to other sectors. The ST led by industrial sector resulted in an increase in the urban population from 34.80 percent in 2000 to 40.03 percent in 2013.

6.3.2 Analysis of Urban Living Standards

Ghana

Figure 6.2 depicts the impact of urbanization on LS in Ghana. For example, we observe that the impact of urbanization on access to improved water sources has been very impressive. The population coverage changed from

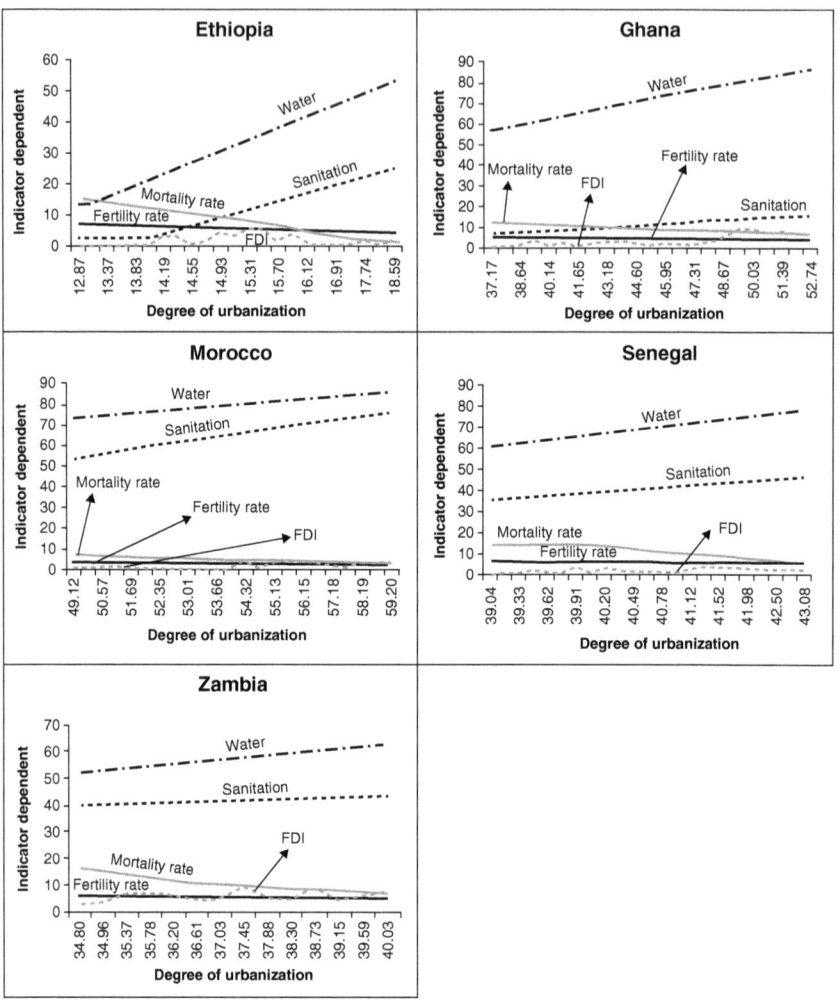

Figure 6.2 Urbanization and living standards

57.10 percent in 1991 to 86.50 percent in 2013. However, the impact of other factors was much less compared to Ethiopia. The population with improved sanitation facilities did not change much. It increased from 7.30 percent in 1991 to 14.70 percent in 2013. The high DU was expected to attract more FDI; but in case of Ghana, it was fluctuating until 2007 and has been declining since then. The share of FDI to GDP (9.52 percent) was highest in 2008 and declined to 6.75 percent in 2013.

The impact of urbanization on health services has not been very impressive. The mortality rate declined from 12.31 in 1991 to 6.65 per 100 live births. Similarly, fertility rate also declined from 5.51 in 1991 to 4.21 per woman in 2013 but with a much lower pace than that of Ethiopia. While the health parameters in Ethiopia and Ghana were similar in 2013, their degrees of urbanization were very different. The urban population in Ghana is 52.74 percent while in Ethiopia it is just 18.59 percent. Despite the fact that ST tends to be moving in the right direction in Ghana, its impact on urbanization and LS indicators are not as impressive as they need to be.

Morocco

The impact of urbanization on access to improved water resources and sanitation facilities is quite significant. The percentage of the population with access to improved water increased from 73.30 percent in 1991 to 85.10 percent in 2013, while the percentage of population with access to improved sanitation also increased from 53.80 percent to 76.50 percent during the same period. The accessibility of these services is very high. It may be attributed to DU and GDP per capita. In fact, they are highly correlated. The per capita income in highly urbanized countries is high. As far as the impact of urbanization on FDI is concerned, it is lower than Ghana, suggesting that urbanization has not succeeded in attracting FDI.

The health indicators in Morocco are comparable with many other countries. The impact of urbanization is significant. Mortality rate changed from 7.65 in 1991 to 2.97 per 100 live births in 2013. Similarly, fertility rate rose to 2.54 per woman in 2013. It is clear that SC contributed to positive urbanization and that in turn improved the socioeconomic indicators and quality of life of the citizens in Morocco.

Senegal

The impact of urbanization on living standard is depicted in Figure 6.2. It can be seen from the figure that the percentage of population with access to improved water sources increased from 60.70 percent in 1991 to 77.00 percent in 2013. The population with improved sanitation facilities increased from 36.00 percent to 46.60 percent during the same period. For the ratio of net FDI to GDP, the Senegalese government was able to attract more FDI as DU increased. The FDI to GDP ratio changed from −0.13 in 1991 to 2.08 percent in 2013 by registering an annual growth rate of 5.90 percent.

The impact on health services has also been positive: mortality rate declined from 13.87 in 1991 to 5.25 per 100 live births by registering a decline of 4.70 percent annually. Similarly, the fertility rate declined from 6.52 in 1991 to

5.13 births per woman. Although fertility has changed substantially in Senegal, it is higher than other sample countries, with the exception of Zambia.

Zambia

It can be seen from Figure 6.2 that basic services in terms of water and sanitation improved marginally. The percentage of population with access to improved water sources increased from 53.00 percent to 63.80 percent while population with improved sanitation facilities marginally increased from 40.60 percent to 43.50 percent.

Zambia was successful in attracting FDI. The ratio of net FDI flow to GDP increased from 3.38 percent to 7.83 percent. This may be attributed to the recent focus on the industrial sector. The health sector experienced an improvement in its services. This is substantiated by the decrease in mortality rate from 16.31 to 7.02 per 100 live births. Similarly, the fall in fertility rate was from 6.10 to 5.43 births per women, still highest among the sample countries.

6.4 The Differential Impacts of Growth on the African Urban Consumer

A diversified urban economy creates and support high-quality employment that enables citizens enjoy the urban dividend. Our premise, as is evident in Chapter 3, is that sustainable urbanization and dynamic industrialization tend to go in tandem with economic ST that puts people at the center of development. Structural economic transformation and inclusive growth is central to Africa's Agenda 2063 at the core of which is the pursuit of economic diversification, industrialization and value addition. The analysis in this book shows that over the long term, there is significant positive correlation between levels of urbanization, LS and economic growth. However, as demonstrated earlier, the eradication of poverty and inequality remains an unfinished assignment, even while several countries are growing and diversifying their economies, nonetheless. Where urbanization is planned, there is a strong propensity to rising productivity (through migration of workers from agricultural work to different urban jobs), increasing demand and investment in diverse sectors. Moreover, when cities grow in ways that promotes the "urban divide," majority of urban dwellers are shut out of the promise of the urban dividend.

A new consumer class is emerging demanding better types of services, stimulating the construction of basic urban services such as rails, roads and water systems. Recent studies show that since 2000, Africa's annual private infrastructure investments have tripled, with a yearly average of $19 billion from 2006 to 2008 (McKinsey, 2010). As productivity rises, Africa's urban workforce has expanded in quality, estimates putting the working age at above 500 million and set to rise to 1.1 billion by 2040.

However, where cities develop without proper planning, the result is unsustainable urbanization that either makes cities unlivable materially or creates unbridgeable chasms of inequity. Take the case of some African cities.

Kinshasa is the capital and largest city of the DRC. Kinshasa ties with Johannesburg for the status of the second-largest city in SSA and the third-largest in the whole continent, only after Lagos and Cairo. In Kinshasa the cost of living is very high in comparison to cities of comparative GDP per capita. Accommodation, health care, transportation, communication, education, alcohol, groceries, recreation and restaurant meals are very expensive. Kinshasa, for example, is 98.9 percent more expensive than Houston, Texas, for groceries, 117.2 percent more expensive for household costs than Kuala Lumpur and 93.4 percent more expensive for transport costs than Dubai.

The population of Kinshasa is 11.5 million, while the inflation rate is 6.6 percent (2019 estimate). Due to administrative boundaries, over 60 percent of the city's land is rural in nature. The economy of the DRC has vast potential due to its natural resources and mineral wealth; nevertheless, the economy of the DRC has declined drastically since the mid-1980s.

The security risk for both the rich and poor in the DRC is high. Risks include petty crime, violent crime and armed robberies. Medical care is extremely limited thus, very costly and medical evacuation is often necessary.

Addis Ababa, on the other hand, has experienced very significant change due to government's drive for industrialization. However, the cost of living for professional migrants in Addis Ababa is overall average, in comparison to other places in the world. Accommodation, clothing, communication and appliances are comparatively high. Addis Ababa is, for example, 0.8 percent more expensive than Houston, Texas, for groceries, 57.9 percent more expensive for household costs than Kuala Lumpur and 34.8 percent more expensive for transport costs than Dubai. Although not a consumption city like Luanda and Abuja, the skewed nature of growth leaves many of the cities vulnerable on the other side of the divide.

Known for its commercial and cultural hub, Addis Ababa stands 7,726 feet (2,355 meters) above sea level, making it the third-highest capital in the world. With an estimated population of about 4 million, the city experiences an annual growth rate of 3.8 percent. Addis Ababa is a diplomatic hub of Africa with a huge presence of expatriates from nearly every country and diverse economic activities.

The economy of Ethiopia is based on agriculture, which accounts for half of GDP, 60 percent of exports and 80 percent of total employment. The security risk for foreigners in Ethiopia is medium, but high for the majority living in the border areas. The population of Addis Ababa is 7.8 million while the inflation rate is 15.4 percent (2019 estimate).

The city has undergone a construction boom with tall buildings rising in many places. Also, various luxury services have become available and the construction of shopping malls has recently increased. Some people have labeled the city the spa capital of Africa. A vast open-air market known as the Mercato, on the western side of the city, is the site for trade of leather, metal and textile goods from flourishing craft industries, and regional agricultural produce such as coffee, tobacco and dairy foods. It is the largest open market in Africa.

Overall, urban dynamic has not always been positive for the African consumer. The phenomenon of consumption cities has characterized the process of ST. For example, Luanda illustrates such a phenomenon. Angola's capital of Luanda is Africa's second-largest oil producer and more expensive compared to other cities in the country especially in the face of increased migration to urban centers. Angola's GDP per head is US$5725.33 (Trading Economics, 2019a) in 2018 when adjusted by PPP.

Luanda may not be the most expensive city in the world for the local population, but the thriving oil economy, limited supply of luxurious housing and a high demand for it among expatriates makes housing expensive. Affordable housing in Luanda is, in many cases, substandard, for the average Angolan as two out of three of Luanda's 2.8 million residents live in squalor in a country urbanizing at the rate of 4 percent annually. Although the country is oil and mineral rich, trade with the country does not translate to increased wages and salaries for the local population, which has led to the revision of customs tariff and tax regulations.

The cost of living in Luanda can best be described as astronomical. Luanda topped the Mercer Cost of Living Survey as the most expensive expat destination in the world in 2013, 2014 and 2015. The destruction and devastation caused by nearly thirty years of war have left Angola with little infrastructure to produce and manufacture goods, and even less arable land to use for basic agricultural development. As a result, nearly everything is imported and costly.

The cost of accommodation keeps increasing due to a glaring undersupply and overdemand. Low bed capacity and a lack of the kind of secure housing that can be used to entice expats abroad have set rental prices extraordinarily high. Lifestyle and preference determine what will be spent on food. Fresh local produce is available at a reasonable price, but bigger supermarkets where much of the products are imported are more expensive. Eating out is also quite expensive and not something that most people do on a regular basis.

In sum, domestic consumption contributes significantly to growth in African countries but the non-exporters of manufactures risk being "consumption cities" and down the line will run into severe balance of payment crisis as has happened recently with the collapse of the oil market. African cities added more than 10 million people in the past decade while real consumer spending grew by 3 percent to 5 percent annually since 2000, and 90 percent of all households have some discretionary income. As a result, consumer-facing sectors such as retailing, banking and telecom have grown rapidly. Urbanization has also prompted a construction boom that created 20 percent to 40 percent of all jobs over the past decade (McKinsey, 2010).

6.4.1 Comparative Analysis

The comparative analysis of the sample countries is presented in Table 6.6. The table shows the base-year value of the indicators and the growth rates. The base year was 1991 in all the countries except Zambia in which it is 2000.

From the table, we observe a positive and highest growth rate of value-added share in services sector in all the countries except Zambia in which the industrial sector recorded the highest growth rate. Although the services sector experienced a negative growth rate (−0.07 percent) in Zambia, the value-added share of the sector is still highest (56.50 percent in 2013). The results show that ST in Ethiopia, Ghana, Morocco and Senegal is led by the services sector while in Zambia it is the industrial sector. Another noticeable fact is that the share of the agriculture sector declined in all the sample countries. The increase in the value-added share in services sector and decline in agriculture share is the right direction of SC.

However, the neglect of manufacturing and industrial sector runs contrary to conventional wisdom of ST. The countries need to reorient their economic policies so that manufacturing and industrial sectors remain competitive in the era of globalization. The industrial sector is being skipped by all the sample countries, excluding Zambia. The manufacturing sector was given due attention in Ethiopia where the value-added share of the sector increased with increasing urbanization. In general, urbanization has not contributed to industrial and manufacturing sectors. Although ST is led by services sector, it has equally resulted in rising urbanization and higher per capita income. The growth of urbanization was between 0.43 in Senegal and 1.59 percent in Ghana while GDP per capita growth was between 1.17 in Senegal and 4.61 percent in Zambia.

A comparative analysis of the impact of urbanization on social sector suggests that urbanization has contributed both negatively and positively. On the negative side, higher rates of urbanization have led to slum formation, including overcrowding and poor hygiene living where there is infrastructure deficit. On the positive side, where cities make adequate investment in infrastructure, citizens gain access to public goods. This is substantiated by the

Table 6.6 Comparative Statistics

Indicators		Country →	Ethiopia	Ghana	Morocco	Senegal	Zambia
Structural Change (Share of value added)		Sector	Services	Services	Services	Services	Industry
		Base-year share	31.03	37.46	49.18	57.52	26.31
		CAGR	1.82	2.26	0.64	0.37	2.62
		Share in 2013	43.19	48.11	56.55	60.57	33.85
Urban population		Base-year percent	12.87	37.17	49.12	39.04	34.80
		CAGR	1.55	1.59	0.78	0.43	1.12
GDP per capita in USD constant 2005		Base year	129.05	385.56	1479.76	677.30	582.62
		CAGR	3.94	2.84	2.90	1.17	4.61
Social sector	Sanitation coverage	Base year per cent	2.60	7.30	53.80	36.00	40.60
		CAGR	12.69	3.19	1.57	1.17	0.54
	Water coverage	Base-year percent	13.40	57.10	73.30	60.70	53.00
		CAGR	6.50	1.88	0.66	1.09	1.44
Health services	Mortality rate	Base-year percent	20.02	12.31	7.65	13.87	16.31
		CAGR	−5.21	−2.73	−4.24	−4.70	−6.35
	Fertility rate	Base-ear percent	7.19	5.51	3.91	6.52	6.10
		CAGR	−2.2	−1.19	−1.94	−1.10	−0.88

Source: Author's calculation

finding that more people gain access to improved water sources and sanitation facilities. The findings are in line with other studies carried out in the context of Africa. For instance, Kariuki et al. (2013) in their study of urbanization in Africa reported that upgrading of electricity, water, sanitation, roads and drainage did improve the effectiveness of service delivery.

Morocco achieved a very high growth of sanitation coverage (1.57 percent) despite having a high percentage in the base year. It may be due to ST and high per capita income in the base year. On the other hand, Zambia has not succeeded much though its base-year value is comparatively high. Ethiopia, whose base-year sanitation coverage was just 2.60 percent, achieved remarkable success in providing improved sanitation facilities. The provision of these services seems to be a function of ST and base-year value of the services. For instance, in Ethiopia, the percentage of population with improved water sources increased by 6.50 percent annually because base-year coverage was very low. On the other hand, in Morocco, the growth rate was lowest (0.66 percent) due to highest base-year value of 73.30 percent. Health services follow a similar trend to that of water and sanitation services. As a result, the mortality and fertility rate declined with an increase in the DU.

6.5 Summing Up

The findings of this chapter suggest that with the exception of Zambia, all the countries have experienced a services sector–led SC. The manufacturing sector declined in all except Ethiopia while industrial sector also declined in all except Zambia. The two important sectors, that is, manufacturing and industrial sectors are stagnating, which is against conventional SC. The true benefits of ST could be reaped only if the workforce moves from low-productive to high-productive sectors. This is not happening in most African countries. At the same time, urban population is growing in all the countries. The growth of urban population without proper basic services would lead to slums. To avoid such a situation, countries need to focus on appropriate economic as well as human resource development policies. The appropriate human development policies would transform youths into skilled workforce, thus providing them opportunity to be employed in high-value-added activities. The points are shared by other studies in Africa. For instance, Turok (2014), in his study on urbanization and Africa's economic revival, also indicated that slowing the level or rate of urbanization should not be an important goal of policy makers. African governments should not seek to accelerate or restrict rural–urban migration but should rather focus on strengthening the economic and employment base of cities and ultimately improving the quality of urbanization. The country-specific policy implications are presented below.

In Ethiopia, although the value-added share of manufacturing has increased with increasing DU, the share of the sector is very small compared to other sectors. The findings show a decrease in productivity of the sector, while employment share has increased over time suggesting that additional workforce is being absorbed in low activities of the sector. This situation needs to be addressed by appropriate economic and human development policies.

Although the share of industrial sector increased in Ghana, the association is statistically insignificant. The labor productivity in the sector also increased with increasing DU in the later period of the study suggesting that the sector is performing well. The productivity of the manufacturing sector registered a positive growth with fluctuating share of value added, while employment share of the sector also declined suggesting that productivity growth may be due to layoff of the existing workforce. This is a real concern for the Ghanaian economy, and the government needs to reorient its policies to improve the sector.

The value-added share of industrial sector in Morocco declined (CAGR: −0.06 percent) with an increasing urban population. However, labor productivity and employment registered positive growth of 0.72 and 1.86 percent annually. This phenomenon suggests that additional workforce is employed in low-value activities of the sector. The situation could be improved among other policy measures by providing appropriate training to youths toward employabilities in high-value activities. This in turn is expected to augment productivity of the sector leading to high share of the value added. The manufacturing sector, on the other hand, registered a negative growth of value added as well as employment share (−0.68 and −0.72 percent, respectively), though the productivity grew marginally (0.77 percent).

The value-added shares of industrial and manufacturing sectors in Senegal are negatively associated with the DU suggesting that additional urban population is employed in low-value-added activities. This is substantiated by the fact that productivity in both the sectors declined (CAGR: −0.10 and −2.26 percent in industry and manufacturing, respectively). Another case in point is the increase in employment share, which experienced an annual growth of 3.44 and 2.61 percent, respectively. As recommended for other countries, the government needs to concentrate on training and skill development for these sectors to enable youth employment in high-value activities.

The performance of the industrial sector in Zambia is in the right direction of ST, but decline in value-added shares of manufacturing and services sectors (CAGR: −2.61 and −0.07 percent, respectively) is the real concern. Like many other countries, the productivity and employment shares of manufacturing sector marginally improved but did not result in increasing labor productivity. As for the services sector in Zambia, labor productivity and employment shares went in the opposite direction. The decline in employment share in the services sector needs to be controlled. The findings recommend Zambia to pay due attention to manufacturing and services sectors by means of appropriate economic and human resource development policies.

It is clear from the findings that all the countries need to have in place appropriate human development policies.

Chapter 7

CONCLUSIONS AND RECOMMENDATIONS: MAPPING AFRICA'S GROWTH PATHWAYS

7.1 Introduction

This concluding chapter serves to summarize the findings of the various chapters. The main conclusion that can be drawn is that when countries engage with policies and practices that deepen ST in ways that foster economic and industrial diversification, the broad outcome is quantitative improvements in TFP. This in turn lead to socioeconomic development and a rise in living standards. In this book, we analyze the relationships between SC, industrialization, urbanization and the resulting socioeconomic outcomes in African countries.

The central theoretical underpinning of the book is ST while the analytical subthemes, making up the book, can be identified as key variables of productivity growth, industrialization, urbanization, poverty and employment. When capital and labor move from low-productivity to high-productivity sectors, SC fuels economic growth and raises productivity. African countries with "dual" economies, this being both modern and traditional sectors, have the potential to significantly increase their productivity and growth through these movements and see resulting gains in resource allocation efficiency, even when within-sector productivity is not changing much. The book employs labor productivity as the measure of productivity, because TFP could not be used due to the lack of data.

The main sources of productivity growth are either in the main the adoption of advanced technologies or upgradation of skill of the workforce. Both inputs are expected to result in higher productivity. In other words, productivity growth could be treated as an outcome of technology transfer or the development of endogenous skills through training and learning.

In the narrative of ST, two dynamics take place: "the rise of new industries (i.e. economic diversification) and the movement of resources from traditional industries to these newer ones. Without the first, there is little that propels the economy forward. Without the second, productivity gains don't diffuse in the rest of the economy."[1] The study is concerned with understanding SC dynamics and the resulting effects on job creation, living standards and the efficiency of productive cities through manufacturing productivity growth that benefit majority of citizens. We did not treat SC as an endogenous factor as it has bidirectional relationship with many indicators of economic development but also has unidirectional relationship with few. For instance, poverty is expected to influence SC and not the other way around.

The evidence from all these analytical exercises show that African countries have witnessed considerable but varying forms of SC over the past few decades. There are three distinctive features of growth in the several African countries. The first being that economic growth is proceeding without the expected job creation. Second, urbanization has been rapid, but this has not been accompanied by the expected industrialization. Third, these countries have largely skipped the industrial phase transiting rather directly from agriculture to low-value services. The countries that earlier recorded some level of industrialization have subsequently experienced premature deindustrialization. Our conclusion is that the massive rates of unemployment that characterizes African economies is rather structural in nature resulting from this unconventional pathway described above. This suggests that countries may well record economic growth, whether through within-sector productivity increase or through SC, but this may not necessarily lead to employment, an important concern for long-term development.

Below we present the main issues and the implications for African development from the individual chapters.

7.1.1 Introduction and Methodology

The chapter introduces the topic of ST and analyzes its impact on economic growth with empirical measures. It reviewed relevant but selected literature given this is a wide field. The detailed literature survey enabled us identify gaps in existing studies of the SC and economic development. The unique contribution of the book was stated in the chapter including the relationship of ST or SC with urbanization and living standards. We analyzed to some depth, what Dani Rodrik termed "premature deindustrialization" in African countries and as well what we in this book term "premature transition to the service sector."

---

[1] Dani Rodrik and Margaret McMillan (2011), paper prepared for a joint ILO-WTO volume.

Perhaps for the first time, advanced statistical techniques were used to quantify SC. In the estimation of composite score of SC sectors were included: agriculture, mining, manufacturing, utilities, construction, "trade, restaurants and hotels services," "transport, storage and communication services" and "finance, insurance, real estate and business services."

7.2 The Structural Transformation Pathways

7.2.1 Structural Transformation and Employment

The chapter focuses on the nature and patterns of economic growth and job creation. SC in terms of shifts in employment was analyzed in detail. The emergence of modern sectors is expected to result in movement of labor from a traditional sector, such as agriculture. In conventional SC models, it is expected that surplus labor from low-value-added sectors will be fully absorbed in new sectors resulting in employment including newly graduating youths from universities. However, our findings in this book corroborate some recent studies that in a large number of African countries labor is being absorbed in low-value-added activities of modern service sectors resulting in little or no value addition. The role of human capital and skills development, institutions and policies would be crucial in harnessing the benefits of SC.

Our findings show differences across countries when we relate employment, wealth and ST. In the Africa situation, while SC contributes significantly to overall GDP, it does so with little contribution to jobs. Economists generally distinguish between three different types of unemployment. Frictional unemployment exists when a lack of information prevents workers and employers from becoming aware of each other. It is usually a side effect of the job search process and may increase when unemployment benefits are attractive. Structural unemployment occurs when changing markets or new technologies make the skills of certain workers obsolete and as we analyzed in this book, when people move from rural to urban areas where industrial opportunities are nonexistent. Finally, cyclical unemployment is a result of the cyclical nature of the economy and occurs whenever there is a general downturn in business activity. Structural unemployment, which is the most prevalent in the African context, tends to create more sustained and chronic unemployment in the long term, and when not addressed could result in a higher natural employment rate.

The most important factor responsible for the incidence of SC and unemployment is the absence of appropriate skills both for entrepreneurship and for the high-value-added activities, which result from SC. In order for countries to raise and augment productivity that generate employment in any sector would require commensurate skill-formation agenda.

An important finding is that compared with the two other sectors, the services sector in SSA is a low-skill set of activities driven largely in the main by the presence of low-skill labor. This is different from the relatively more technology-intensive manufactures and knowledge-intensive environment in emergent Asia, and the advanced industrial countries. In other words, Africa's services sector is not driven by skill-based performance, but rather the sector is operating within low-cost, low-value telecom and other segments. This suggests that services value added and its effects on real economic growth might not be sustainable. Therefore it can be said that the sector is characterized by low-skill activities devoid of significant manufactures with products comprising, mainly, office and stationery supplies, musical instruments and parts, records, tapes and similar low-value telecom products.

The dominance of services and the stagnation of industry have resulted in Africa's persistent structural unemployment. In our analysis of urbanization and SC, we observe deep-seated obstacles or inefficiencies in African urban labor markets, such as a mismatch between the characteristics of labor demand and supply in terms of necessary skill sets. This may result from shifts in the composition of urban economies from industry to services, or from low-skilled to high-skilled occupations, and may also require a combination of demand- and supply-side policy responses.

We recommend that governments should proactively promote skill-development programs that particularly target the youth as this age group constitutes the future generation of workers and the potential actors of change. Policy makers should therefore expand access to education opportunities at all levels and adapt technical, vocational and higher education to changing labor market requirements.

7.2.2 Inter- and Intra-Sectoral Productivity Growth

The chapter analyzed productivity growth during 1991–2013. The entire study period was divided into smaller periods to capture productivity growth more effectively. Four major sectors, namely, agriculture, manufacturing, industry and services, were included in the study. The shift-share analysis technique was applied to quantify the contribution of intra-sectoral changes and SC in productivity growth. The shift-share analysis technique was used to identify the share of productivity growth within sector and due to SC.

Conventional ST is accompanied by productivity growth. However, recent empirical evidence suggests that in some instances this could take place without much change in labor productivity; this is the case with many African countries. One of the principal reasons for this phenomenon is the peculiar urban dynamics that occur through the movement of unskilled labor from rural to urban settings in search of factory jobs that are absent. This leads in the main to underemployed and unemployed people stuck in informal economies in African cities that have been described in this book as "Consumption Cities." This is very common in economies that depend largely on export of natural resources. Nonetheless, the contribution of SC to productivity growth was in large measured positive in a few countries, namely, Ghana, Nigeria and Tanzania, contrary to the situation in Asian countries that are almost all higher than that of Africa. The findings of this book suggest a need for specific policies that facilitate productivity growth. A distinguishing characteristic of successful nations is that explicit economic and industrial policies have been implemented to ensure the absorption of surplus labor from agriculture into other sectors leading to high-value-added jobs. Consequently, productivity growth in other sectors leads to sustained positive economic growth and structural employment. The capacity of bureaucracies needs to be strengthened for proper policy coordination that allows economic and social institutions complement rather than negate each other. An important source of economic inefficiency is the lack of institutional coordination involving economic actors that often do not collaborate.

7.2.3 Urbanization and Economic Development

In this chapter we quantify the share of value added by each sector of an economy, followed by the use of factor analysis to quantify SC. Using various sources of data, the study measures urbanization rates and subsequently, the association of urbanization and ST. The varying patterns of urbanization and ST in various countries reveal the close and unique relationships that hitherto had not been paid much attention in the academic literature. Clearly, the findings provide important lessons to be learnt by African countries in the ways human migration connect with ST.

As with the other key development drivers analyzed in this book, empirical findings relating ST to urbanization point to the need for specific policies to leverage the relationship. It was found that urbanization correlates strongly with rising GDP at the early stages of development, but this relationship weakens beyond urbanization levels of over 70 percent. This implies that high levels of urbanization alone are a prerequisite for wealth creation, but in actuality other complementary factors are required in tandem. Clearly, requisite initiatives include appropriate urban policy, planning, design, management and governance, as well as the existence of institutions capable of addressing the challenges associated with rapid urbanization.

The empirical analyses reveal that the relationship between ST, urbanization and development is positive in all countries across the region. In a number of countries, urbanization correlates with economic development only up to a point such as with Botswana and Ethiopia. The broader finding is that rapid urbanization in SSA is not characterized by the same levels of economic performance recorded in other regions. For Asian countries, the analysis suggests that urbanization and economic development are positively correlated without any threshold at which the relation weakens. China serves as a striking example of a country where ST is evidently strongly positively correlated with urbanization. Unlike several African economies, the surplus of labor coming from agriculture was not absorbed in low-value-added activities but rather in highly productive sectors of manufacturing and high-value-added services. This is the case also with the relatively superior economic success of a country like Malaysia with recorded over time, high levels of urbanization in tandem with declining employment level in agriculture.

This book therefore provides strong empirical foundation to what is sometimes anecdotal: that ST does not occur without urbanization, but not all urbanized countries experienced high economic development and ST. This suggests that not all types of urbanization are beneficial but only sustainable urbanization. Urban areas should be properly managed to raise urban productivity in ways to take advantage of agglomeration economies and economy of scale that cities offer. Explicit policies are needed to nurture the growth of highly productive activities, particularly manufacturing and its connection to services. This book shows that the progress of countries will depend in large part on the productivity of urban areas and the extent to which urban growth is managed to nurture the growth of high-productivity activities through agglomeration economies.

The strategy for creating an "urban engine of growth" includes the adoption of sustainable urban plans and legislation, the promotion of urban industrial agglomerations to build productive cities, the implementation of policies stimulating high growth rate of manufacturing output and the adoption of policies raising the share of employment in industry, which leads to high per capita incomes.

7.2.4 Structural Transformation and Industrialization

African countries may have recorded impressive economic growth, but they have had far less success in managing the process of industrialization, the factor critical for rapid catch-up. Historically, manufacturing has been a main source of technology-driven productivity growth and organizational innovation. The manufacturing sector, especially its capital goods subsector, also has the ability to generate other productive inputs. Accordingly, economies characterized by strong manufacturing sectors are more resistant to external shocks. Long-term development, therefore, will be conditional on the industrial performance of economies. This chapter systematically analyzes the peculiarities of emerging industrialization. The DU is measured as the share of value added by the three major sectors (industry, manufacturing and services) of the total value added.

In addition, the chapter provides evidence that a number of African countries have become highly urbanized without significant transition of their sectoral structures towards manufacturing and, in most cases, directly skipping to services.

From our earlier work (Oyelaran-Oyeyinka and Lal, 2016), most of the dynamic Asian countries that achieved long-term growth are characterized by urban sectors that are driven by manufacturing and services-led growth. In developing countries, 86 percent of growth in value added between 1980 and 1998 came from the urban sector—manufacturing and services (Montgomery et al., 2003). Sustainable urban and structural shifts come about through proper planning, and are supported by enforceable legal mechanisms. When properly managed alongside industrialization and planned urban space, it leads to higher productivity and, eventually, rising living standards and better quality of life.

From our analysis, ST in Africa is marked by significant productivity shifts in only a few countries, namely, Botswana, Ghana and South Africa. The services sector has been very important in the industrialization of Asia unlike in Africa, where services activities are characterized by low value activities. The services sector has been built upon a strong manufacturing sector in Asia. This has in turn resulted in an equally robust high-value-added services sector.

The growing dominance of the services requires policy attention to ensure that the sector contributes effectively to long-term economic growth. One clear policy pathway is to invest systematically in order to progressively raise the capabilities of the sector through explicit investment in manpower and skills development. Inevitably, in the medium and long term, African countries will have to build up the capacity of their manufacturing sector to support the services sectors. In other words, the two sectors will have to develop in tandem for sustained long-term benefits of the economy. For example, critical sectors that act as pillars to services, such as telecommunication, thrive in an environment with a strong capital goods sector. The sector houses a diverse set of firms that manufacture machinery used to create capital goods, such as electrical equipment, aerospace and satellite systems. In economics, capital goods are tangible property, which are deployed to produce other goods or services within a certain period. Machinery, tools, buildings, computers or other kinds of equipment that are involved in production of other things for sale are capital goods.[2]

7.2.5 Poverty Pathway Analysis

This chapter focuses on poverty and its connection to SC. SC may result in prosperity, but if managed improperly, may lead to poverty. Growth-inducing change depends, in large part, on the direction of economic and human resource development policies. For instance, intra-sectoral technological changes may lead to productivity growth but might result in loss of employment. If the surplus labor in one sector is not absorbed in another one, it would result in an increase in unemployment. Consequently, joblessness leads to poverty increase. However, having proper human resource development policies in place and by providing appropriate training to raise skills, displaced labor in one sector can be absorbed in other sectors. This would result in prosperity.

We analyzed the changes in poverty levels in the process of ST; it is found that both factors are strongly and negatively affected in Africa. This association between poverty reduction and ST is one that shows no dissimilarity in all countries.

In Africa, there is an inverse relationship between SC and poverty level as well as poverty gap: when the proportion of workforce employed in high-value-added sectors increased, poverty level decreased. For instance, in South Africa, the share of employment in high-value-added sectors was 69.59 percent and only 19.10 percent of population was below poverty line in 2010, while in Tanzania, the share of such employees was 11.68 percent and the poverty level was 84.74 percent in 2000. Our findings imply that ST offers great potential to reduce poverty in Africa.

This study also suggests that we have to start thinking differently about the informal sectors and slums, which are the physical manifestations of poverty. About 70 percent of the total population in large African metropolis lives in slum communities. There is a negative correlation between informal employment and GDP per capita; hence, informal growth tends to be growth-reducing in developing countries. Thus, informal workers tend to be less well-off than those who work and live in more formal settings. Significantly, the emergence of unplanned cities tend to come with informality, illegality and

---

[2] https://www.google.com/search?q=composition+of+the+Capital+goods+sector&rlz=1C1GCEB_enDE819DE819&oq=composition+of+the+Capital+goods+sector&aqs=chrome..69i57j33l5.19738j0j8&sourceid=chrome&ie=UTF-8.

slums, which is why urban growth in poorer developing countries is strongly associated with slum growth. This can be remedied with appropriate planning and delivery of affordable housing and urban basic services. Urban and economic policies will do well to address urban inequality that has arisen as a result of differentiated wealth concentration in cities.

Overall, this book demonstrates that African policy makers should examine critically and avoid growth paths that are characterized by low-productivity activities—whether SC is stuck in the primary sector, or in low-value services.

Charting the pathway of growth allows us to get to the root of a country's structure, and in the end makes it possible to propose policies to attenuate volatilities and economic shocks that characterize mineral dependence and to promote diversification in the long term.

7.3 Can a Services-Led Growth Pathway Prosper Africa?

According to (UNCTAD, 2015b), the development potentials of tertiary activities on the continent, the services sector in Africa on average accounts for about 50 percent of total output. In some countries, the services sector contribution to total output is over 70 percent. Transport, storage and communications subsectors have been growing most rapidly among other sectors and they provide essential impetus for economic development in Africa. Growth of services averaged over 5 percent during 2002–12. While the average share of services in Africa's real output increased from 45 percent in 2004 to 49 percent in 2012, the share of manufacturing in total output decreased in most African countries over the same period (with 30 countries experiencing declining manufacturing contribution to real output). This incidence indicates that the growth in services is neither characterized by enough backward and forward linkages with manufacturing activities, nor is there evidence of complementarities between service sectors and manufacturing sectors.

Compared with global growth in services, Africa's growth in services more than doubled the global average during 2009–12. However, Africa's growth in services was lower at 4.6 percent than the developing countries' average at 5.4 percent. In effect, Eastern and Western African subregions experienced stronger growth in services than other subregions. Transport, storage and communications subsectors grew at 5.8 percent; next, wholesale trade, retail trade, restaurants and hotels subsectors grew at 5.0 percent and finally, other activities grew at 4.0 percent during the period. In Burundi, Chad, the Congo, Côte d'Ivoire, Equatorial Guinea, Ethiopia, Ghana, Nigeria, Rwanda and Togo, the services sector grew fastest at over 8 percent, driven largely by domestic demand. Only two countries, Ethiopia and Rwanda, were services exports-dependent during the period.

However, with respect to employment contribution, agriculture remains the largest employer of labor on the African continent, despite the fact that the services sector currently accounts for 32.4 percent of total employment on the average. While the share of services employment varies from country to country, it is pertinent to note that the sector accounts for as much as two-thirds employment in some African countries. Over the next 15 years to 2030, the spiraling rate of urbanization in Africa, coupled with its population structure and rising incomes are factors expected to trigger further expansion of the services sector.

Despite the impressive growth of Africa's service sector over the past decade, a greater concern is that most of the thriving subsectors are non-tradable services. This further limits Africa's contribution to global trade in services, a meager 2.2 percent contribution. Challenges confronting the development of Africa's service sector include high energy and transportation costs, regulatory and policy bottlenecks, and primary-sector dependence, which limit investment toward developing service sector potentials. There is also a growing need to make service infrastructure in Africa accessible, qualitative, affordable and competitive (Oyelaran-Oyeyinka and Lal, 2016).

Across all developing countries, the rise in services contribution increased from 51.9 percent in the period 2001–4 to 52.8 percent during 2009–12. Countries engaged in manufactured exports had the greatest increases in services contribution at 61 percent. This was followed by services exporters at 57.0 percent, and the least increase was seen among fuel exporters at 33.9 percent. In Africa, the share of services in real output increased from 45.8 percent in 2001–4 to 49 percent in 2009–12.

It is apparent that oil-exporting economies are less dependent on services exports as five out of six least services-dependent economies in Africa (Equatorial Guinea, followed by Liberia, Angola, the Congo, Chad, and Libya) are Africa's top oil exporters. In Equatorial Guinea the share of services in real output was less than 5 percent during the period 2009–12.

Unlike the African variety, the modern services sector is not characterized by low productivity, as has been well documented in the growth literature on developed economies. Wolf (2005) shows that in 30 OECD member countries, services value-added share have steadily increased. While traditional services (social and personal services and hotels and restaurants) continue to have registered relatively weak productivity growth rates, modern services (transport, financial intermediation, and telecommunication services) are characterized by far higher growth rates. Notably, modern services have registered growth rates comparable to those of some high-growth industries within manufacturing.

The heterogeneity of the services sector is also confirmed in the work by Jorgenson and Timmer (2011) for a sample of EU countries, the United States and Japan. Maroto-Sanchez and Cuadrado-Roura (2009) have also identified important disparities in terms of productivity levels and performance across services sectors, with communications and transport in the European countries or wholesale and retail and financial services in the United States showing improvements comparable more than manufacturing to growth, jobs and poverty reduction in developing countries, although this has still not been widely accepted (*The Economist*, 2011).

What does all of this mean for development in Africa? The promise of the services revolution is that the latecomers to development do not have to wait for their turn to get started after China and other East Asian Tigers become uncompetitive. The globalization of services provides another opportunity for them to find niches beyond manufacturing, where they can specialize, scale up and achieve explosive growth, much like the East Asian Tigers did in manufacturing. The core of the argument is that as the services produced and traded across the world expand with globalization, the possibilities for low-income countries to develop based on their comparative advantage expand. That comparative advantage can just easily be in services as in manufacturing.

Although the same set of general non-distortionary policies is as important for services as for manufacturing, specific strategies for services matter. Services, just like manufacturing, need more investments in physical infrastructure (a stronger communication/transport backbone), human infrastructure (skills and education), good entrepreneurship and trade connectivity. Services are becoming an active component of industrial policy in many developing countries. Local industry associations now give services a seat at the policy table in many developing countries. Policy makers are no longer one-dimensional and just focused on manufacturing-based growth. So, latecomers to development also need a much broader growth agenda than the East Asian Tiger did. Some caution, however, should be exercised in how one interprets the evidence presented here.

The likelihood is that services-led growth may not be as sustainable as manufacturing-led growth due to the high skill-intensive nature of tradable services. Consequently, services-led growth can only be self-sustaining in the region when African countries develop the requisite skills, capacities and capabilities of their population to fill up opportunities that growth in skill-intensive services (such as computer and IT services, banking and financial services, communications, business services) provide.

A recent examination of sustainable services-led growth using data from 48 countries in SSA, supports the notion that services-led growth must be driven by knowledge and skill-based performance in order for it to be sustainable. During 1980–2013, real growth in SSA was more of a function of services growth than of manufacturing growth, and services growth has been the largest driver of real growth. Findings of the study show that current services value-added in SSA's finance and insurance, construction, computer and ICTs subsectors are generated through low-tech and low-knowledge-intensive activities (Gehl-Sampath and Ayitey, 2015). Interestingly, contrary to what subsists in the rest of the world, for Africa, agriculture and services growth have been found to be more poverty-reducing than industry and services growth; therefore, services growth is an indicator of progress since it contributes to output and employment. This is because services sector, riding on the wings of increased investments in basic infrastructure, provides wide-reaching employment opportunities than extractive industries.

7.4 Making a Case for Industrial Manufacturing in Africa

Our conclusion in this book is that African industrialization will consequently lead to the creation of productive jobs for, and raise income for, broad swathes of the African society. This belief holds among policy makers that charting a pathway for industrialization has been the concern of African leaders and policy makers. SSA has undergone mixed experiences for the majority of the past 45 years; therefore, a turning point is required for sustained economic progress of the continent. The region's GDP between 2001 and 2010 grew at an average of 5.2 percent a year while per capita income grew at 2 percent a year, up from –0.4 percent in the previous 10 years. Further, net flows of FDI totaled about US$33 billion during the same period, this is almost five times the US$7 billion total between 1990 and 1999—and export growth was robust (World Bank, 2011).

Conventional ST has not taken place in Africa and generally, but growth cannot be sustained without positive ST, which is the transition of an economy from low-productivity and labor-intensive economic activities (like subsistence agriculture and the informal sector) to higher-productivity and skill-intensive activities (like modern industrial agriculture and manufacturing). Economy-wide growth therefore depends mostly on the rate at which resources can migrate from the traditional to the modern sectors; this has not been strongly experienced in the African context. Generating skilled jobs at a pace rapid enough to absorb the unemployed in the labor market remains an enormous challenge, especially for developing economies. This is due to the large turnout of the young, new entrants into the labor market every year, the lack of appropriate employment opportunities in poor economies and the low quality of education and training without a proper link to the labor markets.

Latin American economies experienced a strong process of labor force reallocation, with decreases in the participation of agriculture and an increase in the share of labor in manufacturing and services. Investment is still low in Africa with less than 15 percent of GDP, and ST will only occur when there is an associated investment in skill development, particularly in areas that are causing the economy of the continent to lag. Therefore, in order to achieve its development objectives and to be relevant in the global value chain, Africa needs to harness its natural resources for skill development for its youthful population considering the benefits that skill development brings. Skill development unleashes the dynamism of Africa's unexploited entrepreneurship potential, creating opportunities for increased job and wealth creation. It is also vital for Africa's global engagement in trade and commerce and is required in manufacturing.

Besides investment, the role of the state and policy is also crucial for the African continent to experience ST. Historically, to stimulate economic growth and in return of multilateral and bilateral loans, most sub-Saharan countries have adopted several policies. The SAPs imposed by multilateral organizations and unfortunately adopted by Africa raised questions on the appropriateness and efficacy of measures such as trade liberalization and their lasting impact on the industrial development of Africa (Lall, 1995; Stein, 1992; Stewart et al., 1992).

Economic growth driven by several industrial development strategies has been substantial in several developing countries. The considerably high standards of dynamic growth set by the Asian Tigers and other NIEs have enabled their progress, and they are catching up with traditional industrial world leaders. Howbeit, African industry can be summarized as economies dominated by low-productivity agriculture and petty service activities with a rise of certain consumer-based industrial activities and services at the expense of manufacturing. Others include mining, the exploitation of crude oil and services, and basic commercial services.

Manufacturing underpins economic development, employment and social stability; the Goal 9 of the SDGs encompasses three aspects of sustainable development. These are infrastructure, industrialization and innovation. The physical systems and structures that are important to the operation of a society are offered by infrastructure, while industrialization supports economic growth, creates job opportunities and reduces income poverty. Innovation, on the other hand, improves the technological capabilities of industrial sectors and stimulates the development of new skills. The Goal 9 is therefore a goal for sustainable industrial development, which is harnessed by innovation and infrastructure provision to bring the desired benefits and to drive ST.

Investment in research and development is pertinent for innovation and the creation of new and more sustainable industries. Global expenditure on research and development as a proportion of GDP was 1.7 percent in 2013 with wide disparities. For developed regions, expenditure on research and development was 2.4 percent of GDP, 1.2 percent for developing regions;

for the LDCs and landlocked developing countries, expenditure was below 0.3 percent. A similar pattern was observed in the number of researchers per 1 million inhabitants. While the global average was 1,083 researchers per 1 million inhabitants, the ratio ranged from 65 per 1 million in the LDCs to 3,641 per 1 million in developed regions (United Nations Sustainable Development Goal (UN SDG 9), 2015).

7.4.1 Rationale for Manufacturing in Africa

Although African countries started promoting industrialization mostly after gaining political independence, it occurred mainly in the 1960s. There is a need for renewed commitment to industrialization as part of a broader agenda for economic diversification, resilience to shocks, the development of productive capacity for high and sustained economic growth and the creation of employment opportunities and substantial poverty reduction. Research suggests that economic development needs SC. Case studies have also shown that commodity export can result in high, but not sustained, economic growth. On the other hand, high, rapid and continued economic growth in modern economic development have been associated with industrialization; specifically, growth in manufacturing production (Szirmai, 2009). Africa requires high and sustained economic growth in order to make significant progress in reducing poverty; thus, the need for ST.

Generating productive jobs and sustainable livelihood is one of the major challenges the African countries currently face. Commodity export cannot meet this need; therefore, a corresponding process of agricultural productivity growth and development of nonagricultural employment opportunities in both industry and services is required. To achieve the Millennium Development Goal 1 and SDG 1 of ending poverty, African countries have to go through the process of ST. This would involve a decrease in the share of agriculture and an increase in the share of industry and modern services in output, with a shift between and within sectors from lower-productivity to higher-productivity activities.

The major difference in growth between Asia, Latin America and Africa can be explained by the variation in the contribution of SC to overall labor productivity (McMillan et al., 2014). While Asian countries have experienced productivity-enhancing SC, both Latin America and Africa have experienced productivity-reducing SC. The African region, therefore, needs to engage in growth paths that generate jobs on a large scale to cater for marginal labor supply, considering its young and progressive population. There is a need to move away from jobless growth strategies and toward inclusive growth paths that are labor-intensive and create learning opportunities for young people.

The new industrial strategies in African countries must address premature industrialization through technology, infrastructure and macroeconomic policies.

7.4.2 Manufacturing Potentials of Africa

The industrial sector comprises manufacturing, mining and construction. However, in reality, the manufacturing sector is the component of industry that possesses greater opportunities for sustained growth, employment and poverty reduction in Africa. Manufacturing is characterized by the physical or chemical conversion of materials, significant alteration, renovation or reconstruction of goods, substances or components into new products. The materials transformed are raw materials that are products of agriculture, fishing, forestry, mining or quarrying or output of other manufacturing activities. However, recent literature on export performance of African countries suggests that the continent has losing international markets largely to Asian countries (Ng and Yeats, 2002). Africa has traditionally performed well in the export of raw agricultural materials, but it has lost much of this space at the same time as it has also been overtaken in the export of semi-processed and agro-processed goods (Fukase and Martin, 2017; Sandrey, 2018). These countries have been able to sustain a rapid transition out of poverty due to an increase in productivity in their agricultural sector. This happens in large measure due to the poor manufacturing capacity that underpins both agricultural processing and as well high-value modern services.

The strategic position of manufacturing in the development process includes the place of research and development, which is vital for technological advancement and innovation—all of which are important for economic development. Manufacturing is the main channel for technological diffusion to other sectors of the economy, such as services and agriculture, providing strong linkages with them. For example, manufacturing has strong linkages with the efficiency and productivity of the services sector components and demand impetus for growth of the agricultural sector with forward and backward linkages thereby contributing to employment and output, and domestic investment in the development process.

According to Engel's law, the share of manufactures increases as per capita income rises while the share of agriculture in total household expenditure falls. This indicates that manufactures portend major opportunities for export market expansion and an engine of growth in merchandise trade. What a country produces and exports is important as trend has shown that countries that export dynamic manufactured products over the past three decades have derived remarkable increase in merchandise trade with high income elasticity of demand (UNIDO and UNCTAD, 2011).

Dearth of manufacturing activities is always a major point of debates on Africa's rise as very few countries have succeeded in lowering poverty and attained a high standard of living based on services alone without transfer of labor to the factories. Although manufacturing is beginning to be a significant contributor to overall GDP, with the emergence of new industries in various countries, agriculture and services are still dominant. According to the World Bank, up to eighty million jobs may leave China and several other Asian manufacturing jobs could migrate to Africa due to wage pressures. If labor productivity growth continues in Africa and infrastructure and skills are built up, the region stands to reap huge economic advantages.

Unlike traditional agriculture and traditional services, industrial manufacturing and modern agriculture provide greater opportunities for employment creation and the potential to absorb labor, which is limited or displaced in the agriculture sector. For this reason, the development of the manufacturing sector should not be seen and done as an alternative to, and at the expense of, the agricultural sector. This is because modern agriculture contributes tremendously and is integral to industrial development as it has comparative advantage for industry and also through the supply of wage goods that enhance the competitiveness of domestic firms in global export markets (UNIDO and UNCTAD, 2011). Therefore, policy makers have to construct mutually supportive linkages between the industrial and non-industrial sectors of the economy.

Several investments are making their way to Africa such as an affiliate of SRAM Corporation, the world's second-largest cycle-components maker; it plans to invest in Ethiopia that will create more than a hundred manufacturing jobs. Huajian, a Chinese shoemaker employing over four thousand individuals, is also in Ethiopia; H&M, a multinational Swedish retail-clothing firm, and Primark, an Ireland-based one, both source a lot of material from Ethiopia. Meanwhile Ayka-Addis, a Turkish-owned textile and garment factory with over six thousand staff is the largest firm in Ethiopia's apparel industry. Madécasse, a New York-based chocolatier, with over 650 workers in Madagascar, is already turning raw cocoa into expensively wrapped milky and nutty bars. General Electric, an American conglomerate, is building a 250-million-dollar plant in Nigeria to make electrical gear. Mobius Motors, a Kenyan firm started a few years ago by Joel Jackson, a Briton, is building cheap, durable cars for rough roads.

Domestically owned manufacturing is also growing. This includes Seemhale Telecoms of South Africa, which is planning to make cheap mobile phones for the African market. Angola, with the help of Brazil, intends to build its own arms industry while African craftsmen are owning clothing lines and gracing major fashion runways. Several other businesses are recipients of growth outside the manufacturing sector. They include the spread of big retail shops encouraging light industry.

Ethiopia is implementing a deliberate plan for economic miracle by providing a veritable ground for manufacturing through leveraging on their abundance of cheap labor, low-cost electricity and cotton-growing potential, which has made it the newest frontier of the global garment trade and a substitute to China, where wages are quickly becoming uncompetitive. This has also triggered plans for government-financed industrial parks across the country. The development initiative focused on utilizing government's savings into investments in critical areas for long-term growth such as roads, railways, electricity, agriculture, healthcare and education. Along with foreign aid, the government has mobilized domestic resources outside of a commodities-driven context at a scale never seen in Africa through improving tax collection, shutting out foreign banks and refusing to privatize telecommunications. Also, 34 public universities and 1,350 postsecondary technical schools were established to enhance vocational training as part of a new German-inspired system. These boosted public investment from 5 percent of GDP in the early 1990s to 19 percent in 2011, which was the third-highest rate in the world. It also powered robust economic growth and improvements in human development and reduced poverty, although foreign investment is being held back due to excessive bureaucracy which impedes the ease of doing business.

Signed by America's congress in 2000, the African Growth and Opportunity Act has boosted trade in African-made goods. However, African countries just like Ethiopia need to make deliberate effort to scale up infrastructure and improve the business climate and investment in other industrial needs. They should also take advantage of their good mix of favorable demography, urbanization, an emerging middle class and strong services. Africa, just like India, can generate more jobs and wealth from the service sector while gradually building its manufacturing sector.

REFERENCES

Ackah-Baidoo, P. (2016). "Youth Unemployment in Resource-Rich Sub-Saharan Africa: A Critical Review." *Extractive Industries and Society* 3(1): pp. 249–61.

AfDB (2011). "Enhancing Capacity for Youth Employment in Africa. Some Emerging Lessons." *African Development Brief* 2(2).

AfDB (2012). "Annual Report 2012." Online, available at: https://www.afdb.org/fileadmin/uploads/afdb/Documents/Publications/Annual_Report_2012.pdf.

(2016). "Jobs for Youth in Africa: Catalyzing Youth Opportunity across Africa." Online, available at: https://www.afdb.org/fileadmin/uploads/afdb/Images/high_5s/Job_youth_Africa_Job_youth_Africa.pdf.

AfDB, OECD and UNDP (2016). "Sustainable Cities and Structural Transformation." African Economic Outlook 2016. Online, available at: https://www.un.org/en/africa/osaa/pdf/pubs/2016afrecooutlook-afdb.pdf.

AfDB, OECD, UNDP and UNECA (2013). *African Economic Outlook: Structural Transformation and Natural Resources*, special thematic edition. Online, available at: https://www.un.org/en/africa/osaa/pdf/pubs/2013afrecooutlook-afdb.pdf.

African Economic Outlook (2012). "Promoting Youth Employment." Online, available at: http://www.africaneconomicoutlook.org/en/theme/youth_employment/education-skills-mismatch/.

(2017). "Entrepreneurship and Industrialisation," p. 163.

Amsden, A. H. (1989). *Asia's Next Giant: South Korea and Late Industrialization*. New York: Oxford University Press.

(2007). *Escape from Empire: The Developing World's Journey through Heaven and Hell*, edn. 1, vol. 1, p. 94. Cambridge: MIT Press.

Amsden, A. H., and Chu, W. W. (2003). *Beyond Late Development: Taiwan's Upgrading Policies*. Cambridge: MIT Press.

Anyawu, J. C., and Augustine, D. (2012). "Towards Inclusive African Labor Market: Empirical Analysis of Gender Equality in Employment and Its Implications for Policy". Online, available at: https://scholar.google.com/scholar?q=Anyawu,+J.+C.,+and+Augustine,+D.+(2012).+%E2%80%9CTowards+Inclusive+African+Labor+Market&hl=en&as_sdt=0&as_vis=1&oi=scholart (accessed on March 31, 2016).

Arouri, M. E. H., Youssef, A. B., Nguyen-Viet, C., and Soucat, A. (2014). "Effects of Urbanization on Economic Growth and Human Capital Formation in Africa." PGDA Working Paper No. 119.

Asian Development Bank (2012). "Youth Employment in Asia: 12 Things to Know." Online, available at: http://www.adb.org/features/12-things-know-2012-youth-employment.

Atiyas, I. (2015). "Structural Transformation and Industrial Policy." *Policy Perspective* no. 16: p. 1220.
BBC Africa (2014). "Made in Africa: Is Manufacturing Taking Off on the Continent?" By Akwagyiram A. BBC Africa. Online, available at: http://www.bbc.com/news/world-africa-27329594.
Birdsall, N. (2006). "The World Is Not Flat: Inequality and Injustice in Our Global Economy." UNU World Institute for Development Economics Research (UNU-WIDER), WIDER Annual Lecture 9. Online, available at: https://www.cgdev.org/sites/default/files/archive/doc/commentary/speeches/Birdsall_WIDERpaper.pdf.
Brixiová, Z., Ncube, M., and Bicaba, Z. (2015). "Skills and Youth Entrepreneurship in Africa: Analysis with Evidence from Swaziland." *World Development* 67: pp. 11–26.
Calvès, A. E., and Schoumaker, B. (2004). "Deteriorating Economic Context and Changing Patterns of Youth Employment in Urban Burkina Faso: 1980–2000." *World Development* 32(8): pp. 1341–54.
Center for Strategic and International Studies (2018). "Meeting Challenges by Bridging Stakeholders. CSIS." Online, available at: https://www.csis.org/analysis/urbanization-sub-saharan-africa.
Chang, H. J. (2005). *Why Developing Countries Need Tariffs—How WTO NAMA Negotiations Could Deny Developing Countries' Right to a Future*. Geneva: South Centre.
    (2009). "Industrial Policy: Can We Go Beyond an Unproductive Confrontation?" A Plenary Paper for *Annual World Bank Conference on Development Economics*, June 22–24. Seoul: World Bank.
    (2011). "Institutions and Economic Development: Theory, Policy and History." *Journal of Institutional Economics* 7(4): pp. 473–98.
Chemengich, M. K. (2010). *Impact of African Growth and Opportunity Act on the Textile and Apparel Industry of Kenya*. Online, available at: http://actifafrica.com/documents/ACTIF%20report%20on%20the%20Impact%20of%20AGOA%20in%20Kenya_Margaret%20Chemengich_2010.pdf.
Cornwall, J. (1977). *Modern Capitalism: Its Growth and Transformation*. New York: St. Martin.
Curzon, P. V. (1981). *Industrial Policies in the European Community*. New York: St. Martin's.
DFID (2016). "Supporting Economic Transformation: Developing Export-Based Manufacturing in Sub-Saharan Africa." Policy Summary, March 2016. Online, available at: https://set.odi.org/wp-content/uploads/2016/05/Export-Based-Manufacturing-in-Africa_Summary.pdf.
Duranton, G. (2008). "Viewpoint: From Cities to Productivity and Growth in Developing Countries." *Canadian Journal of Economics / Revue canadienne d'économique* 41(3): pp. 689–736.
ECA (2013). "Services Trade in Africa: Opportunities & Challenges." Presentation by Laura Páez, September 12–13, 2013, Addis Ababa.
The Economist (2011). "The Service Elevator: Can Poor Countries Leapfrog Manufacturing and Grow Rich on Services?" Online, available at: https://www.economist.com/finance-and-economics/2011/05/19/the-service-elevator.
    (2012). "Education in South Africa Still Dysfunctional. Standards Still Leave a Lot to Be Desired." January 21, 2012.
Eggenberger-Argote, N. (2005). *Informal Sector Support and Poverty Reduction*. Bern: Swiss State Secretariat for Economic Affairs.
Elhiraika, A. B. (2008). "Promoting Manufacturing to Accelerate Economic Growth and Reduce Volatility in Africa." African Economic Conference: Globalisation, Institutions and Economic Development of Africa, November 12–14, Tunis, Tunisia.

Ellison, G., Glaeser, E. L., and Kerr, W. R. (2010). "What Causes Industry Agglomeration? Evidence from Coagglomeration Patterns." *American Economic Review* 100(3): pp. 1195–213.

Engerman, S. L., and Sokoloff, K. L. (1997). "Factor Endowments, Institutions, and Differential Paths of Growth among New World Economies." In S. H. Haber (ed.) *How Latin America Fell Behind*, pp. 260–304. Stanford, CA: Stanford University Press.

European Commission (2009). *Promoting Sustainable Urban Development in Europe: Achievements and Opportunities*. Brussels: European Union.

Ewusi, K. (1987). *Structural Adjustment and Stabilisation Policies in Developing Countries: A Case Study of Ghana's Experience in 1983–1986*. Tema: Ghana Publishing Corporation.

Fagerberg, J., and Verspagen, B. (2002). "Technology-Gaps, Innovation-Diffusion and Transformation: An Evolutionary Interpretation." *Research Policy* 31: pp. 1291–304.

Fay, M., and Opal, C. (2000). *Urbanization without Growth: A Not So Uncommon Phenomenon*, vol. 2412. Washington, DC: World Bank.

Fosu, A. K. (2013). "African Economic Growth: Productivity, Policy Syndromes and the Importance of Institutions." *Journal of African Economies* 22(4): pp. 523–51.

Fransman, M. (1982). *Industry and Accumulation in Africa*. Portsmouth, NH: Heinemann.

Freeman, R. (2008). "Labour Productivity Indicators. Comparison of Two OECD Databases, Productivity Differentials and the Balassa-Samuelson Effect." OECD Statistics Directorate Website, available at https://scholar.google.com/scholar?q=Freeman,+R.+(2008).+%E2%80%9CLabour+Productivity+Indicators.+Comparison+of+Two+OECD+Databases,&hl=en&as_sdt=0&as_vis=1&oi=scholart.

Fukase, E., and Martin, W. (2017). "Agro-Processing and Horticultural Exports from Africa," IFPRI Discussion Paper Series.

Gehl-Sampath, P., and Ayitey, D. (2015). "Challenges and Opportunities to Structural Transformation: Africa's Service Sector." In P. Gehl-Sampath and B. Oyelaran-Oyeyinka (eds.), *Sustainable Industrialization in Africa: A New Development Agenda*, 46–65. London: Palgrave Macmillan.

Godfrey, Nick, and Zhao, Xiao (2014). "The Contribution of African Cities to the Economy and Climate: Population, Economic Growth, and Carbon Emission Dynamics," Technical Note. Drawing on Data from Oxford Economics and LSE Cities for the New Climate Economy. New Climate Economy.

Gollin, D., Jedwab, R., and Vollrath, D. (2016). "Urbanization with and without Industrialization." *Journal of Economic Growth* 21(1): pp. 35–70.

Hansda, S. (2005). "Sustainability of India's Services-Led Growth: An Input Output Analysis of the Indian Economy." Online, available at: http://129.3.20.41/eps/ge/papers/0512/0512009.pdf (accessed on April 10, 2016).

Harvey, D. (2009). "Reshaping Economic Geography: The World Development Report 2009." *Development and Change* 40(6): pp. 1269–77.

Hausmann, R., Hwang, J., and Rodrik, D. (2007). What You Export Matters. *Journal of Economic Growth* 12(1): pp. 1–25.

Heshmati, A., and Rashidghalam, M. (2016). "Labour Productivity in Kenyan Manufacturing and Service Industries." *East Africa Research Papers in Economics and Finance*, IZA Discussion Paper No. 9923.

Hirschman, A. O. (1958). *The Strategy of Economic Development*. Yale Studies in Economics: 10. New Haven, CT: Yale University Press.

IFPRI (2018). "Mechanized: Transforming Africa's Agricultural Value Chains," available at: https://www.ifpri.org/publication/mechanized-transforming-africas-agriculture-value-chains (accessed on January 8, 2020).

Iheduru, O. M. (1999). *The Politics of Economic Restructuring and Democracy in Africa*. Westport, CT: Greenwood.

ILO (2000). "Resolution Concerning Statistics of Employment in the Informal Sector," adopted by the Fifteenth International Conference of Labour Statisticians (January 1993) in *Current International Recommendations on Labour Statistics*. Geneva: International Labour Office.

(2008). "Employment for Social Justice and a Fair Globalization: Overview of ILO Programmes." Online, available at: http://www.ilo.org/wcmsp5/groups/public/@ed_emp/documents/publication/wcms_140957.pdf.

(2011). *Key Indicators of the Labour Market (KILM)*. Geneva: ILO.

(2015a). "Five Facts about Informal Economy in Africa." Online, available at: https://www.ilo.org/africa/whats-new/WCMS_377286/lang--en/index.htm.

(2015b). *Global Employment Trends for Youth 2015*. Geneva: ILO.

ILO (2016). *World Employment and Outlook: Trends 2016*. Geneva: ILO.

(2016a). *Women at Work: Trends 2016*. Geneva: ILO.

(2016b). *World Employment and Outlook: Trends 2016*. Geneva: ILO.

(2018). *Women and Men in the Informal Economy: A Statistical Picture*. Geneva: ILO.

(2019). *World Employment and Social Outlook: Trends 2019*. Geneva: ILO.

IMF (2015). *World Economic Outlook: A Survey by the Staff of the International Monetary Fund*. Washington, DC: IMF.

Islam, S. Nazrul, and Iversen, K. (2018). " 'From Structural Change' to 'Transformative Change': Rationale and Implications." UNDESA/ ST/ESA/2018/DWP/155.

Jedwab, R., and Osei, R. D. (2012). "Structural Change in Ghana 1960–2010." Online, available at: https://www2.gwu.edu/~iiep/assets/docs/papers/Jedwab_IIEPWP 2012-12.pdf.

Jedwab, R. , Gollin, D., and Vollrath, D. (2013) "Urbanization with and without Industrialization." Working Paper Series IIEP-WP 2014–1, Institute for International Economic Policy (IIEP), Washington, DC: George Washington University, available at: www.gwu.edu/~iiep/assets/docs/papers/Jedwab_IIEPWP_2014-1.

Jorgenson, D. W., and Timmer, M. P. (2011). "Structural Change in Advanced Nations: A New Set of Stylised Facts. *Journal of Economics* 113(1): pp. 1–29.

Kaldor, N. (1966). *The Causes of the Slow Rate of Economic Growth of the United Kingdom: An Inaugural Lecture*. Cambridge: Cambridge University Press.

(1967). *Strategic Factors in Economic Development*. Ithaca, NY: Cornell University Press.

Kathuria, V., and Raj, R. S. N. (2010). "Manufacturing an Engine of Growth in India – Analysis in the Post-Nineties." Submitted for Conference on Frontier Issues in Technology, Development and Environment, March 19–21. Chennai, India: Madras School of Economics.

KPMG (2012). "The Role of Cities in Africa's Rise." Available at: https://www.africanbusinesscentral.com/wp-content/uploads/2015/07/The-Role-of-Cities-in-Africas-Rise-KPMG.pdf.

Krugman, P. (1994). "Competitiveness: A Dangerous Obsession." *Foreign Affairs* 7(2): pp. 28–44.

Lall, S. (1995). "Structural Adjustment and African Industry." *World Development* 23(12): pp. 2019–31.

Lall, S., and Wangwe, S. (1998). "Industrial Policy and Industrialisation in sub-Saharan Africa." *Journal of African Economies* 7(1): pp. 70–107.

REFERENCES

Lele, U. (2014). "Today's Structural Transformation Is a More Mixed Story than in the Past." Online, available at: Dani Rodrik's weblog http://rodrik.typepad.com/dani_rodriks_weblog/2014/05/todays-structural-transformation-is-a-more-mixed-story-than-in-the-past.html.

Lewis, W. A. (1954). "Economic Development with Unlimited Supplies of Labour." *Manchester School* 22(2): pp. 139–91.

(1978). *Growth and Fluctuations 1870–1913*. London: Allen and Unwin.

Maroto-Sánchez, A., and Cuadrado-Roura, J. (2009), Is Growth of Services an Obstacle to Productivity Growth? A Comparative Analysis. *Structural Change and Economic Dynamics* 20(4): pp. 254–65.

Marti, D. F., and I. Ssenkubuge (2009). "Industrialization and Industrial Policy in Africa: Is It a Policy Priority?" South Centre Research Paper No. 20.

McKinsey Global Institute (2010). "Lions on the Move: The Progress and Potential of African Economies." McKinsey Global Institute. Online, available at: https://www.mckinsey.com/~/media/McKinsey/Featured%20Insights/Middle%20East%20and%20Africa/Lions%20on%20the%20move/MGI_Lions_on_the_move_african_economies_full_report.ashx.

(2010). "What's Driving Africa's Growth?" Online, available at: https://www.mckinsey.com/featured-insights/middle-east-and-africa/whats-driving-africas-growth.

(2012). "Help Wanted: The Future of Work in Advanced Economies." Discussion Paper. Online, available at: https://www.mckinsey.com/~/media/McKinsey/Featured%20Insights/Employment%20and%20Growth/Future%20of%20work%20in%20advanced%20economies/Help_wanted_future_of_work_full_report.ashx.

McMillan, M., and Rodrik, D. (2011). "Globalization, Structural Change and Productivity Growth." NBER Working Paper No. 17143, paper prepared for a joint ILO-WTO volume, Cambridge, MA: National Bureau of Economic Research.

McMillan, M., Rodrik, D., and Verduzco-Gallo, I. (2014). "Globalization, Structural Change, and Productivity Growth, with an Update on Africa." *World Development* 63: pp. 11–32.

Mendes P. F., Bertella, M. A., and Teixeira, F. A. (2014). "Industrialization in Sub-Saharan Africa and Import Substitution Policy." *Brazilian Journal of Political Economy* 34(1): pp. 120–38.

Montgomery, Mark R., Stren, Richard, Cohen, Barney, and Reed, Holly E. (eds.) (2003). *Cities Transformed: Demographic Change and Its Implications in the Developing World*. Washington, DC, National Academics Press.

Morris, M., Kaplinsky, R., and Kaplan, D. (2012). '"One Thing Leads to Another" – Commodities, Linkages and Industrial Development: A Conceptual Overview.' MMCP Discussion Paper No. 12 (revised).

Mumo, N. (2010). "Africa's Industrialization Debate: A Critical Analysis." *Journal of Language, Technology & Entrepreneurship in Africa* 2(1): pp. 146–64.

Muraguri, P., Ortiz, S., and Soler, D. (2018). *Kenya Country Report*. Navarra Center for International Development. Spain: Institute for Culture and Society, University of Navarra.

Ng, Francis, and Yeats, Alexander (2002). "What Can Africa Expect from Its Traditional Exports," Africa Region Working Paper Series, No. 26, June. Washington, DC: World Bank.

Nigeria Bureau of Statistics (NBS) (2018). "Nigerian Gross Domestic Product Report (Q3, 2018)."

Nixson, F. (1990). "Industrialization and Structural Change in Developing Countries." *Journal of International Development* 2(3): pp. 310–33.

The Observatory of Economic Complexity (OEC) (2018). "China." Web page https://atlas.media.mit.edu/en/profile/country/chn/.

OECD (2008). "OECD Compendium of Productivity Indicators," p. 11. Available at: https://www.oecd-ilibrary.org › industry-and-services › oecd-compendium (accessed on January 11, 2020).

——— (2013). *African Economic Outlook 2013: Structural Transformation and Natural Resources*, Paris: OECD Publishing, p. 14. Online, available at: https://doi.org/10.1787/aeo-2013-en.

——— (2015). "OECD Economic Surveys: South Africa," p. 6. Online, available at: http://www.oecd.org/eco/surveys/South-Africa-OECD-economic-survey-overview.pdf.

OECD and United Nations (2011). *Economic Diversification in Africa: A Review of Selected Countries*. Paris: OECD Publishing.

Ohno, I., and Ohno, K. (2012). "Dynamic Capacity Development: What Africa Can Learn from Industrial Policy Formulation in East Asia." In A. Noman et al. (eds.), *Good Governance and Growth in Africa: Rethinking Development Strategies*, ch. 7, pp. 221–45. Oxford: Oxford University Press.

Oseifuah, E. K. (2010). "Financial Literacy and Youth Entrepreneurship in South Africa." *African Journal of Economic and Management Studies* 1(2): pp. 164–82.

Overman, H. G., and Venables, A. J. (2005). "Cities in the Developing World." CEP Discussion Papers dp0695, Centre for Economic Performance. London: London School of Economics and Political Science.

Oyelaran-Oyeyinka, B. (2012). "Institutional Capacity and Policy for Latecomer Technology Development." *International Journal of Technological Learning* 5(1/2): pp. 83–110. 10.1504/IJTLID.2012.044878.

——— (2014). *Rich Country Poor People; Nigeria's Story of Poverty in the Midst of Plenty*. Ibadan: Technopol.

Oyelaran-Oyeyinka, B., and Lal, K. (2015). *Urbanization and Structural Transformation: An Empirical Analysis*. UN-Habitat Occasional Issues Paper. Nairobi: United Nations Human Settlements Programme.

——— (2016). *Structural Transformation and Economic Development: Cross Regional Analysis of Industrialization and Urbanization*. London: Routledge.

Pack, H., and Saggi, K. (2006). "The Case for Industrial Policy: A Critical Survey." *World Bank Research Observer* 21(2): pp. 267–97.

Páez, L., Karingi, S., Kimenyi, M., and Paulos, M. (2010). "A Decade (2000–2010) of African-U.S. Trade under the African Growth Opportunities Act (AGOA): Challenges, Opportunities and a Framework for Post AGOA Engagement." Online, available at: https://www.brookings.edu/wp-content/.../agoa_full_report.pdf.

Reich, R. B. (1991). *The Work of Nations: Preparing Ourselves for 21st-Century Capitalism*. New York: A. A. Knopf.

Rodrik, D. (2015). "Premature Deindustrialization." *Journal of Economic Growth* 21(1): pp. 1–33.

Rodrik, D., and McMillan, M. (2011). "Globalization, Structural Change, and Productivity Growth." In M. Bachetta and M. Jansen (eds.), *Making Globalization Socially Sustainable*, pp. 49–84. Geneva: International Labor Organization and World Trade Organization.

Romer, P. M. (1986). "Increasing Returns and Long-Run Growth." *Journal of Political Economy* 94(5): pp. 1002–37.

Rosen, J. W. (2016). "Made in Africa: Will Ethiopia's Push for Industrialization Pay Off?" Online, available at: http://www.ayyaantuu.net/made-in-africa-will-ethiopias-push-for-industrialization-pay-off/.

Rosenberg, N. (1982). *Technology and Economics*, New York: Cambridge University Press.

Sandrey, R. (2018). "Agriculture and the African Continental Free Trade Area," TRALAC. Online, available at: https://www.tralac.org/publications/article/13757-african-agricultural-production.html (accessed on January 11, 2020).

SIDA (2006). "Fighting Poverty in an Urban World: Support to Urban Development." Online, available at: http://www.sida.se/contentassets/6107b402eb5444b0ba156af2741a815d/fighting-poverty-in-an-urban-world_1056.pdf.

Smith, A. (2007). "Of the Wages of Labour." In *An Inquiry into the Nature and Causes of the Wealth of Nations*. Book 1, ch. 8, p. 32. Online, available at: https://www.ibiblio.org/ml/libri/s/SmithA_WealthNations_p.pdf.

Stein, H. (1992). "Deindustrialization, Adjustment, the World Bank and the IMF in Africa." *World Development* 20(1): pp. 83–95.

Stewart, F., Lall, S., and Samuel, W. (eds.) (1992). *Alternative Development Strategies in Africa*. London: St. Martin's.

Stoneman, C. (1982). "Industrialization and Self-Reliance in Zimbabwe." In Fransman, M., (ed.), *Industry and Accumulation in Africa*. Portsmouth, NH: Heinemann.

Sundaram, J. K., Schwank, S., and von Arnim, R. (2011). "Globalization and Development in Sub-Saharan Africa." DESA Working Paper No. 102 ST/ESA/2011/DWP/102.

Szirmai, A. (2009). "Industrialisation as an Engine of Growth in Developing Countries, 1950–2005." UNU-MERIT Working Paper, 2009–10. The Netherlands: United Nations University.

(2009). "Industrialization as an Engine of Growth in Developing Countries." UNU-MERIT Working Papers ISSN 1871–9872.

Taylor, J. B. (2003). "New Policies for Economic Development." Contribution in Annual World Bank Conference on Development Economics: The New Reform Agenda, April 29–30. Washington, DC: World Bank.

Teal, F. (1999). "Why Can Mauritius Export Manufactures and Ghana Not?" *World Economy* 22(7): pp. 981–93.

Todaro, M. P. (1989). *Economic Development for the Third World*. New York: Longman.

Trading Economics (2019a). "Angola." Online, available at: https://tradingeconomics.com/angola/gdp-per-capita-ppp.

(2019b). Unemployment Rate. Online, available at: https://tradingeconomics.com.

Tregenna, F (2009)." Characterising Deindustrialisation: An Analysis of Changes in Manufacturing Employment and Output Internationally." *Cambridge Journal of Economics* 33(3): pp. 433–66. Online, available at: https://doi.org/10.1093/cje/ben032.

Turok, I. (2004). "Cities, Regions and Competitiveness." *Regional Studies* 38(9): pp. 1069–83.

Turok, I., and McGranahan, G. (2013). "Urbanization and Economic Growth: The Arguments and Evidence for Africa and Asia." *Environment and Urbanization* 25(2): pp. 465–82.

UNCTAD (2006). "Least Developed Countries Report 2006: Developing Productive Capacities." Online, available at: http://unctad.org/en/Docs/ldc2006_en.pdf (accessed on April 21, 2016).

(2011). *The Least Developed Countries Report 2011: The Potential Role of South-South Cooperation for Inclusive and Sustainable Development*. New York: United Nations.

(2015a). *Economic Development in Africa Report 2015: Unlocking the Potential of Africa's Services Trade for Growth and Development*. Geneva: United Nations Conference on Trade and Development.

(2015b). "World Investment Report 2015: Reforming International Investment Governance." Online, available at: http://unctad.org/en/PublicationsLibrary/wir2015_en.pdf (accessed on April 20, 2016).

(2017). "Diamond Exports from Botswana and Sierra Leone: The Role of Institutions in Mitigating the Impact of Commodity Dependence on Human Development." Background document to the Commodities and Development Report 2017. Online, available at: https://unctad.org/en/PublicationsLibrary/suc2017d9_en.pdf.

UNDESA (2015a). "Towards Integration at Last? The Sustainable Development Goals as a Network of Targets." DESA Working Paper No. 141 ST/ESA/2015/DWP/141.

(2018). "68% of the World Population Projected to Live in Urban Areas by 2050, says UN." United Nations Department of Economic and Social Affairs. Online, available at: https://www.un.org/development/desa/en/news/population/2018-revision-of-world-urbanization-prospects.html.

UNDP (2014). "Human Development Index, Trends 1980–2013." Online, available at: http://hdr.undp.org/en/content/table-2-human-development-index-trends-1980-2013.

(2015). "Human Development Report 2015: Work for Human Development." Online, available at: http://hdr.undp.org/sites/default/files/2015_human_development_report_1.pdf.

data. Online, available at: http://hdr.undp.org/en/content/database.

UNECA (1997). *Technological Capability Building in the South: Lessons and Opportunities for Sub-Saharan Africa*. United Nations Economic Commission for Africa. Addis Ababa: Economic Commission for Africa.

(2011). *Economic Report on Africa 2011: Governing Development in Africa—The Role of the State in Economic Transformation*. Addis Ababa: United Nations Economic Commission for Africa (UNECA).

(2013). "Services Trade in Africa: Opportunities & Challenges." Regional Meeting on Promoting Services Sector Development and Trade-led Growth in Africa. Presentation by Laura Páez, September 12–13. Addis Ababa: United Nations Economic Commission for Africa.

(2015). *Economic Report on Africa: Industrialization through Trade*. Addis Ababa: UNECA.

UN-Habitat (2010). *State of the World's Cities 2010/2011: Bridging the Urban Divide*. United Kingdom: Earthscan.

(2012). "The Economic Role of Cities." Global Urban Economic Dialogue Series. Available at: https://oldweb.unhabitat.org › books › economic-role-of-cities.

(2014). *State of African Cities 2014: Re-Imagining Sustainable Transitions*. London: Routledge.

(2015). *Sustainable Urban Development in Africa*. Nairobi: United Nations Human Settlements Programme, p. 8.

(2016). "Urbanization and Development: Emerging Futures. Key Findings and Messages." World Cities Report. Online, available at: http://wcr.unhabitat.org/wp-content/uploads/2017/02/WCR-2016_-Abridged-version-1.pdf.

UN-Habitat and DFID (2002). *Sustainable Urbanisation: Achieving Agenda 21*. Nairobi: UN-Habitat.

UNIDO and UNCTAD (2011). *Economic Development in Africa Report 2011: Fostering Industrial Development in Africa in the New Global Environment*. New York: United Nations. Online, available at: https://unctad.org/en/docs/aldcafrica2011_en.pdf.

UNIDO (1983). *Industry in a Changing World*. ID/CONF.5/2, ID/304. New York: United Nations.

(2009). "Structural Change in the World Economy: Main Features and Trends." Research and Statistics Branch Working Paper 24/2009. Vienna: UNIDO.

(2009). "Breaking in and Moving Up: New Industrial Challenges for the Bottom Billion and the Middle-Income Countries." Industrial Development Report 2009, Vienna: United Nations.

(2012). *Promoting Industrial Diversification in Resource Intensive Economies*. Vienna: UNIDO.

(2015). "Social Inclusion and Structural Transformation Concepts, Measurements and Trade-Offs." Inclusive and Sustainable Industrial Development Working Paper Series WP 17 | 2015. Online, available at: https://www.unido.org/api/opentext/documents/download/9929075/unido-file-9929075.

(2016). *International Yearbook of Industrial Statistics*. United Kingdom: Edward Elgar.

UNIDO and UNCTAD (2011). "Fostering Industrial Development in Africa in the New Global Environment." Economic Development in Africa Report 2011. Special Issue. New York: United Nations.

United Nations (2013). "A New Global Partnership: Eradicate Poverty and Transform Economies through Sustainable Development." The Report of the High-Level Panel of Eminent Persons on the Post-2015 Development Agenda. Online, available at: https://www.un.org/en/development/desa/policy/untaskteam_undf/HLP%20P2015%20Report.pdf.

United Nations Department of Economic and Social Affairs, Population Division (2014). World Urbanization Prospects: The 2014 Revision, Highlights (ST/ESA/SER.A/352). New York: UNDESA.

United Nations Sustainable Development Goal 9. Online, available at: https://sustainabledevelopment.un.org/sdg9.

USDA (2012). "Ghana Exporter Guide." Online, available at: https://gain.fas.usda.gov/Recent%20GAIN%20Publications/Ghana%20Exporter%20Guide%202012_Accra_Ghana_11-2-2012.pdf.

Vollgraaff, R., and Thukwana, N. (2018). "AfDB Seeks to Plug Africa $170 Billion Infrastructure Needs." Online, available at: https://www.bloomberg.com/news/articles/2018-05-08/afdb-seeks-funds-to-plug-africa-170-billion-infrastructure-gap.

Winter, Sidney G., and Nelson, Richard R. (1982). *An Evolutionary Theory of Economic Change*. Cambridge: Harvard University Press.

Wolf, M. (2005). *Why Globalization Works*. New Haven, CT: Yale University Press.

World Bank (2000). *World Development Report 2000/2001: Attacking Poverty*. Washington, DC: World Bank.

(2009). *Systems of Cities: Harnessing Urbanization for Growth and Poverty Alleviation*. Washington, DC: World Bank.

(2011). *World Development Indicators 2011*. Washington, DC: World Bank.

(2014). "Global Poverty Indicators." Poverty & Equity Data Portal. Online, available at: http://povertydata.world bank.org/poverty/home/.

World Bank data. Online, available at: https://databank.worldbank.org/source/world-development-indicators.

World Bank Group (2013). *Africa's Pulse: An Analysis of Issues Shaping Africa's Economic Future*, vol. 7. Washington, DC: World Bank.

(2015). "Manufacturing FDI in Sub-Saharan Africa: Trends, Determinants, and Impact." Online, available at: https://www.worldbank.org/content/dam/Worldbank/Event/Africa/Investing%20in%20Africa%20Forum/2015/investing-in-africa-forum-manufacturing-fdi-in-sub-saharan-africa-trends-determinants-and-impact.pdf.

(2016). *Africa's Pulse: An Analysis of Issues Shaping Africa's Economic Future*. Africa's Pulse No. 14, October 2016, World Bank Other Operational Studies 25097. Online, available at: https://openknowledge.worldbank.org/bitstream/handle/10986/25097/108582. pdf?sequence=7.

(2017). "The World Bank in Africa: Sub-Saharan Africa's Growth Is Projected to Reach 3.1 Percent in 2018, and to Average 3.6 Percent in 2019–20." Online, available at: https://www.worldbank.org/en/region/afr/overview.

(2018). "The World Bank in Tunisia." Web page, available at: https://www.worldbank.org/en/country/tunisia/overview.

(2019). "The World Bank in Africa." Web page, available at: https://www.worldbank.org/en/region/afr/overview.

INDEX

Abuja 53, 123
Accelerated Industrial Development of
    Africa (AIDA) policy 47
Addis Ababa 28, 123–24
African Development Bank (AfDB) 11, 89
African Economic Outlook (AEO) 14
African Growth and Opportunity Act 145
African Union Commission (AUC) 48
Agenda 2063 122
agglomeration diseconomies 68
agglomeration economies 55, 56, 59,
    76, 134
Agreement on Textiles and Clothing 19, 48
agriculture, share of 99, 102
agriculture/agricultural sector, 18–21, 50
  in Botswana 45
  and employment 34, 98
  exports 23
  in Kenya 23, 42
  labor productivities in 46
  in Nigeria 30, 43, 63
  products 19
  resources 5
  in South Africa 22, 99
  in Tanzania, 29–20, 45, 99
  in Tunisia 23
  in Uganda 29
Alexandria 28
Algeria 17
Angola 38, 124, 144–45
  enclave-driven institutional structures 12
  oil and gas exports and lack of
      economies diversity 17
  urbanization 52
Asia 14, 29, 135
  imports 6

  labor productivity 53
  urbanization level 53
Asian Tigers 50
automobile industry 22
Ayka-Addis 74, 144

Bangladesh 19
banking 17, 19, 33, 107, 125, 139
Botswana 16, 21
  agriculture 45
    employment share of 103
  employment 96, 98
  industrialization policy, 44–45
  manufacturing value added 48
  mineral dependency 13
  productivity growth, 78–79, 82
  service-led economic development 31
  services sector 102
  urbanization
    and labor productivity 66
    and living standards (HDI) 63, 65–66
Burundi
  manufacturing value added 48
  services sector growth in 34
business process outsourcing services 24

Cairo 28, 54
call centers 22
Cameroon 18
  manufacturing value added 47
capacity-building programs 24
Cape Town 28
capital accumulation 27, 28
capital goods 36, 134, 135–36
capital intensity, and urban manufacturing,
    27–28, 43, 102

Chad
    oil and gas exports and lack of economies diversity 17
    services sector growth in 34
Chenery, H. B. 3
China 6, 19, 73, 134, 139, 144
    exports of 14
    productivity 72
    services sector in 30
    urbanization 52
cities 5, 77. *See also* urbanization
    and costs 58
    demographic dividend in 60
    demographic pressure in 58
    ghost cities 53
    and global GDP 54
    productive cities efficiency 130
    proximity advantages, 55–56
    role in national economies 59
    secondary cities 60
    unplanned cities 136
    water and sanitation facilities 56, 58, 59, 111, 120, 121, 122, 126–27
coffee exports 14, 23
collateral registries 88
commercial banks 88
commercial services 19, 141
commodity export 20, 47, 48, 142
commodity trade across borders 31
communications 137
comparative advantage 139, 144
compound annual growth rate (CAGR), 24–25, 96–98
construction and engineering 22
consumer spending 28, 39, 109, 125
consumer-based industrial activities and services 49, 141
consumer-facing sectors 21. *See also* banking; retail sector; telecommunications
consumption cities 6, 12, 28, 52, 55, 124–25, 133
    spatial structures 28
consumption–production nexus 28
Côte d'Ivoire 11
    manufacturing value added 47
    services sector growth in 34
creative labor, 34–35
credit bureaus 88
crude oil, exploitation of 19, 141

Cuadrado-Roura, J., 138–39
cyclical unemployment 95, 131

Dakar 28
Dar es Salaam 54
debt, 37–38
deindustrialization 6, 11, 30
    premature 5, 92, 130
demand, lack of 8
Democratic Republic of the Congo 19, 28, 123
    import substitution policy 37
    natural resources and financial economic growth 20
    oil and gas exports and lack of economies diversity 17
    services sector growth in 34
developing countries
    repercussions due to informal sector 57
    role of cities in national economies 59
development banks 88
diamonds 13
    export of 6
domestic markets 43, 76
dual economies 9, 129
Durban 28

East Africa 38
East Africa Community (EAC) 45
East Asian Tigers 139
economic backwardness 47, 49
economic diversification 4, 18–19, 20–21, 122
    in Botswana 44
    in Kenya 23
    lack of 17
    in South Africa 22
    in Tunisia, 23–24
economic growth 5, 25, 27, 130
    contributing factors, 61–62
    and employment 130
economic growth pathways 5, 11
Economic Recovery Program (ERP) 43
economy of scale 134
economy transitions, 34–35
Egypt
    youth employment 93
    youth unemployment 92
electricity 39, 59, 73, 75, 85, 145

INDEX

employment, 7–8, 9, 25, 89
  in Botswana's agriculture sector 100
  creation 91
  diminished opportunities for skilled
    workers 4
  and economic growth 90
  in mining, shares of 102
  opportunities, and enclaved economy 15
  and redistributive growth 107
employment shares 13
  in agriculture 46
  of agriculture 103
  in agriculture and industry
    Ghana, 79–80
  in industry and manufacturing
    Botswana 79
  Kenya 80
  in manufacturing sector 48
  Nigeria, 80–81
  South Africa 81
  Tanzania 82
  for Tanzanian manufacturing and
    services sector 101
enclave economies 4, 12
  and commodity markets 16
  consequences of, 14–15
  and employment 16
  and employment opportunities 15
  and natural resource (*see* natural
    resources)
endogenous industrial capabilities, lack of 6
energy 73
Engel's law 143
entrepreneurial skills, lack of 92
Equatorial Guinea 38
  oil and gas exports and lack of
    economies diversity 17
  services sector growth in 34
Ethiopia 11, 19, 21, 28, 123–24, 145
  employment in 96
  industrialization 76
  labor productivity 73, 74–75
  manufacturing value added 48
  national minimum wage 76
  natural resources and financial
    economic growth 20
  productivity growth 82
  sanitation facilities 126
  services sector growth in 34

textile 73
urbanization
  and labor productivity 66
  and living standards (HDI) 63, 66
  and manufacturing 127
  and productivity, 114–15
Europe 139
export-led growth
  Tanzania 45
export-oriented industrialization
  Botswana 44
export-oriented policies 13
exports 37, 143
  fish exports 14
extensive scale economies 12
external economies of scale 55
external price shocks 4, 15

Faso, Burkina 92
financial crisis 89
  impact on South Africa 22
financial institutions 88
fiscal decentralization 59
food processing 5, 24
foreign direct investment (FDI) 7, 16, 39,
  76, 83, 85
  greenfield FDI 14
  and incentives 86
  and infrastructure 85
  and institutions 85
  and productivity, 84–86
  rate of return on 21
formal employment 90
frictional unemployment 95, 131
fuels 25

Gabon 17
garment exports 19
gender-based employment 91, 93–94
General Electric 144
geographic location 6, 24
Ghana 18, 21
  economic evolution of 18
  Economic Recovery Program (ERP) 43
  employment in 96, 98
  employment share of agriculture 103
  enclave-driven institutional structures 12
  Ghana Shared Growth and
    Development Agenda (GSGDA) 44

Ghana (cont.)
  Growth and Poverty Reduction Strategy 44
  import substitution policy 37
  industrial sectors 18
  industrialization policies in, 43–44
  labor productivity in, 79–80
  manufacturing value added 48
  mineral dependency, 13–14
  poverty 44
  Poverty Reduction Strategy 44
  productivity growth, 79–80, 82, 133
  radical import liberalization 44
  services sector
    and employments 100
    growth 34
  share of manufacturing 44
  urbanization
    and labor productivity 67
    and living standards, 119–21
    and living standards (HDI) 67
    and manufacturing, 127–28
    and productivity, 114–15
  youth employment 92
ghost cities 53
ghost towns 53
global unemployment 89
globalization of services 139
gold export 6
government intervention 49
government-financed industrial parks 145
Green Revolution 5, 29
gross value added (GVA) 78

high-productivity sector 68, 72, 129.
  See also manufacturing
high-productivity services 107
high-value-added activities 8
high-value-added services sector 135
H&M 73, 144
home-grown companies 28
Hong Kong 14
housing 59
housing market 53
Huajian 75, 144
human capital investment 4, 73, 107, 131
  and productivity, 86–87
  underinvestment in 15
human resource development policies 136
hydropower 19

Ibadan 28
Import Substitution Industrialization (ISI)
  model, 37–38, 42, 47, 72
  Botswana 44
  Ghana 43
  Nigeria 42
  Tanzania 45
income
  inequalities in 4, 12
  inequity in 108
India 19, 33, 145
Indigenization Decree 42
Indonesia
  manufacturing and services 17
  productivity 72
industrial development, struggles 5
industrial growth, and urbanization 27
industrial manufacturing 5, 12–13, 144
industrial policy 7, 73
Industrial Policy Action Plan II
  (IPAP II), 40–41
industrial sector 125, 127–28
  and non-industrial sector, linkages
    between 144
industrialization 3, 4, 8, 11, 13, 25, 27,
  47–48, 83, 122, 130, 134–36,
  140–42, 141
  Ethiopia 76
  failure of, 48–49
  and manufacturing 46
  and poverty reduction 106
  premature 143
  and share of employment in
    manufacturing sector 48
  significance of 36
  structural change 46
  and transformation of economy 34
industrialization policies, 35–40
  in Botswana, 44–45
  in Ghana, 43–44
  import substitution policy, 37–38, 44,
    45, 47, 72
  in Kenya 42
  in Nigeria, 42–43
  objectives 36
  in South Africa, 40–42
  Structural Adjustment Program, 38–39
  and structural transformation, 36–37
  in Tanzania 45

informal economies 28, 90, 133
  and urbanization 57
informal employment 90, 95
  and GDP per capita 136
informal sectors 72, 136
  employment, 107–8
  unemployment 95
  and youth employment 92
informal services sector 50, 69
informal-service subsectors 5
information and communications technology (ICT)
  based operations 96
  in Tunisia 24
infrastructure 19, 141, 143
  deficit 57
  development of 83
    and productivity 87
  energy and transport 6
  lack of 6
innovation 7, 141
  and productivity, 83–84
institutional framework establishment 7, 83
inter- and intra-sectoral productivity growth, 132–33
International Labour Organization (ILO) 94
International Monetary Fund (IMF) 38
international trade 45
intra-African trade 5, 19
intra-sector productivity 78
  in Botswana 79
  in Ghana 79, 80
  in Kenya 80
  in Nigeria, 80–81
  in South Africa 81
  in Tanzania 81
intra-sectoral technological changes, and employment 136
investment
  in human capital 7, 83
  in industrial infrastructure 27
  in physical capital and infrastructure 7
  in research and development 141
investment rates 13
investments
  in infrastructure 59
Islam, S. Nazrul 2, 3
Iversen, K. 2, 3

Japan 30
Jedwab, R. 52
job creation 130
jobless growth 1, 2, 3, 90, 142
Johannesburg 28, 53, 54
Jorgenson, D. W. 138

Kano 28
Kariuki 126
Kenya 18, 21
  abolition of quota system 99
  agricultural products exports 14
  challenges 23
  economic diversification in 23
  economic recovery strategy 42
  employment 96, 98–99, 103
  employment share of agriculture 101
  employment share 42
  employment share of agriculture 103
  export-led industrialization 42
  industrialization policy in 42
  labor productivity in 80
  liberal economic reform 42
  manufacturing value added 47, 48
  private sector 23
  productivity growth in 80, 83
  urbanization
    and labor productivity 67
    and living standards (HDI) 67
Khartoum 28
Kilamba 53
Kinshasa 54, 123
Kuala Lumpur 53

labor- and skill- intensive industrial activities 7
labor demand and supply 103
labor force reallocation. *See* labor migration
labor markets reforms 84
labor migration 27, 50, 55, 140
labor productivity 7, 9, 13, 29, 46, 71, 73, 77–78, 129, 144
  in agricultural and nonagricultural sectors 46
  in Botswana, 78–79
  factors of low level of 72
  in Ghana, 79–80
  in Kenya 80

labor productivity *(cont.)*
  in manufacturing 40
  in Nigeria, 80–81
  in South Africa 81
  in Tanzania, 81–82
  and urbanization 55, 62, 64–65, 116
labor-intensive growth 41, 142
Lagos 28, 52, 53, 54
Lall, S. 38
landlocked developing countries 142
latecomer economies 47, 49, 139
Latin America 140
learning-by-doing labor 35
least developed countries (LDCs), 19–20, 142
  challenges 19
  commodity exports 19
  manufacturing value added, 19–20
  technology-related exports 19
leather industry
  in South Africa 22
  in Tunisia 24
legal reforms, 59–60
Lesotho 48
liberal economic reform 42
Libreville 52
Libya 17
life expectancy 28
  in cities 56
living standard 144
living standards 8, 25, 57, 106, 130
  and employment 109
  in modern cities 27
  urban living standards 56
    Ghana, 119–21
    Morocco 121
    Senegal, 121–22
    Zambia 122
low-end services sector 72
low-productivity sector 5, 49, 71, 72, 129, 141. *See also* agriculture sector; services sector
low-skill labor 132
low-value-added activities 131
Luanda 28, 52, 53, 54, 124

macroeconomic policies 143
Madagascar
  import substitution policy 37
  manufacturing value added 48

Madécasse 144
Malaysia 134
  productivity 72
Mali 19, 20
manufacturing, 12–13, 29, 127
  Botswana, 44–45
  declining share of employment in 72, 73
  and diversification 40
  domestically owned manufacturing, 144–45
  and employment 91
  FDI in 85
  Ghana 102
  and growth 31, 108
  improvement of productivity in 7
  Kenya 102
  in Kenya 23, 42
  Morocco 128
  Nigeria 99, 102
  in Nigeria 43
  potentials, 143–45
  and productivity 40, 134–35
  rationale for, 142–43
  share of
    in Africa's GDP 48
    Ghana 98
  South Africa 102
  in South Africa 22, 99
  and structural change 40
  and sustainable development 107
  in Tanzania 45, 99
  in Tunisia 23, 24
manufacturing activities, dearth of 144
manufacturing performance
  and value of commodity export 48
manufacturing value added (MVA) 47, 48
  share of 49
manufacturing-based economies 4
Maroto-Sanchez, A, 138–39
Mauritius 47, 48
McMillan, M. 5
Mercato 124
merchandise trade 20, 37, 48, 143–44
metals 22
micro insurance 88
microenterprises 95
microfinance institutions 88
middle-income stage 35
migrations/migrants 51, 144
  and urbanization 57

Millennium Development Goal 142
mineral and oil dependency 4
mineral-dependent economies
   external relationships of 15
minerals 25
mining sector 19, 39, 141
   Nigeria 30, 99
   South Africa 22
mobile financial services 88
Mobius Motors 144
modern agriculture 144
modern sectors 131
modern services sector 138
Morocco
   urbanization
      and living standards 121
      and productivity, 116–17
Mozambique 18
multifactor productivity (MFP) 9, 71, 78, 129

Nairobi 28, 53
   slums 57
natural resources 25
   exports of 6, 51
   and sustainable growth, 16–18
New Economic Geography 56
new growth path policy 40, 41
Newly Industrializing Economies (NIEs) 50
Nigeria 11, 15, 21, 28
   agriculture 101
   banking 17
   employment in 96, 99, 102
   employment share of agriculture 103
   enclave-driven institutional structures 12
   export-led industrialization 43
   foreign private-sector-led initiatives 43
   import substitution policy 37
   industrialization policies in, 42–43
   labor productivity in, 80–81
   manufacturing and services 17
   natural resources 17
   Niger Delta 15
   oil and gas exports and lack of economies diversity 17
   oil dependency 14
   productivity growth in, 80–81, 82, 133
   service-led economic development 31
   services sector growth in 34

share of agriculture 99
share of employment 43
structural transformation in 30
telecoms 17
trade policies 43
unemployment in 90
urbanization 52
   and labor productivity 67
   and living standards (HDI) 63, 67
nonagricultural sectors, labor productivities in 46
nonrenewable resources 25
non-tradable services 34, 52, 72, 138
North Africa
   economic growth 91
   gender employment 93

offshoring 24
oil and gas exporters 17
oil and gas industries 39
oil and mineral
   dependency, 13–16
   exporters in SSA 12
   resources 39
oil export 6, 138
oil industry 15
oil production 14
oil refineries 15
opportunity deprivation 107
organizational innovation 134
overconsumption 4, 15
own-account operations 95

petrochemicals processing 15
petty service activities 49, 141
Phillips Van Heusen (PVH) 73
physical capital 83
policy reforms 19
   innovation and technological advancement 84
political decentralization 59
poor industrial skills 6
poverty 8, 9, 44, 130, 136–37
   negative effects, 105–6
   reduction 105, 107, 110, 136, 142
power supply. *See* electricity
premature deindustrialization 5, 92, 130
premature industrialization 143

premature transition to the service
    sector 130
Pretoria 28
Primark 144
primary commodity exports 48
private sector
    in Egypt 93
    in Ethiopia 76
    in Kenya 23
    in Nigeria 43
    in Tunisia 24
privatization
    in Kenya 42
    in South Africa 40
production, copying of 35
production cities 52
productive activities 53
productive cities 6
productive sectors 39
productive urban employment 40
productivity 13, 31, 71, 77
    based growth 35
    decline in 6
    and financing and resource
        mobilization, 87–88
    foreign direct investment, 84–86
    growth of 78
    and human capital investment, 86–87
    and infrastructure development 87
    and innovation and technological
        advancement, 83–84
    manufacturing and agriculture,
        compared 27
    reducing structural change 72
    shift share analysis 78
    sources of change in 78
    of urban areas 134
productivity growth 7, 8, 9, 71, 129, 133
    in Botswana, 78–79, 82
    in Ethiopia 82
    in Ghana, 79–80, 82
    in Kenya 80, 83
    labor productivity (*See* labor
        productivity)
    in Nigeria, 80–81, 82
    in South Africa 81, 83
    in Tanzania, 81–82, 83
    and urbanization 60

productivity measures 71, 77
public investment 41, 75, 145

Rabat 28
rapid urbanization, 56–58, 61,
    130, 133–34
real estate development projects 53
reallocation-effect 78
regional integration 87
regulation 19
repetitive labor, 34–35
Republic of Korea 14
    services sector in 30
resources
    based exports 49
    dependent economies, 18–21
    migration, and economy 140
    natural resources and finance economic
        growth 20
    reallocation of 52
restaurants and hotels 137
retail sector 13, 16, 19, 34, 39, 72, 73, 107,
    125, 137, 139
Rodrik, Dani 5, 130
rural development model (RRD) 47
rural economies, 19–20, 27
rural–urban landscapes, 28–29
rural–urban migration 127
Rwanda 11, 85
    manufacturing value added 48
    services sector growth in 34

savings rate 13
sector diversification, lack of 15
Seemhale Telecoms 144
Sen, Amartya 3
Senegal 11, 18
    urbanization
        and living standards, 121–22
        and productivity, 117–18
Seoul 53
service-led structural transformation 5
services, share of 138
services employment, share of 34
services growth 33
services sector 7, 11, 13, 29, 45, 135
    in Botswana 45
    and employment 98, 99, 138

GDP share for 50
  in Ghana 44
  growth in 33
  inter-sectoral linkages 33
  in Japan 30
  in Kenya 23, 42
  local 19
  in Nigeria 30, 43, 99
  nontradable services 34
  and productivity 107
  shares of 102
  in South Africa 99
  in sub-Saharan Africa 132
  in Tanzania 45
  in Tunisia 24
  in Uganda 29
  in Zambia 125
services value added 132
services-led growth, 30–35, 137–40
shift-effect 78
shoes industry 24
Sierra Leone 19
  natural resources and financial economic growth 20
Singapore 14
skilled labor force, dearth of 86
skill-formation agenda 132
skill-intensive activities 53
skills 8
  absence of 131
  development 49, 131, 141
  development programs 132
  and employment 94
  upgradation of 9, 129
slums 136
  unmitigated formation of 28
small- and medium-sized enterprises (SMEs) 12
Smith, Adam 105
social services 50
socioeconomic development 8
South Africa 11, 101, 136
  agro-processing in 22
  automobile industry in 22
  call centers 22
  construction and engineering industry 22
  economic diversification in 22

employment 96, 99, 103
employment creation 41
employment share of agriculture 103
enclave-driven institutional structures 12
financial sector 22
financial services 22
geological projects 22
impact of financial literacy on youth entrepreneurship in 92
industrial action plan 41
Industrial Policy Action Plan II (IPAP II), 40–41
industrialization policies in, 40–42
knowledge economy 41
labor productivity in 81
manufacturing share in employment 101
manufacturing value added 47, 48
metals 22
mineral dependency 14
new growth path policy 40, 41
productivity growth in 81, 83
service-led economic development 31
services sector in 21
trade liberalization 40
unemployment problems 22
urbanization
  and labor productivity 67
  and living standards (HDI) 63, 67
youth unemployment, 92–93
Southern Africa Development Community (SADC) 45
SRAM Corporation 144
stagnant economic development 6
state investments 7
  in infrastructure 73
steered urbanization 59
storage 137
structural adjustment program (SAP) 18, 38–39, 42, 47, 50, 141
  consequences of 43
  Nigeria 43
structural transformation/change 4, 9, 11, 25, 29–30, 46, 51, 68, 130
  and change of productivity 29
  comparative analysis of 30
  dynamics of, 129–30
  and employments 7, 89, 96–103, 131–32
  and human well-being 2

structural transformation/change (cont.)
   and industrialization policies 36
   and labor productivity 51
   and learning 49
   and living standard 5
   and living standards 111
   and manufacturing 27, 40
   movement of the workforce 29
   in Nigeria 30
   and productive sectors 39
   and productivity 135
   and productivity changes 51
   and productivity growth 52, 82
   productivity-enhancing 142
   productivity-reducing 142
   role in industrialization and economic development, 48–49
   and skill development 49
   and social development 3
   in Uganda 29
   and urban markets 28
   and urbanization 51
structural unemployment 8, 94–95, 95–96, 103, 131
structural-change effect 78
sub-Saharan Africa 4, 13, 53, 139, 140
   economic growth in 11, 91
   GDP per capita 61
   growth process 40
   informal sector 72
   international demand for resources 39
   labor productivity in 62
   share of manufactures exports of 48
   shares of global manufacturing 39
   slums 57
   structural transformation in 13
   women employment, 93–94
surplus labor 136
sustainable development 3
Sustainable Development Agenda, 2030 94
Sustainable Development Goals 91, 105, 141, 142
sustainable urbanization 3, 59, 68, 134
Swaziland 92
   manufacturing value added 48

Taiwan 30
Tanzania 11, 18, 22, 136
   agriculture in, 29–20
   employment in 96, 99, 103
   employment share of agriculture 103
   globalization export-oriented strategy 45
   import substitution policy 37
   in industrialization policies 45
   international trade 45
   labor productivity in, 81–82
   manufacturing value added 48
   National Trade Policy 45
   productivity growth in, 81–82, 83, 133
   share of employment 45
   urbanization
      and labor productivity, 67–68
      and living standards (HDI), 67–68
tea exports 14
technological advancement 7, 9, 27, 129, 143
   and productivity, 83–84
technology-driven productivity growth 134
telecommunications 16, 17, 19, 39, 59, 125, 132
textile industry 24
Thailand
   exports of 14
   productivity 72
Timmer, M. P. 78, 138
Tnisia 96
Togo 34
total factor productivity (TFP). See multifactor productivity (MFP)
tourism 19
   Kenya 23
   South Africa 22
   Tunisia 24
trade globalization 84
trade liberalization 40
transition economies, 18–19
transnational corporations, 14–15
transport 137
   infrastructure 85
Tunisia 21
   aeronautical and automotive components 24
   business process outsourcing services 24
   capacity-building programs 24
   economic diversification, 23–24
   and Europe 24
   exports of 24
   food processing 24

free-trade area 24
macroeconomic policies 24
offshoring 24
service-led economic development 31
structural reforms 24
textile industry 24
trade policies 24
Turok 127

Uganda 18, 22, 28
  employment in 96
  structural transformation in 29
  urbanization
    and labor productivity 68
    and living standards (HDI) 68
unemployment and underemployment, 91–92, 107, 131, 133
  cyclical unemployment 95, 131
  demand side of skills 94
  gender employment, 93–94
  impacts of 50
  informal employment 95
  in South Africa, 89–90
  structural unemployment, 95–96
  supply side of skills 94
  youth employment, 92–93
United Nations Development Programme 110
United Nations Research Institute for Social Development 16
United Republic of Tanzania 28
United States 139
unsustainable urbanization 6
urban advantage, 5–6, 58–60
urban consumers, 122–27
  comparative analysis, 125–27
  Morocco, 126–27
  Senegal, 125–27
  Zambia, 125–26
urban development corridors 60
urban divide 122
urban efficiency 59
urban governance 59, 69
urban growth 110, 134
urban hierarchies 60
urban inequalities 58
urban manufacturing, capital intensity, 27–28, 43, 102
urban markets 28

urban migration, 57–58
urban mortality rates 28
urban opportunities and challenges, 55–58
urban population, 53–54, 55, 68, 110
urban poverty 58
urban productivity 134
urban sprawl 28
urban unemployment 90, 94
urbanization 2, 4, 8, 9, 11, 25, 51, 76, 127, 133–34. *See also* cities
  consumption cities (*See* consumption cities)
  in developing countries 28
  and development 56
  in development policy 54
  and economic development 6, 68
  and employment opportunities 55
  funding 59
  and GDP, 54–55, 56, 60–61, 133
  and ghost towns/cities 53
  growth and development 54
  and infrastructure deficit 57
  and labor productivity 6, 55, 60, 62
    in Botswana 66
    in Ethiopia 66
    in Ghana 67
    in Kenya 67
    in Nigeria 67
    in South Africa 67
    in Tanzania, 67–68
    in Uganda 68
  and living standards 59, 63–64, 68
    in Botswana 63, 65–66
    in Ethiopia 63, 66
    in Ghana 67, 119–21
    in Kenya 67
    in Morocco 121
    in Nigeria 63, 67
    in Senegal, 121–22
    in South Africa 63, 67
    in Tanzania, 67–68
    in Uganda 68
    in Zambia 122
  and natural resource exporting 51, 52
  and productivity 68
  and productivity analyses
    Ethiopia, 114–15
    Ghana, 114–15
    Morocco, 116–17

urbanization (*cont.*)
    Senegal, 117–18
    Zambia, 118–19
  rapid, 56–58, 61, 130, 133–34
  regional analysis, 60–62
  and services sector 138
  and share of value added 135
  and structural transformation, 2–3, 60, 132, 134
    in Ethiopia 112
    in Ghana 112
    in Morocco 113
    in Senegal 113
    in Zambia 114
  and structural transformation 110

value addition 122
value-added sectors 84
value-added shares 102
  of industrial and manufacturing sectors in Senegal 128
  of industrial sector in Morocco 128
van Ark 78
vocational training 145

well-being 106
  measures of 108
wholesale trade 137
Wolf, M. 138
women employment 93
World Bank 38, 106, 110, 144

youth employment 90, 92–93, 103
youth unemployment 91
youthful population 5

Zambia 18
  enclave-driven institutional structures 12
  import substitution policy 37
  industrial sector in 125, 128
  manufacturing value added 47
  services sector, labor productivity and employment shares 128
  urbanization
    and living standards 122
    and productivity, 118–19
Zimbabwe
  import substitution policy 37
  manufacturing value added 47

www.ingramcontent.com/pod-product-compliance
Ingram Content Group UK Ltd.
Pitfield, Milton Keynes, MK11 3LW, UK
UKHW041919140426
5217IPUK00013B/230